Sir Joseph Banks

Sir Joseph Banks

18th Century Explorer, Botanist and Entrepreneur

Charles Lyte

DAVID & CHARLES
Newton Abbot   London   North Pomfret (Vt)

British Library Cataloguing in Publication Data

Lyte, Charles
  Sir Joseph Banks.
  1. Banks, *Sir* Joseph
  2. Botanists – England – Biography
  581'.092'4   QK31.B/

  ISBN 0–7153–7884–8

© Charles Lyte 1980

Typeset by Trade Linotype Ltd, Birmingham
and printed in Great Britain
by Redwood Burn Ltd, Trowbridge and Esher
for David & Charles (Publishers) Limited
Brunel House   Newton Abbot   Devon

Published in the United States of America
by David & Charles Inc
North Pomfret   Vermont 05053   USA

CONTENTS

*This book is dedicated to the memory of my Father,
Edwyn Lyte, who loved the eighteenth century*

I am deeply indebted to Dr Averil M. Lysaght for her advice and guidance, Mr W. L. Banks for his help and encouragement, and for the unfailing and invaluable help of the staffs of the Natural History Museum Botany Library, the Natural History Museum Zoological Library, the Lindsey County Library, Lincoln, the National Library of Wales, and McGill University, Montreal. I am also grateful to the Hon Victor Montagu for allowing me to examine his Banks papers, and above all to the fortitude and patience of my wife Sarah, and my children.

CHAPTER 1

THE BEGINNINGS
OF A BOTANIST

Outside the large, comfortable house in Argyll Street in Westminster the steady, chilling February rain filled the open drains and deepened the mud, muting the rumble and clatter of passing waggons and carriages. But in the house in Argyle Buildings lights burned from the kitchens to the attics.

William Banks, a heavily built, bluff Lincolnshire landowner, prowled round the fine reception room, pausing only to warm himself at the fire, while beyond the closed doors maids scurried up and down the stairs answering the commands of the physician and midwife who were attending his wife's first confinement.

The year was 1744 and in the eighteenth century a birth was as much a time for anxiety as it was for joy, for too often it was a finely fought battle between birth and death, and wealth was no guarantee against the loss of a child or mother, or indeed, both. William Banks was naturally anxious, but he had less cause for worry than many, for his wife of two years, Sarah, was a strong, determined woman unlikely to wilt under the pain and exhaustion of childbirth, and there was no cause for concern because she produced a big, bawling, baby son—the new heir to the considerable Banks' fortune.

They named the boy Joseph after his great-grandfather, a tough, astute attorney and property owner who did much to establish the family's great wealth. Cradled in the arms of the wet-nurse they saw a child whose future must have seemed to them as established and dependable as the acres of their great Lincolnshire estates. He would become a county magnate, a politician and an amateur antiquarian in the now firmly established Banks' tradition.

What they could not have guessed for one moment was that he would be the father of one of Britain's greatest colonies, lift science out of the alchemist's den and plant it firmly in the laboratory; that he would sail round the world on an historic voyage of adventure and discovery, and become a trusted and admired confidant of the King of England. Only as a politician would he fail the family tradition by resolutely turning his back on a parliamentary career.

Joseph Banks was not born into the aristocracy. His family roots were firmly buried in sound yeoman stock, but the Banks outlook was not so rural as to be blunted to the advantages of commerce and the growing importance of industry. Over the generations it had combined excellence in farming with even more profitable business enterprises.

The family could be traced back to one Simon Banke, who married a Yorkshire heiress in the reign of Henry III, but it was not until 1702 that the Banks' fortunes were soundly established in Lincolnshire. This was the year that Joseph's great-grandfather—always known as Joseph Banks the First—bought the Holland Estate from Sir George Humble for £9,000 and moved into the county. Twelve years later he bought the Revesby Estate for £14,000, and this became the family seat. In 1726 he added the Marsh Estate.

Moving from Scofton in Nottinghamshire, Joseph the First soon found his place among the hierarchy of Lincolnshire, and played a prominent part in the affairs of the county. He sat in Parliament for both Grimsby and Totnes, although political life appears to have been something of a secondary interest.

Above all he loved his estates and his home at Revesby Abbey, and was fascinated by the local history. It was through this latter interest that he became an antiquary of some distinction, an enthusiasm which was apparently genetic, passing down to his great-grandson. One can detect something of his keenness from a letter to a fellow antiquary, Dr William Stukely, in which he regrets the doctor cannot visit him because

I would show you a sight of eight religious houses, very great ones, in twelve miles riding, in the nearest road from my house to Lincoln, all within two hundred paces of the road. Revesby Abbey, Tattershall College, Kirkstead, Stickswould, Axholme, Barney, Stanfield and Barlings Abbeys.

He had studied them all. Revesby Abbey itself, by now merely the outline of a ruin, had been founded in 1142, and was affiliated to Rivaulx Abbey. It passed from the monks to Charles Brandon, Duke of Suffolk, as reward for the part he played in putting down a Lincolnshire uprising.

Joseph the First died in 1727. He was only sixty-two and would doubtless have lived much longer had he not fallen from the roof of

Revesby where he had climbed to inspect new building and repairs. Even the fall did not kill him outright. He lingered on for some time before dying from his injuries.

He was succeeded by his son, another Joseph, who fourteen years earlier had married Anne Hodgkinson, the daughter and heiress of a rich Derby merchant, thus bringing even greater wealth to the Banks' family.

Joseph the Second had a solid and respectable, if unspectacular, career. He served the county, was Member of Parliament for Peterborough, and he too become an accomplished antiquary; he added considerably to the family home and rebuilt Revesby Church. He did, however, become a Fellow of the Royal Society, the great fellowship in which his grandson was to play so prominent a part.

His comfortable life was not untinged by tragedy, for his heir, another Joseph, died in his early twenties, as yet unmarried. He himself did not long outlive his eldest son, for at the age of forty-five he died of 'an atrophy', possibly some form of cancer, and the great estates passed to his second son, William.

Like his grandfather and father before him he went into politics, and sat as the Member for Grampound, and was active in the county, serving for a time as Deputy-Lieutenant of Lincolnshire. But his real interest lay in agriculture, and in particular in draining the fens. It was a profitable enterprise which enriched the already bountiful Revesby Estates. So great was William's passion for farming that he spent as little time as possible in London, living in his Argyll Street house only when parliamentary duties demanded his presence.

In the eighteenth century Members of Parliament were not required to spend the greater part of their time cooped up in the House of Commons, and unless they were seeking real political power and high office, there was little need to live in any permanent way in London. William Banks had no particular political aspirations, indeed he resented being away from Revesby and his beloved fens. It was hardly surprising then that as soon as he was old enough to travel, the infant Joseph was taken home to the family seat.

For the first nine years of his life Joseph grew up in Lincolnshire, a great open county of fine farmland, rivers, streams, mysterious blow-wells—deep flowing pits of clear water which were believed, incorrectly, to be bottomless—woods, and the vast, rather sinister fens with their endless acres of whispering reeds from whose depths could be heard the muffled boom of the wild fowlers' guns.

He enjoyed tremendous freedom, and was at his happiest with a gun or fishing rod in his hand and a dog at his heels. There was no lack of game with the fields, woods, bogs and marshes teeming with partridges and pheasants, woodcock, snipe, wild duck, teal, widgeon, green and golden plovers, as well as wood pigeons and hares, rabbits and wild geese. But the most exciting sport was found in the trackless wastes of water and reeds where it was all too easy for the inexperienced to be lost.

In Joseph Banks's boyhood the fens were known as 'the aviary of England' and 'the great magazine of wild-fowl in this kingdom'. The wildfowlers who lived in and made their living from the fens—a rather remote, wild breed of men—brought an astonishing number and variety of birds to market. This withdrawn, independent tribe of hunters would emerge from their wilderness with their boats loaded with lapwings, knots, dotterels, seagulls, plovers, woodcock, redshanks, pigeons, terns, snipe, stints, ruffs and reeves, partridges, bitterns and curlews.

Although an enthusiastic and excellent shot, Joseph's greatest love was fishing. It was a passion that he shared with a neighbouring land-owner, the fourth Earl of Sandwich, the reforming First Lord of the Admiralty, who marred his reputation by his association with the rakes of the Hell-Fire Club at Medmenham, and such notorious political figures as Wilkes.

Banks was still a boy when he first met Sandwich, and although the fourth Earl was considerably older than he, the two struck up a friend-ship that was to mature and endure over the years, and play a very significant part in Joseph's career.

In those early days they went on many fishing expeditions together. With rivers and streams such as the Humber, Trent, Welland and Witham, Nene and Ancholme, and the oddly named Bain, Glen, Lud and Lymm, Eau, Rase and Slea, there was no lack of choice, and the fishing was good with fine trout and carp, almost mythically large pike, and tench and roach, bream and grayling. There was an ancient rhyme which Joseph must have heard many times:

> Ankolme eels and Witham pike,
> In all England are nane syke.

Although there were some fine hunts in the county, Joseph never showed much enthusiasm for riding to hounds, but throughout his life he was a fairly frequent visitor to race meetings in the county, which had a racing history going back to the fifteenth century.

While he was the despair of his tutors who found it almost impossible to keep him at his books, his free, wild country upbringing was perfect training for the arduous travels which lay ahead.

When Joseph was nine his father decided that he must acquire some formal education if he was to be able to take his place in the world as a gentleman, and consequently packed him off to Harrow. His progress at the school was so appalling, and he learnt so little, that after no more than three years his father took him away and sent him to Eton. Thus he achieved a fairly unique double early in life.

At Eton his academic performance hardly improved. After attending the school for two years his form master, one Edward Young, wrote to William Banks complaining that Joseph had returned late to school after the Christmas holidays, and as if to make the point that this was more serious in Joseph's case, he went on to deplore his performance in Greek and Latin, his apparent disregard for academic work, and his seeming passion for playing.

Having accepted William Banks's explanation that Joseph's late return to school was due to 'the badness of roads and weather', Edward Young wrote again :

It gives me great pleasure to find you think Master Banks improved. To be able to construe a Latin author into English with readiness and propriety is undoubtedly no less necessary than to be able to turn an English one into Latin. They ought indeed to go hand in hand together. And I hope we shall by degrees bring Master Banks to a tolerable perfection in the former; tho' the point, which I have been hitherto chiefly labouring, is to improve him in the latter, because of his great deficiency in that respect when he came to us.

Young, who was clearly not as impressed with Joseph's progress as was his father, presses home the need for the boy to work harder at his lessons, and he urges William to

. . . take the trouble to write to him, to show the great necessity there will be for him to exert particular diligence at this time; and I will likewise take all opportunities of inculcating the same to him. For you can't but be sensible that there is a great inattention in him, and an immoderate love of play, (I hope you will excuse my giving you my opinion of him so freely, as I cannot think it right to deceive you in a point of so much consequence to his welfare) which we must endeavour to get the better of in some degree, or it will be a constant obstacle to his improvement. This sometimes occasions quarrels between us; tho' in other respects we agree extremely well together; as I really think him a very good-tempered and well disposed boy.

Despite the rugged conditions at Eton when Joseph went there as an Oppidan, there was a great emphasis on excellence in learning, particularly the classics which dominated the curriculum. Homer, Lucian, Virgil, Horace and Ovid ruled the scene, although Milton and Pope had been added to the reading list. There was also arithmetic, algebra and geography. Joseph seems to have shone in none of these. Indeed his Eton friend, Lord Brougham, was fond of recalling in later years that 'my friend Joe cared mighty little for his book, and could not well understand any one taking to Greek and Latin'.

For a strong, active, fun-loving boy, Eton in the eighteenth century had many distractions from books. Apart from football, cricket and fives, there was a huge selection of popular games such as shirking walls (a kind of fives), and scrambling walls, which appears to have been the prototype of the famous Eton wall-game. There was battledore, peg-top, peg-in-the-ring, hopscotch, marbles and kites, tops, humming-tops and hunt the hare. You could break the rules and attempt to slide down the stairs from the cloister to the college kitchen.

If all else failed you could always prosecute the running feud between the Collegers, foundation scholars who were lodged in the College and were normally poor boys, and the Oppidans, the sons of wealthy parents, who lived in lodgings in the town of Eton. 'Hoops' was the seemingly innocent way of starting a battle between the two groups. They would advance on one another merrily bowling their hoops until they were within striking distance and then club one another with their heavy hoop sticks.

The Collegers had every right to resent the privilege of the Oppidans who lived in relative comfort in private lodgings and were well fed. Although the Collegers no longer had to sleep in the Long Chamber in extraordinary misery, the new dormitories introduced in the late eighteenth century were hardly better. As late as 1788 there was little glass in the windows and during hard winters the boys would wake to find their beds covered with snow.

Food was monotonous and limited; mutton, bread and beer, and some potatoes. In 1785 plum pudding on Sunday was introduced, but only because it was financed out of a bequest. A leg or shoulder of a small Southdown sheep was considered sufficient for eight boys, a loin for six, and a neck for four. The boys served themselves, but in such a strict order of seniority that junior boys often found themselves left with little more than a polished bone. One junior Colleger of the period recalled in later years that he often had to make do with dry bread, or bread dipped in cold gravy, and a few mashed potatoes.

As late as 1834 a critic wrote: 'The inmates of a workhouse or a gaol are better fed and lodged than the scholars of Eton.'

But it was a hard and brutal age, and hardship came as second nature to most. Joseph only just missed one of the school's most barbarous customs, that of battering a ram to death on the annual election day for new scholars for Cambridge. But every year throughout his time, ram pasties were served at the high table in hall during the Election Monday dinner, just so that nobody should forget the bloody tradition of the past.

Joseph was popular with his fellows at Eton. He was a sturdy, courageous boy, qualities that he needed since his academic work did not improve and he must have been a frequent candidate for the flogging block on Fridays, the day set aside for punishing slothful and poor performers.

What made life doubly difficult was that on the one hand the school was still governed by the rigid and demanding sixteenth-century Consuetudinarium of William Malim, while on the other hand there were so many delightful distractions, particularly for a boy brought up in the country. He could follow in the footsteps of the great Isaac Walton, and Sir Henry Wotton, a famous Provost of Eton, and fish where they did together at Black Potts below the shooting fields. At least when he was accused of frittering away his time he could quote Sir Henry who said of fishing that it was 'an employment for my idle time, which was then not idly spent'.

But there were no excuses for what was undoubtedly the most popular sport—poaching. Using guns, snares, nets, ferrets, hounds and dogs, the boys used to raid the royal estates at Windsor. Apart from the game, which was always welcome, there was the sheer excitement of trying to outwit the game-keepers who made no distinctions for Etonians—they shot at them just the same as at any other poachers. Many a boy crawled back to school suffering from gunshot wounds.

They were a rough, tough bunch, the Etonians of the eighteenth century. Brawling with bargemen was a favoured pastime, as was driving—fast, furiously and dangerously—bull-baiting, badger-baiting, dog-fights, and cat and duck hunts.

A sport that Joseph loved and excelled in was swimming. Like other Oppidans he bathed near an oak in the lower shooting fields, while the Collegers had to make do with a spot further up the river, diving into the water from a wooden bridge which linked Eton with Windsor.

Indirectly it was swimming that was responsible for an almost Pauline transformation in his character that was to shape his entire future, and change him from a big, cheery, not over-bright country gentleman's son into a dedicated scientist, and one of the most acute observers of his age.

Years later as an old man he described the experience to Sir Everard Home, who was not only his doctor, but one of his closest and most constant companions during the last years of his life.

One evening he and Home were sitting together in Banks's London home in Soho Square when he told this story, which was repeated by Sir Everard while delivering the Hunterian Oration in honour of surgery in 1822, two years after Joseph Banks had died.

A year after he arrived at Eton Joseph was found by his form master, Edward Young, reading a book, which in Joseph's case was something of an event. Sir Everard said :

This sudden turn which his mind had taken, Sir Joseph explained to me in the following manner; one fine summer evening he had bathed in the river as usual with other boys, but having stayed a long time in the water he found when he came to dress himself, that all his companions had gone; he was walking leisurely along a lane, the sides of which were richly enamelled with flowers; he stopped and looking round, involuntarily exclaimed, How beautiful! After some reflection, he said to himself, it is surely more natural that I should be taught to know all these productions of Nature, in preference to Greek and Latin; but the latter is my father's command and it is my duty to obey him; I will however make myself acquainted with all these different plants for my own pleasure and gratification. He began immediately to teach himself botany.

Because of the lack of books on the subject, at least at Eton, he made friends with the old women who scoured the hedgerows for the herbs used by druggists and apothecaries, and paid them sixpence for every piece of useful information about plants that they could pass on to him. In this way he laid the foundation of what was to become an encyclopaedic knowledge.

During the holiday following his conversion, Joseph discovered an old copy of *Gerrard's Herbal*, complete with engravings and descriptions, in his mother's dressing room. He took it back to school, and doubtless it was the book that his master found him reading so eagerly.

Once on the path of natural history there was no turning back, and his enthusiasm knew no bounds. He quickly established an insatiable appetite for collecting, an appetite that was to result in an enormous natural history collection. The most impressive part was an herbarium, now in the Natural History Museum in London, and still being used by scientists.

A close friend at Eton was the father of Lord Brougham, the author of *The Lives of Men of Letters and Science who flourished in the time of George the Third*. In later years Lord Brougham recalled:

I have often heard my father say, that being of the same age, they used to associate much together. Both were fond of walking and swimming, and both were expert in the latter exercise. Banks always distinguished him, and in his old age he never ceased to show me every kindness in his power, in consequence of this old connexion.

My father described him as a remarkable fine-looking, strong, and active boy, whom no fatigue could subdue, and no peril daunt; and his whole time out of school was given up to hunting after plants and insects, making a hortus siccus of the one, and forming a cabinet of the other. As often as Banks could induce him to quit his task in reading or verse-making, he would take him on his long rambles; and I suppose it was from this early taste that we had at Brougham so many butterflies, beetles, and other insects, as well as a cabinet of shells and fossils.

Any hopes that Joseph's master might have entertained that the boy had at last turned to the academic life were short-lived, for young Banks made it clear to all that he could not understand anyone taking to Latin and Greek when there was so much to be discovered in nature all around them. And when he went to Oxford he cheerfully ignored the oft-repeated jibe from his fellow undergraduates who used to shout: 'Here is Banks, but he knows nothing of Greek.'

Indeed his reputation at Oxford was that of a pleasure-loving buffoon. According to a scurrilous article in the *Town and Country Magazine*, published in 1775:

To relate his juvenile feats of gallantry, when still at the university, would carry us beyond the line we prescribed for these memoirs. Oxford echoed with his amours, and the bed-makers of . . . College have given the world some testimonials of his vigour.

However vigorous his Oxford affairs may have been they did not deflect him from his avowed ambition to become the leading man of his age in all branches of natural history, and in botany in particular. By the close of his university career the very people who jeered at him for his ignorance of the classics were coming to him to settle arguments on points of natural history.

Joseph's Eton career was cut short when he returned home to be inoculated against smallpox. He reacted severely against the inoculation and was confined to bed. By the time he recovered there was little purpose in his returning to school, and instead he went to Oxford where he became a Gentleman Commoner at Christ Church.

When he arrived in the great university city in 1760, just before he was eighteen, he found that the Chair of Botany was occupied by Dr Humphrey Sibthorp, who was said to have delivered only one lecture on the subject in thirty-five years, and who made it quite clear that he was not going to alter the habit of a lifetime merely to satisfy the whims of a wealthy young undergraduate.

Dr Sibthorp was delighted when Banks announced that he would find a lecturer in botany, and would arrange for him to be paid by his pupils. But such was the low esteem with which the subject was held in Oxford that he was unable to find anyone equal to the task. Far from giving up in despair, however, he hired a horse and rode to Cambridge. There he found Dr Martyn, the Professor of Botany, who told him to talk to a young Jew, Israel Lyons.

Lyons was only about four years older than Joseph. He was the son of a silversmith, and although the family was poor and of humble origins, they had a passion for scholarship. Like Banks, Israel Lyons had taught himself botany as a boy. He was also a brilliant mathematician, and at an early stage attracted the attention and patronage of Dr Robert Smith, Master of Trinity.

The two young men met and struck up an immediate friendship, despite the huge gap between their backgrounds. In Lyons, Banks recognised the source of expertise and knowledge that he so desperately needed if he was to complete his grand design; and, in Banks, Israel Lyons saw the opening through which he could pass to exploit fully his own talents. Ten years after Banks left Oxford, Lyons sailed as astronomer on Captain Phipps' great expedition to the North Pole. He also married well, and but for the fact that he died before reaching middle age would undoubtedly have lived to enjoy a distinguished career.

One of the most attractive features of the eighteenth century was that excellence allowed any man to step across the chasm that separated the classes; Joseph Banks was one of the leading men of property and privilege who devoted his life to sponsoring the careers of men of talent.

The two men returned to Oxford where Banks organised a small group of students to study botany and natural history under Lyons.

Largely financed by Banks, the project was a complete success on two counts—Joseph acquired the scientific training he needed, and at Oxford natural history was accepted as a respectable, rather than dilettante, subject.

His happiness at Oxford was marred only by the sudden death of his father in 1761 from the 'breaking of an Imposthume in his breast', and although he became master of Revesby and the Banks' fortune, he did not legally inherit until he came of age in 1764.

Following the death of her husband, Sarah, Joseph's mother, disposed of the family's London home in Westminster, and took a house in Chelsea.

Turret House in Paradise Row was an attractive Queen Anne building which had formerly been Rothery's School. She could hardly have made a happier choice with the river and good fishing close by, as well as the Chelsea Physic Garden, the forerunner of Kew. Within a short distance of the house there were a number of nursery gardens, and within an easy ride there was the famous Hammersmith nursery of James Lee, who was not only a skilled horticulturist, but also a distinguished botanist.

When he left Oxford in 1763 Joseph spent much of his time at Revesby, with occasional trips to the new London house. Most of his energies were devoted to natural history, although he also had to learn how to run a great estate. He was fortunate in having the support of an extremely competent mother. Before his sudden death Joseph's father had been confined to a wheelchair, and Sarah had had to act for him.

There was a strong bond between mother and son. Joseph's love of nature was clearly inherited from her. During the course of his life he was to have a hand in exploding many old myths that had been nurtured by ignorance. This was another maternal trait. As a distinguished man of science he once wrote in a letter:

I have from my childhood, in conformity with the precepts of a mother void of all imaginary fear, been in the constant habit of taking toads in my hand, and applying them to my nose and face as it may happen. My motive for doing this very frequently is to inculcate the opinion I have held, since I was told by my mother, that the toad is actually a harmless animal; and to whose manner of life man is certainly under some obligation as its food is chiefly those insects which devour his crops and annoy him in various ways.

Toads were widely believed to be poisonous, and in some way the instruments of evil.

Apart from his mother, his sister, Sarah Sophia, was constantly at his side. She was a year younger than Joseph, a tall, gaunt, rather masculine girl with a booming voice and a passion for collecting almost anything that took her fancy from coins to calling cards. Handsome without being beautiful, she tended towards eccentricity, a fact that may have helped to keep her from the altar. She was, however, a contented and fulfilled woman, devoting her life and energy to helping her brother in his work. She tirelessly made fair copies of his journals and documents, no easy task since Banks's handwriting, punctuation and spelling left everything to be desired. Even after he married, Sarah Sophia continued to live with him.

In 1764 Joseph came of age and into possession of his fortune, and it was then, according to Lord Brougham

. . . that the great merits of this distinguished person shone forth. With all the incitements which his age, his figure, and his station naturally presented to leading a life of idleness, varied only by the more vulgar gratifications of sense or of ordinary ambition, and with a fortune which placed these gratifications in ample measure within his reach, he continued steadily devoted to scientific pursuits, and only lived for the studies of the naturalist. He remained out of Parliament; he went little into any society but that of learned men; his relaxation was confined to exercise, and to angling, of which he was so fond, that he would devote days and even nights to it.

His constant fishing companion was still the Earl of Sandwich, both in Lincolnshire and in London, for they were neighbours in both places. They were so keen on the sport that they even worked out a plan to drain the Serpentine so that they could discover what types of fish lived in it. Fortunately for their careers and reputations they were prevented from carrying out the plan which they proposed to execute without permission.

Brougham gives the impression of Joseph as a rather worthy, solitary young man, though in fact he was always gregarious by nature. He enjoyed the theatre, and loved to organise parties, in particular fishing parties for women as well as men, during which everyone feasted on the catch which was cooked on the river bank.

Lord Sandwich was a man of the world and would not have allowed Joseph to become dull for lack of appropriate amusement. Anyway, by this time, through family links, the Banks family had moved into the higher reaches of society. Entertainment in Lincolnshire was not confined to hearty squires and farmers.

William Banks's sister, Margaret, an extremely beautiful woman—
the Duke of Cumberland gave balls in her honour—married the Hon
Henry Grenville. Her daughter Louisa, Joseph's cousin, married the
third Earl of Stanhope. And on his mother's side his aunt, Hannah
Sophia, was the wife of the eighth Earl of Exeter.

So there were fine houses to visit, and grand society entertainments
when the family was in London.

By the time Joseph left Oxford he had shaped fairly clearly in his
mind the plan for his future. It included expeditions and explorations
in search of plants, animals, insects, indeed anything new and valuable
to the growing science of natural history. So the years after leaving
university were a period of preparation, of training to work in the field,
and so unflagging was his zeal that it once nearly landed him in prison.

He went out of London to Hounslow to search for a particular plant
which he believed grew in the area. Dismounting from his horse at the
place where he thought he would discover a specimen he clambered
down into the ditch happily unaware that shortly before at the same
spot a man had been robbed by a highwayman. Once over their fright,
the robbed man and his driver had decided to take the horses out of
their carriage and return to hunt down the thief. Joseph was ferreting
about in the undergrowth when the two came galloping up, and on
sighting him decided he must be the villain. Before he could explain,
he was trussed up and carted off to London where he was charged at
Bow Street with the robbery. It took some time and eloquence to
persuade the magistrate, Sir John Fielding, that he was innocent.

Living so close to the Chelsea Physic Garden, Joseph was able to
cultivate the friendship of Phillip Miller, the crabby but brilliant
custodian of the garden. Like James Lee, Miller was a brilliant botanist
and author of the classic *Gardener's Dictionary*. He allowed Joseph
to study the large collection of foreign plants which grew in the garden.

Banks also searched out the leading naturalists of the time: men
like Thomas Pennant the zoologist; the Rev John Lightfoot, an admired
botanist; Dr Charles Lyttleton, Bishop of Carlisle and a noted antiquary; Dr Charles Morton, Librarian of the British Museum; and
William Watson, a doctor who also had a fine reputation in physics
and astronomy. By listening to their conversation his understanding of
science was immensely widened, and clearly they were impressed by
him, for they were among the men who nominated him to the Royal
Society in April 1766 when he was only 23—the same month that he set
sail for Newfoundland and Labrador, the first of his great adventures.

CHAPTER 2

EXPLORING
IN ESKIMO-LAND

By the time he came into his huge inheritance at the age of twenty-one, Joseph Banks was determined to travel, not as a dilettante, but as a serious explorer. His family and friends assumed that by 'travelling' he meant that he was going to take the well-worn trail of the Grand Tour to Paris and Lyons, Rome and Venice, with, perhaps, a little gentle botanising along the way. They were horrified when he announced that he would go to Newfoundland and Labrador to hobnob with Eskimos rather than the literati of Europe.

Even the well-educated and cultured of the eighteenth century saw in the untamed wilds of the new world unspeakable terrors and dangers —disease, murderous Indians, and savage beasts. Banks came under tremendous pressure to change his mind. He was foolhardy and selfish; he was jeopardising the glittering career of a man of wealth and taste; his widowed mother and fatherless sister would be abandoned to the world without the support of a man. There were many tears and much persuasion, but he stood firm against all the arguments and arm-twisting.

Years later, writing in 1813 to William Hooker (who was to become Sir William Hooker, the first of the great Hookers of Kew), who had been talked out of going on an expedition to Java, Banks recalled the pressures he had been under to abandon his first major journey. Angrily he wrote to Hooker:

But, pressed as you are, I advise you to submit and sacrifice, if you can, your wish for travelling, to the importunities of those who think they can guide you to a more serene, quiet, calm, sober mode of slumbering away life than you propose for yourself. Let me hear from you how you feel inclined to prefer ease and indulgence to hardship and activity. I was about twenty-three when I began my peregrinations. You are somewhat older, but you may be assured that if I had listened to a multitude of voices that were raised to dissuade me, I should have been now a quiet country gentleman, ignorant of a number of things I am now acquainted with.

The choice of Newfoundland and Labrador was not part of some careful scientific design, but the product of circumstances. His mother was a deeply religious woman, and after moving to Chelsea she came into contact with the Moravians, a religious sect who had a house nearby.

The Moravian Church (Unitas Fratrum) had been founded in Bohemia. It had grown out of the reform movement started by John Huss, and was influenced by the teachings of John Wycliffe and the Lollards. Presbyterian in character, its members were pacifists who pursued an exemplary moral life. Their philosophy was utterly simple, declaring as they did that 'the Holy Scriptures are our only rule of faith and practice'.

After enjoying a good deal of popular and influential support, and possibly because of that, they became the victims of cruel persecutions, and many members of the brotherhood had to flee from their homeland. Groups settled in various parts of Europe, including England, where they arrived in 1735.

Although aliens, the Brethren were to prove exceedingly useful to the British in their campaign to control Newfoundland and Labrador and their important and rich cod fisheries. With a rapidly expanding home population the abundant supply of dried cod, and oil manufactured from the fish's liver, was vital to the British economy. The fisheries were equally important to the French, and for years British and French fishermen had contested the rights and harbours in the area.

By the early 1760s the British were getting the upper hand, but a vital key to success was winning the hearts and minds of the Eskimo tribes who inhabited the coast and islands. This was where the Moravians came in. The Brethren had decided that they should take Christianity to the Eskimos. They had contacted tribes in Greenland and learned the language.

In 1752 an attempt was made to establish a mission on the coast of Labrador. Four missionaries sailed in a trading vessel, the *Hope*, which was commanded by a Moravian sailor, Erhardt. With the help of the ship's crew they built a house in a sheltered harbour, and were left there while the *Hope* sailed north in search of a cargo.

Erhardt made contact with Eskimos who asked him to trade with them. He left his vessel with a small party of sailors, but they never returned. After waiting for some days, Goff, the Mate of the *Hope*, finally abandoned his captain and shipmates, and returned to the mission. Because he was shorthanded for the journey home he took off the missionaries to make up numbers. A year later Goff returned to the mission only to find the house in ruins.

In 1764 and 1765 the Moravians returned to Labrador, on this occasion being carried in the British fisheries protection vessel, the *Niger*. Apart from trying to establish contact with the Eskimos, they were also involved in a survey of part of the coast. Both missions were successful, and led to a lasting Moravian influence in the area.

While not a particularly religious man, Joseph Banks liked the Moravians. He admired their high moral standards, and their hardiness in trying to take Christianity to lands as inhospitable as Labrador and Newfoundland.

With growing fascination he listened to their accounts of the Eskimos, of great islands of ice, and of an undisturbed land rich in plants and animals. He was determined to see it for himself and make the first scientific collection of its flora and fauna.

The problem of getting to Newfoundland and Labrador was solved by two close connections with the navy. The one was his great friend and adviser, Lord Sandwich, and the other Constantine John Phipps, who became the second Lord Mulgrave.

Phipps was almost exactly the same age as Banks, and they had become fast friends at Eton. Constantine Phipps left Eton to join the navy, serving as a cadet under his uncle, the great Augustus John Hervey. By the time Banks was planning his expedition, Phipps was a serving lieutenant, and becoming himself increasingly interested in exploration. He listened enthusiastically to Banks's plans, and when Joseph suggested that he should join him he leapt at the idea.

In all probability it was Phipps who suggested that they should take passage with one of the naval fishery protection vessels which spent the summer cruising in the cod waters, not only keeping the French and British fishermen from one another's throats, but also beating off French privateers.

The Navy co-operated and it was agreed that the two young men should sail in HMS *Niger*, due to leave Plymouth in the spring of 1766. The Niger, which was commanded by Captain Sir Thomas Adams, who had taken the Moravians to Labrador the year before, was a small, crowded vessel of 679 tons. She carried thirty-two guns and a crew of 220 men, all crammed into a mere 125ft by 35ft 2in.

Although it has been assumed that Phipps was a lieutenant on the *Niger*, this was not so. Both he and Banks were signed on as supernumeraries.

During the weeks before the ship was due to sail, Banks planned his equipment with the eye to detail and the disregard for cost that was to mark all his later voyages. He assembled a small library of botanical and zoological books, quires of paper and presses for his plant collections, spirits for preserving zoological specimens, butterfly nets, and a variety of nets and trawls for collecting marine life. Guns, fishing rods and notebooks were added to the growing pile of gear.

All was ready and packed by 7 April 1766 when he set off on the journey to Plymouth. Phipps was picked up at Salisbury.

Despite the rigours of the lurching coach journey to Plymouth they were soon sight-seeing and collecting, in the time until the ship sailed.

On 11 April they made up a party to visit Mount Edgecumbe, the magnificent home of Lord and Lady Edgecumbe. Banks admired the views from the Mount, and the fine local stone from which the buildings were constructed, but was critical that not enough of 'the modern taste' had been employed in its building. He was far more interested in a small pond in the grounds which contained goldfish with curiously bulging eyes 'standing out from their heads on each side as the eyes of lobsters and crabs are formed. . . .' And he noted the wild plants growing among the rocks and the cultivated plants in the gardens.

A persistent south-east wind made it impossible for the *Niger* to get under way, so the following days were spent botanising, and collecting along the tideline and sifting through rockpools. Banks journal reads:

. . . Found a kind of sea polype which we had never seen before. . . . We found also among the rocks an amphibious insect which for want of another name I shall call the Sea Hog Louse.

Among the rocks he found wild madder, stinking Gladwin (*Iris foetidissima*), rock samphire and deadly nightshade, but was disappointed that there were no rare plants. He spotted the first swallows of the year, and found small fish in the rock pools 'not unlike the stone loach of our freshwater rivers'. Waiting for a fair wind became a limbering-up exercise for the serious collecting ahead.

By the seventeenth, ten days after leaving London, Banks was in a high state of frustration. He wrote:

At seven this morn we were called up by the winds being fair to get the ship out of Hammoaze. Accordingly at half past eight we broke loose and in about an hour came to moorings between Drake's Island and the land. On Saturday next, God willing, we sail for Newfoundland.

The next few days were occupied with more sightseeing—gardens, and a visit to William Cooksworthy's china factory, where the owner was using the fine white clay from St Austell, now the centre of a rich industry producing china clay.

At half-past one on 22 April the anchors were raised, the sails set, and the *Niger* was carried out to sea by a fresh east-north-east wind. With a steady wind and only a gentle swell coming off the Atlantic the journey started well. Banks found an insect on board, and fished for seaweed with a grappling hook. He saw sharks scavenging round the vessel, and 'shoals of Porpusses'.

Five days out the almost idyllic conditions deteriorated. For two days the *Niger* was tossed about by a savage gale, and Banks discovered that he was a poor sailor. On the twenty-ninth he wrote : 'These two last days we have had hard gales. I have been too sick to write.'

During the following seven years in which he travelled thousands of nautical miles in small sailing ships, Banks never overcame sea-sickness. Once in the teeth of a gale he was prostrated, unable to write up his journals, and indifferent to the undiscovered wonders of nature.

With the return of calm weather there was a search for a mysterious island—Rodney's Island—which was claimed to have been sighted about 700 miles off the Lizard. But despite the landbirds wheeling about the ship and a lookout at the masthead, there was nothing to be seen but the unrelieved grey of the heaving Atlantic. Rodney's Island remained what it had always been—a seaborne mirage.

May came calmly on the ocean, and Banks passed his time leaning out of the quarter-gallery window scooping seaweed and jellyfish from the surface of the water with a landing net. But the calm was short-lived, and within the first week of the month the vessel was struck by fresh storms, and Banks was once again too ill to collect or write.

By 8 May the temperature had dropped dramatically and the first iceberg was sighted. Banks was captivated by its beauty. It was sighted at ten at night, and although there was no moon, 'the ice itself appears like a body of whitish light. The waves dashing against it appear much more luminous.' The following morning the ship was sailing among seven icebergs. 'We steer very near a small one which from its transparency and the greenish cast in it makes a very beautiful appearance. . . .'

Exactly twenty days from leaving Plymouth the expedition arrived at St John's in Newfoundland. The following morning Banks was ashore, and although it was still too early in the spring for many plants to be ready for his presses, the weather was extraordinarily warm. There were fine fir trees to be noted, however, and large numbers of mosses and lichens.

St John's, in 1766, was a rough and squalid town dependent on fishing. Apart from a naval and military presence, the bulk of the population was made up of French and British fishermen. At the height of the fishing season about 10,000 Frenchmen and some 30,000 British crowded the small town. It was, Joseph Banks said:

. . . the most disagreeable town I ever met with . . .

It is very difficult to compare one town with another, tho' that probably is the best way of conveying the idea. St. John's however, cannot be compared with any I have seen. It is built upon the side of a hill facing the harbour, containing two or three hundred houses and near as many fish flakes interspersed, which in summer time must cause a stench scarce to be supported. Thank heaven we were only there spring and fall before the fish were come to the ground and after they are gone off.

For dirt and filth of all kinds St. John's may, in my opinion, reign unrivalled as it far exceeds any fishing town I ever saw in England. Here is no regular street, the houses being built in rows immediately adjoining the flakes, consequently no pavement. Offals of fish of all kinds are strewed about. The remains of the Irish men's chowder, who you see making it, skinning and gutting fish in every corner.

As everything here smells of fish, so you cannot get anything that does not taste of it. Hogs can scarce be kept from it by any care, and when they have got it are by far the filthiest meat I ever met with. Poultry of all kinds, ducks, geese, fowls and turkies, infinitely more fishy than the worst tame duck that ever was sold for a wild one in Lincolnshire. The very cows eat the fish offal and thus milk is fishy. This last particular indeed I have not met with myself, but have been assured it is often the case.

Apart from the heaps of rotting fish entrails and bones, there were great stacks of salted cod drying in the sun and wind, and huge vats of putrefying cod livers slowly being converted into high quality lamp oil.

If ever there was living proof of 'where there's muck, there's money', St John's was it, for it was money, or in some cases the lack of it, that held the settlers. For the merchants and boat owners there was money to be made, but for the hired hands there was the trap of debt.

After long hours of fishing with hand lines and being tossed about on rough icy seas, more often than not soaked to the skin, the fishermen's only solace was beer, which was sold to them at exorbitant prices by their employers. At the end of the season they were so in debt they could not afford the fare home, and were forced to spend the harsh winter months trapping and sealing.

Newfoundland and Labrador were not pleasant places, but for a naturalist they were a rich hunting ground. Even in the neighbourhood of St John's, which had been stripped of timber to build the town, Banks made useful collections, but his hopes of an early spring and an even richer haul of plants, were dashed nine days after landfall when he trekked inland to the little settlement of Petty Harbour. There he was cut off by snow which fell so heavily that it lay five feet thick on the ground in a day.

For the remainder of May and the first ten days of June, he collected in the St John's area, and on 11 June left for Croque, the settlement north of the Long Range mountains. There he was reunited with Constantine Phipps, who was building a house and laying out a garden. As Croque was used as a watering point for the fishery protection vessels it seems likely that he was building under Admiralty orders, and this would account for him being able to obtain leave of absence to make the trip.

The house was called Crusoe Hall, and Phipps was supervising the work with frenzied activity. 'He works night and day and lets the mosquitoes eat more of him than he does of any kind of food, all through eagerness' Banks noted approvingly.

Returning from an abortive hunt for a polar bear which had been spotted with two cubs, Banks was just in time to hitch a lift on a shallop—one of the heavy sailing boats used for fishing—to Englee in the mouth of Canada Bay, which was a part of Newfoundland dominated by the French fishermen, who had been armed by their home government. Joseph arrived at a time when a violent clash seemed imminent between the British and French fishermen. At Conche they found a lone British fishing vessel which was being harrassed by four French boats. The French were preventing the British boat from catching bait, and the skipper warned that if 'proper precautions were not taken mischief would certainly ensue, as the French sent out arms, allowing two muskets to each bait boat.'

Not only were the French being aggressive and threatening, they were also trading illegally with the Eskimos. It is not clear whether the trade was in guns, or liquor, or merely illegal because it broke the British monopoly.

Throughout June Banks collected indefatigably, and was almost continuously on the move. Despite his youth and strength, the strain began to tell. On 22 June he wrote in his journal:

At three o'clock came to the ship very compleatly tired as we had not pulled off our clothes since we came out nor lodged anywhere but in the aft cuddy of our boat.

The result of exhaustion and strain was that in July he was taken ill with a fever and confined to bed. He was unable to collect, or even to write up his journal.

In August, obviously depressed and debilitated by illness, he wrote that he had been confined

... for the greatest part of that month (July) to the ship, incapable of collecting plants at the very season of the year when they are most plentiful. Some few, indeed, I got by the diligence of my servant, who I sent often out to bring home anything he thought I had not got. He also shot several birds for me, but my situation was far too weak and dispirited by my illness to examine systematically any thing. That has made my bird tub a chaos, of which I cannot give so good an account as I could wish, and has left many blanks in my plants which I fear I must trouble my good friends in England to fill up.

But Banks did not remain plunged in gloom for long. During the first week of August he was back on his feet, although unsteadily, collecting insects and plants. He must have been very weak, because he noted in his journal: 'I was baffled by every butterfly who chose to fly away for some time till my strength returned and which it did in an uncommonly short time.'

Fit once again he took a boat to Bellisle de Gris, saw a bear near Conche, and arrived at Croque in time to join the ship which was bound for Chatteaux Bay and Labrador. They were hardly under way before running into a violent gale, but to Banks's great relief this time he did not suffer from sea-sickness 'which has so much harrassed me always before in the least degree of rough weather'.

During the voyage to Chatteaux Bay he wrote to his old Eton and Oxford friend, William Phelp Perrin:

This morn I wrote to Solander in a storm, tonight I write to you in a Newfoundland fog. This, indeed, is not of the thickest as I believe a man may see twenty yards from his nose. If it was I defy the devil to see ten.

We are now in our passage from Newfoundland to the coast of Labrador and a deuce of a rough one we have had, as, indeed was our passage out, which was one continued puke to me, tho' now I have quite got the better of it, as you would say if you was with me, for now tis a calm to what it was in the morn, yet I cannot keep my seat without being moored head and stern, as we seamen call it. That is my legs against a ledge and my back against the mizzen mast.

On the journey out from England, Banks was so crippled by sea-sickness that at one point he lashed himself to a gun so that he could stay on deck without going overboard.

He described the horrors of that outward journey to Sir Everard Home, who repeated the story in his Hunterian orations:

Early in the voyage it blew a gale which made him dreadfully seasick, and unable to keep his legs upon deck: determined not to go below he made himself fast to a gun, by means of ropes knotted and twisted in all different ways he could contrive. In this situation he was making the most solemn vows, that nothing again would tempt him to go out to sea; these were interrupted by the mizzen-topmast coming rattling down the shrouds, immediately over his head; this sudden alarm put a stop to the sea-sickness, his mind being wholly occupied in disengaging himself, and trying to escape from the impending danger.

Apart from wishing to make the first significant biological collections in the area, Banks was passionately keen to meet the Eskimos, or Indians, as he and everyone else commonly called them. Simple, unsophististicated and uncivilised people exerted an extraordinary attraction to him. It was not the fascination of the peepshow for something bizarre or fearful, but an earnest desire to understand them. The fact that he did not encounter Eskimos in the wild—he did in fact meet some who were later brought to London—was a source of lasting regret to him, but he did listen avidly to any first-hand, or even second-hand, accounts of them.

For information about Indians he also had to rely on other people's accounts, and it is hardly surprising that he did not make contact with the Indians themselves as they and the fishermen were in a constant state of war. At St Peter's Bay he noted in his journal:

Our people who fish in those parts live in a continual state of warfare with them, firing at them whenever they meet them, and if they chance to find their houses, or wigwams, as they call them, plundering them immediately, tho' a bow and arrows and what they call their pudding is generally the whole of their furniture.

They in return look upon us in exactly the same light as we do them, killing our people whenever they get the advantage of them and stealing or destroying their nets wheresoever they find them.

He learnt that the Newfoundland Indian could discharge arrows at great speed and with deadly accuracy, that they built their canoes with birch bark sewed together with deer sinews, and that when they scalped a man they took all of his hair and the skin of his face down to the upper lip.

But the people he really wanted to see, the Eskimos, remained as elusive as ever. Although he was to be disappointed, he never gave up hope. In a jaunty letter to his sister, Sarah Sophia, written from Chatteaux Bay in August, he said :

We are here in daily expectation of the Eskimaux ladies here. I wish with all my heart they were come as I might have sent you a sealskin gown and petticoat—perfumed with train oil, which to them is as sweet as lavender water . . .

Although his stay in the wild part of Canada was relatively short, and, indeed, shortened more than it need have been by his illness, Banks still found time to relax. He enjoyed some fine days' sport fishing for trout and salmon in the rivers and there was good and abundant shooting. The sea fishing, too, was impressive. Early in September he measured and weighed a giant halibut which was brought aboard the ship. It weighed 284lb 'which was only 14lb less than an ox killed for the ship's company', measured 6ft 11in from nose to tail, and was 3ft 10in wide.

There was even some relatively elegant entertainment to be had. In October the sixth anniversary of King George III's accession to the throne was celebrated with great gusto in St John's. The *Guernsey*, lying in the harbour, was dressed overall, 'and if I may compare great things with small, looked like a pedlers basket at a horse fair where ribbons of divers colours fly in the wind fastened to yard wands stuck around it.' Having viewed this brave sight, Banks wrote :

We were all invited to a ball given by Mr Governer, where the want of ladies was so great that my washerwoman and her sister were there by formal invitation. But what surprised me the most was that after dancing we were conducted to a really elegant supper set out with all kinds of wines and Italian liqueurs, to the great emolument of the ladies who ate and drank to some purpose. Dancing it seems agreed with them by getting them into such excellent stomachs.

Apart from being a tireless and meticulous collector of plants, animals, birds, shells and geological specimens, Banks also collected ethnic objects whenever possible, and noted down the minutiae and mundane details about whatever community he found himself among. It was this sharp eye for detail, however apparently insignificant, which makes his journals so fascinating and valuable.

Thus during his Newfoundland and Labrador journey he found time to note down recipes for fish chowder :

The chief food of the poorer and when well made a luxury that the rich, even in England, at least in my opinion, might be fond of. It is a soup made with a small quantity of salt pork cut into small slices, a good deal of fish and biscuit boiled for about an hour. Unlikely as this mixture appears to be palatable, I have scarce met with anybody in this country who is not fond of it.

And there was spruce beer which he saw being brewed from the branches of the black spruce and molasses :

. . . in less than a week it is fit to drink. From this liquor, in itself very weak, are made three kinds of flip, called here Callibogus, Egg Calli and King Calli.

The flip mixing was little more than adding spirits to the anaemic spruce beer.

In great detail Banks described the different methods—British and French—of preparing and preserving the cod catch. He described seal hunts and the brutal massacres of whole herds of great lumbering walruses.

He describes curious rock formations on islands in Chatteaux Bay; the find of a huge horde of ancient whalebone, and speculates on much earlier visits to the area by Europeans. There are notes on vegetable growing and poultry farming at the settlement, and a description of the battle to win control of St John's from the French.

Only storm and illness were able to halt Banks from the ceaseless pursuit of the new, the interesting and the curious.

On 28 October Banks saw the last of St John's as the *Niger* sailed out of the harbour bound for Lisbon. On 5 November a violent storm hit the small vessel with the force of an explosion, and very nearly proved a complete disaster for Banks.

We had a very hard gale of wind off the Western Islands which has almost ruined me. In the course of it we shipped a sea which stove in our quarter and almost filled the cabin with water in an instant, where it washed backwards and forwards with such rapidity that it broke in pieces every chair and table in the place. Among other things that suffered my poor box of seeds was one, which was entirely demolished as was my box of earth with plants in it which stood upon the deck.

The loss of the seeds and the plant box was a heavy blow, but the rest of his collection appears to have survived more or less intact, but one does wonder whether the porcupine, presented to him by a sergeant of marines, was also in the cabin during the flood. Certainly he got the animal back to England, because Pennant saw it, but by then it may well have been dead.

Apart from the box and the seeds the damage was very slight, and he successfully brought home a large and valuable collection of plants, both cryptogams (non-flowering plants) and flowering plants, as well as animals, birds and fishes.

The *Niger* was breaking her journey at Portugal, and on 17 November sailed into the River Tagus. The approach to Lisbon was hardly the friendliest in the world. The edgy Portuguese, Banks observed, had lined the shore with small batteries :

The whole way from the Rock of Lisbon, St Julian's Castle (St Juliao de Barra) mounts a great many guns, but the people must be dreadfully exposed to the shot of any ship that attempted it.

The Bugio lighthouse and the Torre de Belem were all bristling with ordnance.

While the approach to Lisbon was threatening, Banks found the people kind, although he was disappointed that there was no entertaining in Portuguese homes, at least not for foreigners. He put it down to the poor standard of living even among 'their first people living in a style much inferior even to our merchants who reside among them'. But he was offered boxes at the opera and every civility.

He disliked the oppressive laws of the country, and was mildly scathing about the power of the Catholic Church in Portugal, although, perhaps this was little more than a typical response from a Protestant eighteenth-century Englishman.

Banks's journal covering his six weeks stay in Lisbon is slightly disapproving and suggests that he really had a rather boring time.

But this was not strictly true. He visited gardens, and became a member of the English colony's Natural History Society, and rapidly became one of its most popular, if transitory, members. But more importantly he met most of the leading Portuguese scientists of the day, notably the botanists Domingo Vandelli, and João de Luoreiro. The friendships were maintained over the years, and the men were in the habit of exchanging various botanical specimens collected in all parts of the world.

Those meetings with men of science in Lisbon really marked the start of what was to become an important part of Banks's life, that is the international correspondence he maintained with scientists. It was a correspondence that was to grow to mammoth proportions, and cut across the restrictions of diplomatic and inter-government feuding, and even wars.

It might seem naive, but Banks did not believe that politics or national boundaries should in any way interfere with the free exchange of scientific information, or the free movement of men seeking out the new wonders of nature. Had such a generous philosophy been fully accepted civilisation would have been all the richer for it.

At the end of 1766 Banks arrived home. The voyage to Newfoundland and Labrador had confirmed for him that his career would be one of discovery, however arduous and dangerous the journeys. No sooner was he reunited with his family than he was planning fresh expeditions.

Sailing barges bringing cargoes up the Thames to Chelsea gave Joseph Banks his first taste of the world beyond his comfortable London home and the family estates at Revesby Abbey in Lincolnshire, and inspired him later to observe of the Grand Tour: 'Every blockhead does that: my Grand Tour shall be one round the whole globe' (*Kensington Chelsea Public Libraries*)

When the Endeavour dropped anchor at Tierra del Fuego, Banks and Solander were the first to make contact with the timorous natives. It was the first time that Banks demonstrated his remarkable ability to communicate with primitive people

CHAPTER 3

VIA WALES TO THE PACIFIC

During his absence exploring and collecting in Newfoundland and Labrador, Banks was elected a Fellow of the Royal Society. At only twenty-three, he was remarkably young for such a distinction. His critics have been quick to point out that his wealth and position bought his Fellowship, and it was true that in the eighteenth century the Royal Society had more noblemen among its Fellows than practical working scientists. But Banks could justifiably lay claim to being an academically trained botanist, and when the extent of his Newfoundland and Labrador collections became known, no-one could deny that he had proved himself a first-rate field collector.

The *Niger*, with Banks aboard, docked at Plymouth towards the end of January 1766. Apart from getting his collections to safety, he now had to split his time between seeing to the affairs of Revesby, and settling into a recently bought house in New Burlington Street.

On 15 February 1767 he attended his first meeting of the Royal Society. Now he had unfettered access to the best minds in the country, and he revelled in their conversation and company, and most of the Fellows he met were attracted by his apparently boundless energy and enthusiasm. His booming voice and bluntness, from time to time earned him some enemies, when his directness seemed to border on rudeness, but nobody could gainsay his generosity, particularly in making available his collections and library, both of which were rapidly growing.

But however stimulating the company of philosophers, or however diverting the soirées and dinner parties where he would hold the floor with accounts of his recent travels, Banks was soon feeling restless. In the early spring he was in Kent collecting plants, shells and fossils, and gathering information on subjects as diverse as the manufacture of vitriol and the conduct of a court martial.

In May he set off for the West Country, staying for some days with his aunt, Mrs Grenville, at her home at Eastbury. He visited fine country houses, and examined the products of archaeological digs, and as always fresh specimens were collected for his herbarium.

His old friend Thomas Pennant had asked him to visit him in Flintshire, but Banks was suddenly seized with an overwhelming desire to sit at the feet of the great Carl Linnaeus, and to become his student, although he perfectly well understood the Linnean system of classifying plants, animals, birds and fish.

He wrote to Pennant from London :

What will you say to me if I should be prevented from paying my respects to you and North Wales this year, tho' I so fully intend it. Nothing but your looking upon it with the eye of an unprejudiced natural historian can bring any excuse to be heard with patience. Look then with zoologick eyes and tell me if you could blame me if I sacrificed every consideration to an opportunity of paying a visit to our master, Linnaeus, and profiting by his lectures before he dies, who is now so old he cannot long last.

I know you cannot blame me and you will not when I tell you that nothing shall hinder my attendance in Flintshire but such an expedition.

Not only did he plan to study under the old master, but then to go on from Uppsala in Sweden on an expedition to Lapland.

In the event Banks did not go to Sweden, but to Wales instead, a journey that was originally planned on a modest scale but expanded into a long expedition across Wales from south to north, and over the border to Cheshire, Derbyshire, and homeward through Warwickshire, Oxfordshire and Berkshire. In these days of motorways it is a trip that could be completed in a matter of hours, but on eighteenth-century roads by coach and on horseback it was a long and arduous venture. In fact it took Banks from 13 August 1767 until 29 January 1768.

As in all Banks's journeys it was devoted to collecting and observation. He got no further than Bayswater before he was making notes of some particularly fine elders growing near a brewhouse, and receiving gifts of plants from his fellow botanist, the Rev John Lightfoot at Uxbridge.

He called on Dr Sibthorp in Oxford, and paused in Gloucester to tour the Cathedral. In the Forest of Dean he failed to spot any deer, 'but was told that there are a few, tho' they are almost lost, on account of the great number of deerstealers in the neighbourhood' he wrote in his journal.

By 21 August he was deep in Wales and shooting grouse on the hills, and at the end of the month and early in September he was making careful observations on the Welsh method of gathering in the harvest, which he found impressive.

It was while he was in Wales that he met an extraordinary Methodist teacher Hoel (*sic*) Harris.

Harris started life as a village schoolmaster, but managed to obtain a commission in the Militia, but once a captain needed money to support his new position in life. Here Banks takes up the story:

He began to cast about for the easiest way to get some. That of a Methodist Teacher seemed the least troublesome and he immediately began the trade : shrewd and cunning enough he soon became a saint, and so established a one that it was not in the power of anything in the world to alter the opinion the people had conceived of his holiness, which they deemed infallible, as this story fairly proves.

While he was in North Wales preaching he was received into the house of one of the faithful, who caressed him, as everyone did who was happy to receive so great a saint into their houses, a mark of distinction which none but the most pious were honoured with.

The wife of this family was handsome enough to move the passions of our Apostle; what does he, but immediately begins to seduce her, easily effects it, carries her away from her husband, and lives with her three or four years, as great a saint as ever.

He is now situate in the old house, which he may be said to have preached into a very comfortable one by this method : in the course of his excursions he persuaded his disciples that the only way to enjoy true piety and holiness was to come to Trevicca, where he would preach to them and take care to feed, lodge them etc., that they should work for the general stock and live together like a family of love. Of these people, he himself told me, he has more than a hundred and forty in his family, indeed the whole village of Trevicca belongs to him. These have built him a very good house, and now that is furnished they are sent about the country to gentlemen's houses, where they do any kind of jobs that are wanted, bringing their wages constantly to him. Those who are not artificers are employed at home in spinning, combing, weaving, knitting, each according to their abilities and a ware house is kept by him, where their work is disposed of.

As he made his stately progress across Wales, Banks studied ruins, ancient carvings, fossils; he studied the local agriculture and watched men fishing from coracles; he examined the inscriptions on gravestones, and tramped round castles.

His journal of the journey is peppered with minute detail, local history, carefully recorded legends, and scientific observation.

By early December he reached Cheadle where he had an estate, which he found 'in better order than I expected, except that the tenants have lopped the timber more than I should choose they shall in future'.

Most of his stay was involved in estate business and settling a number of disputes that had arisen. But there was time to visit a copper mine owned by the Duke of Devonshire, and he travelled to Worsley to see the work on the Duke of Bridgwater's navigation.

There was weaving at Rochdale to be observed, as well as coal-mining before moving on to Northwich to see the salt works.

Nothing seemed to miss his eye; iron works, wagon building, gun-making, they were all worthy of study.

Everywhere he went curiosities and oddities were produced for his inspection, and by the time he reached Lichfield even Banks was beginning to flag. There he was taken to see a Mr Newton,

... a gentleman who is lately returned from the East Indies with a vast fortune and is consequently called the Nabob. His collection consists of heaps of shells, sometimes whole drawers full of one species, among these some good ones, especially an echinus of a species entirely new to me.

But Banks had to pay dearly for these finds :

As a punishment for the small pleasure I had received from the echinus, I was obliged to admire drawers full of Indian weapons, fly flaps, and pictures of the Nabob and his court, letters from him to Mr Newton in Indian language, and closets full of china. Defend me, I say, from a Nabob's collection unless half an hour at least is given me to use as I list : never, never again to capitulate unless such terms are before agreed upon.

Laden with biological and geological specimens, fossils, flint arrow-heads, ancient coins, gifts, pages of notes, indeed the typical cargo of the curious traveller, Banks must have been glad to return to the comfort of New Burlington Street. The last stretch of the journey had been beset with bad weather, a fact that Pennant sympathised with, although he sagely remarked that the 'perils of snow and ice' would prove a useful preparation for the projected Lapland expedition.

But Lapland was to pale into insignificance when Banks learned of plans for another more exotic journey.

In 1639 a young clergyman with a scientific bent had observed the Transit of Venus when the planet passes in a direct line between the earth and the sun. From his parsonage in Hoole in Lancashire he had tried, and failed, to calculate from the transit the exact distance between the earth and the sun. Such a measurement, it was believed, would be the key to more accurate navigation.

The transit occurred again in 1761, and again the observations were a total failure, but what was known was that the transit would reoccur in June 1769, and after that there would not be another chance to make observations until 1874. It was vital, therefore, that observations in 1769 should succeed. This was recognised by the Royal Society, and discussions on the most promising locations began in 1766. Banks undoubtedly heard about them although it is doubtful as a new Fellow that he would have been asked to take part in them.

One area which particularly appealed to the Royal Society was the Pacific Ocean. Islands in the Ocean were known, but the ships that had visited them either kept poor navigational records, or the governments of their home countries were reluctant to part with potentially valuable information to other nations.

While influential, the Royal Society was a relatively poor organisation. It certainly could not afford to fit out an expedition from its own purse, but it did petition the King for £4,000 and a vessel, and the Government through the Admiralty, decided to back the expedition.

Even before the Pacific destination had been decided, the Admiralty put the project in hand, and it proved to be one of those rare occasions when officialdom made all the right decisions, or at least one that was to have far-reaching and profitable results.

Turning down the Royal Society's nominee to lead the expedition, the Admiralty chose James Cook, a sailor who was little-known outside naval circles, and who had not even been commissioned. However, he had made a considerable reputation for himself as a brilliant navigator and cartographer in Canada.

It was Cook who had carried General James Wolfe and his force through the dangerous waters of the St Lawrence to the successful storming of Quebec, and he had also distinguished himself as a marine surveyor in Newfoundland.

Cook was also one of a growing number of men from working-class backgrounds who were to take their places among the giants of the eighteenth century. His sea-going career began as an apprentice on the small Yorkshire colliers which traded down the east coast. He rose rapidly through the ranks and could doubtless have enjoyed a prosperous career in the merchant navy, but instead he chose to join the Royal Navy as an able seaman, and start again virtually at the bottom of the ladder.

When it came to a choice of a vessel for the projected trip Cook returned to his origins and asked for a Whitby collier, 'cats' as they were known. A man-of-war would have been more commodious and faster, but its draught was too deep, in his view, for the purpose. A flat-bottomed Yorkshire cat, Cook knew, could scape over uncharted reefs and shallows and very likely survive.

Following his advice the Admiralty bought a collier, the *Earl of Pembroke*, and renamed it the *Endeavour*. The tiny ship was destined to sail into history, for not only did the Admiralty want it to carry scientists to observe the Transit of Venus, it also had a greater enterprise in mind—to establish once and for all if there was indeed a great undiscovered continent in the south.

Generations had argued for and against the existence of the Southern Continent. Many old maps of the world included a vague, incomplete profile of Terra Australis Incognita, the Unknown Southern Land, and it was hotly argued that it must exist as a counter-balance to the known great land masses. Certainly it was known that there was land in the Pacific Ocean. The great sixteenth-century Spanish navigators such as Torres and Quiros had penetrated deeply into the Ocean and sighted and landed on many islands. Nearly half way through the seventeenth century the Dutch navigator, Tasman, had discovered Tasmania, and sighted and followed for a distance the western coast of New Zealand. His discoveries added support to the notion of Terra Australis Incognita.

Twenty-two years after Tasman's discoveries the British started taking a serious interest in the Pacific. Although the spirit of adventure was abroad, the reasons were largely practical. There was serious disquiet in the American colonies, which the farsighted could see would only be settled by armed conflict, and Britain might need a new source of cheap colonial wealth. Also the Spaniards had revived their interest in the Pacific, and were endeavouring to blockade the area to exclude other nations from profitable exploration.

Britain's first expedition of two vessels—the *Dolphin* and the *Tamar* —was largely unsuccessful. Two years later Captain Samuel Wallis, commanding the *Dolphin*, a frigate of the sixth rate, sailed accompanied by the *Swallow*. He at least was successful in fixing the position of Tahiti, and this was to prove of greater value than might at first have been supposed.

The groundwork for the Transit of Venus expedition had been well advanced when Wallis returned, and hearing of the scheme declared that he had discovered the perfect location, Tahiti, or King George the Third Island as it had now been named. It had a fine harbour in Matavai Bay, abundant fresh water and food, friendly natives, and good sites for a camp and observatory.

Wallis convinced the Royal Society, and it asked the navy to carry its astronomers to the island. It also made another request, and that was that :

Joseph Banks Esq., Fellow of the Society, a gentleman of large fortune, who is well versed in natural history, being desirous of undertaking the same voyage, the Council very earnestly request their Lordships, that in regard to Mr Banks's great personal merit and for the advancement of useful knowledge, he also, together with his suite, being seven persons more, that is, eight persons in all together with their baggage, be received on board of the ship, under the command of Captain Cook.

There is no doubt that Banks had lobbied furiously to be included in the expedition. He would have done so had it only been a voyage to Tahiti and back, but it is extremely likely that he got wind of the sealed orders that had been passed to Cook, now promoted to a Captain for the expedition.

Cook described his special orders in his *Journal of the Endeavour Voyage* :

I was therefore ordered to proceed directly to Otaheite (Tahiti) and, after the astronomical observations should be completed, to prosecute the design of making discoveries in the South Pacific Ocean by proceeding to the south as far as latitude of 40°; then if I found no land, to proceed to the west between 40° and 35° till I fell in with New Zealand, which I was to explore and thence to return to England by such route as I should think proper.

The orders went even further. They said :

You are also to be careful to observe the nature of the soil and the products thereof, the beasts and fowls that inhabit or frequent it; the fishes that are to be found in the rivers or upon the coast, and in what plenty, and in case you find any mines, minerals or valuable stones, you are to bring home specimens of each, as also such specimens as the seeds of trees, of fruits and grains as you may be able to collect, and transmit them to our secretary that we may cause proper examination and experiments to be made of them.

What better man than Joseph Banks to undertake the scientific side of the expedition. Certainly that was his view when he became aware of the whole purpose of the expedition. He was determined to sail with the *Endeavour*, and he had the means to see his determination fulfilled. He had money and he had influential friends in the Royal Society, and in the person of his old fishing companion, Lord Sandwich, a powerful voice to speak up for him at the Admiralty, a body which was notoriously suspicious of civilians who wanted to join naval expeditions.

In the face of such lobbying it is perhaps not surprising that their Lordships agreed to allow Banks and his party to join in the adventure. No doubt they were also attracted by the fact that Banks was prepared to finance his part of the undertaking, at a cost to himself, it is estimated, of £10,000, an enormous sum in those days.

With the backing now of both the Royal Society and the Admiralty, Banks set about his preparations with his customary enthusiasm and disregard for expense. Once again his family and some close friends were alarmed by the dangers he faced. Certainly he had returned safely from Newfoundland and Labrador, that was at least a well-tried journey, but to circumnavigate the world was something quite different. Once again he was urged to settle for a less ambitious expedition, but he brushed aside the alarms, commenting: 'Every blockhead does that; my Grand Tour shall be one round the whole globe.'

Others entered into the spirit of the adventure and inundated him with advice. Leading among them was his good friend Thomas Pennant. He advised Banks to hide between the pages of his books any pictures made on the voyage to avoid paying customs duty on his return; urged him to take a plentiful supply of umbrellas as a defence against rain and sun; to take as well good oil-skins; and he recommended a good water dog or two, 'also a fleet dog to pull down the guanocos'.

Thomas Falconer wrote tedious letters about geography and geographers, both subjects that Banks found exceedingly boring.

But a great deal of the help he received was valuable, even life-saving. Dr Nathaniel Holme, a naval surgeon who had made a special study of scurvy, the most common and deadly disease among seamen of those days, made him up a quantity of concentrated lemon juice, which Banks drank with brandy as a successful cure whenever he developed symptoms of scurvy.

He scoured London for the best provisioners, finding 'much the best salt beef I have ever tasted' in a butcher in New Crane Street, small beer from a supplier near St Giles, and porter from another man at Wapping New Stairs. There were barrels of salted cabbage, and sheep, fowls and pigs brought aboard for him and his party.

Banks chose his party with care. His number two was Daniel Carl Solander, an outstanding Swedish naturalist who had been a favourite pupil of Linnaeus, and who was currently working for the British Museum.

Sydney Parkinson, John Reynolds and Alexander Buchan were the artists, with Herman Sporing an assistant draughtsman. Two servants— James Roberts and Peter Briscoe—came from Revesby; in addition there were two negro servants and, of course, Banks's two greyhounds.

John Ellis, a naturalist and Fellow of the Royal Society, gave some idea of the extent of Banks's equipment in a letter to Linneaus, informing the master that Solander was to sail in the *Endeavour*.

No people ever went to sea better fitted out for the purpose of natural history, nor more elegantly. They have got a fine library of natural history; they have all sorts of machines for catching and preserving insects; all kinds of nets, trawls, drags and hooks for coral fishing; they have even a curious contrivance of a telescope, by which, put into the water, you can see the bottom to a great depth, where it is clear. They have many cases of bottles with ground stoppers, of several sizes, to preserve animals in spirits. They have the several sorts of salts to surround the seeds; and wax, both beeswax and that of the Myrica.

Despite the organisation involved, seeing that the equipment and stores were correct and in the best condition, supervising the packing and crating as well as making constant visits to the *Endeavour* to oversee the stowing of his cargo, Banks also found time to meet and correspond with fellow naturalists.

It was not only the serious side of life that he attended to. There was a round of dinners and parties, and the taking of fond farewells, some of them very fond indeed. The fondest, without doubt, involved a Miss Harriet Blosset. She was the middle of three daughters of an apparently well-to-do family. Her eldest sister was tall, handsome and somewhat dominating; her youngest demure, mousy and a devout Methodist, while Harriet was pretty, flighty and not over-bright. Such a handsome, romantic figure as Joseph Banks was irresistible to her. Until then a prudent flirt, she now set no limits in her eagerness to please her lover, and Banks, who had a hearty sexual appetite, became infatuated by her. He spent his last night in London with Harriet before sailing. They went to the opera, *La Buona Figliuola* by Niccoló Piccinni—then all the rage—and on to a supper party.

This last night, during which Banks was elated and not a little drunk, was witnessed by Horace Benedict de Saussure, a distinguished Swiss geologist and physicist, and one of the first men to climb Mont Blanc, who was in London at the time with his wife.

In his journal he recalled the evening:

Saw for the first time Miss Harriet Blosset, with Mr Banks, her betrothed. Returned on foot from the opera with them and supped together.

It seems that most of the Blosset family were at the party, for de Saussure continues:

The eldest daughter, tall, decided, agreeable, a great musician, splendid voice, fond of society, polished. The second, Miss Harriet, desperately in love with Mr Banks, from whom she was to part the next day—a hitherto prudent coquette, but now only intent on pleasing her lover, and resolved to spend in the country all the time he is away. The youngest, a Methodist devotee, delighted to pass two or three years in the country with her sister and live out of the world. The mother, a good natured little woman, talking politics. As Banks cannot speak a word of French, I could not judge of his abilities. He seems to have a prodigious zest for natural history . . . Miss Blosset, not knowing that he is to start next day, was quite gay. Banks drank freely to hide his feelings.

And thus Banks left London with a flourish, leaving behind an agitated mother and sister, an anxious and admiring friend, and poor love-struck Miss Blosset, devotedly awaiting his return and distractedly making him fancy waistcoats.

On 16 August 1768, Banks and his entourage, obeying a summons from Cook, set off for Plymouth where the *Endeavour* was moored and ready to set off for the south seas. There was a short delay while final adjustments were made and last-minute baggage stowed.

At three o'clock on the afternoon of the twenty-fifth, the anchors were raised and the *Endeavour* slipped slowly out of Plymouth Sound and made for the open sea. By sunset on that August day she was a tiny dot on a great shining gun-metal sea. Only 106ft long, she seemed barely large enough to hold the ninety-four officers, scientists, seamen and marines crammed aboard her—a little flat-bottomed, three-masted collier wallowing, almost waddling off, on one of the greatest adventures in maritime history.

Banks nicknamed her 'Mrs *Endeavour*', and it was apt, for she was a stout, reliable body who took everything as it came calmly and unhurriedly. She was a craft of 368 tons, about half the tonnage of the *Niger*. At her greatest breadth she was 29ft 3in, and her depth, 11ft.

The start of the voyage was uneventful as the vessel was wafted along by a steady breeze. Banks and Solander observed porpoises and discovered a minute marine insect in some water that was being used to season a cask, but by the twenty-ninth the fair breeze had stiffened into a hard gale. Banks's belief that he had overcome sea-sickness during his trip to Canada was shattered—he was violently ill.

For the following two weeks Banks and Solander collected what they could from the sea, although their endeavours were hampered by Richmond, one of the negro servants, losing a net overboard. The spare nets were in the hold and could not be got at.

On 12 September the first landfall was made at Madeira, although from a naturalist's point of view it was a poor time of the year. Returning from a day on the island Banks wrote :

The season of the year was undoubtedly the worst for both plants and insects, for being the height of the vintage, when nothing is green in the country but just on the verge of small brooks.

Despite the unfavourable conditions he was still able to collect over 300 different plants.

The stay on Madeira also enabled Banks to test one of the two electrical machines he had brought with him. Exactly why he took the machines with him is not clear. The experiment he made lacked any real scientific form. Perhaps it was just that he could never resist any new gadgetry, and the most likely explanation is that he took them along as a hedge against boredom.

The machines, hand-cranked electrometers, produced a current that gave an electric shock that varied in intensity in a thoroughly haphazard way. The machine he used on Madeira had been made by Jesse Ramsden, a famous instrument-maker of the time. Banks was able to use it to take his revenge on the hapless governor of the island. He only had a few days in which to make his collections and observations and one of these was completely wasted waiting for the governor to call.

He recorded :

One day, however, we had a visit from the Governor, of which we had notice before and were obliged to stay at home, so that unsought honour lost us very near the whole day, a very material part of the short time we were allowed to stay upon the island.

We, however, contrived to revenge ourselves upon his Excellency, by an electrical machine which we had on board; upon his expressing a desire to see it we sent for it ashore, and shocked him full as much as he chose.

On 18 September the *Endeavour* was under way again, driven along by a light breeze, which enabled Banks and his party to use casting nets and gather what they could from the ocean. Five days later when they were called on deck to see the Pike of Teneriffe, a rare oceanic fish, which Banks called Scomber Serpens (*Gempylus serpens*), was caught. It was an exciting capture since only one other specimen was known to be in existence, and that was one taken by Sir Hans Sloane some years before during his passage to Jamaica.

A few days later there was further excitement when a young shark, which was following the ship, was hooked and hauled aboard. It carried the added bonus of four sucking fish (*Remora remora*) which joined the *Gempylus* in pickling spirits, while the shark was cut up for the midday meal.

Not withstanding it was twelve o'clock before the shark was taken, we made shift to have a part of him stewed for dinner, and very good meat he was, at least in the opinion of Dr Solander and myself, tho' some of the seamen did not seem to be fond of him, probably from some prejudice founded on the species sometimes feeding on human flesh.

Quite clearly Banks had a very strong stomach, perhaps fortified by his overwhelming curiosity and the willingness to try almost anything new. Throughout the voyage his menus ranged widely over such unlikely delicacies as sharks and vegetable-fed dogs.

October came in calmly. A young, yellow wagtail sought sanctuary on the vessel, and proved so tame that Banks made a pet of it until it was killed by the ship's cat. Swallows were taken, one had died from exhaustion on the deck, and fishing with both lines and nets was fruitful.

With the calms setting in, early in the month Banks and Solander were able to take a small boat and work on the sea around the *Endeavour*. These expeditions were particularly productive, adding handsomely to the growing collection of surface creatures—jellyfish and marine snails, such as *Janthina janthina*, which float in a cluster of air bubbles. At the same time Banks was able to shoot sea birds.

By the sixteenth the boating trips were frustrated by 'a fine breeze of wind', but he was comforted by

. . . the opportunity of seeing a phenomenon I had never before met with, a lunar rainbow which appeared about ten o'clock very faint and almost or quite without colour, so that it could be traced by little more than an appearance which looked like shade on a cloud.

The day after sighting the lunar rainbow Banks was able to get out in his boat, but the trip was completely fruitless and the return of the fresh breezes once again meant further enforced idleness. He felt bored and trapped on the tiny ship. Even an attempt at keep fit exercises had the opposite effect. On the eighteenth he glumly wrote in his journal :

This evening trying as I have often (foolishly no doubt) done to exercise myself by playing tricks with two ropes in the cabin I got a fall which hurt me a good deal and alarmed me more, as the blow was on my head, and two hours after it I was taken with sickness in my stomach which made me fear some ill consequence.

Was Banks really trying to skip with two ropes in a cabin measuring 6ft by 6ft 7in?

A week later, however, there was some light relief when the *Endeavour* 'crossed the line' and the ceremony of ducking the ship's company was performed.

About dinner time a list was brought into the cabin containing the names of everybody and thing aboard the ship, in which the dogs and cats were not forgot; to this was affixed a petition, signed by the ship's company, desiring leave to examine everybody in that list that it might be known whether or not they had crossed the line before. This was immediately granted; everybody was then called upon the quarter deck and examined by one of the lieutenants who had crossed, he marked every name either to be ducked or let off according as their qualifications directed.

Captain Cook and Dr Solander were on the black list, as were myself, my servants and dogs, which I was obliged to compound for by giving the duckers a certain quantity of brandy for which they willingly excused us the ceremony.

Many of the men, however, chose to be ducked rather than give up four days allowance of wine which was the price fixed upon, and as for the boys they were always ducked, of course; so that about twenty-one underwent the ceremony which was performed thus :

A block was made fast to the end of the main yard and a long line reved through it, to which three cross-pieces of wood were fastened, one of which was put between the legs of the man who was to be ducked and to this he was tied very fast, another was for him to hold in his hands and the third was over his head lest the rope should be hoisted too near the block and by that means the man be hurt. When he was fastened upon this machine the Boatswain gave the command by his whistle and the man was hoisted up as far as the cross-piece over his head would allow, when another signal was made and immediately the rope was let go and his own weight carried him down, he was immediately hoisted up again and three times served in this manner which was every man's allowance.

Thus ended the diversion of the day, for the ducking lasted till almost night, and sufficiently diverting it certainly was to see the different faces that were made on this occasion, some grinning and exalted in their hardiness, whilst others were almost suffocated and came up ready enough to have compounded after the first or second duck, had such a proceeding been allowable.

As the *Endeavour* sailed steadily towards the coast of South America so the atmosphere became heavy and humid.

Almost immediately on crossing the tropic the air became sensibly much damper than usual, tho' not materially hotter, the thermometer then in general stood from 80 to 82. The nearer we approached to the calms still damper everything grew. This was perceivable even to the human body and very much so, but more remarkably upon all kinds of furniture : everything made of iron rusted so fast that the knives in people's pockets became almost useless, and the razors in cases not free. All kinds of leather became mouldy. Portfolios and trunks covered with black leather were almost white. Soon after this mould adhered to almost anything, all the books in my library became mouldy so that they were obliged to be wiped to preserve them.

Many of the crew went down with bilious attacks, but Banks remained in perfect health, which he put down to regular bathing.

In the failing evening light of 29 October Banks stood on the deck entranced by one of nature's more spectacular illumination displays.

This evening the sea appeared uncommonly beautiful, flashes of light coming from it perfectly resembling small flashes of lightning, and these so frequent that sometimes eight or ten were visible at the same moment.

Opinions were divided as to the cause of the spectacle. Some seamen said they were caused by fish leaping after lesser prey, others that the light came from blubbers (jellyfish). Banks went fishing for the lights with a landing net. 'They proved to be a species of medusa which when brought on board appeared like metal violently heated, emitting a white light.' Among them were minute crabs which gave off a light like the common hedgerow glow-worm.

The rest of the month and the early part of November passed quietly as the *Endeavour* followed her course to Brazil at a gentle, stately pace—Mrs *Endeavour* at her most dignified. By 6 November soundings proved that they were sailing thirty-two fathoms above coral reefs, and two days later they came up with a fishing boat. Banks and Solander went aboard and traded for fish for the ship's company. Throughout the voyage Banks was to do most of the marketing. For a man who had been condemned both at Eton and Oxford for his inability to learn languages, albeit dead ones, he demonstrated a remarkable talent for making himself understood throughout his many travels.

For the following five days the *Endeavour* cruised down the coast of Brazil to Rio de Janeiro, which was reached on 13 November. Since Britain's relationship with Portugal was good, Cook and the entire ship's company looked forward to a warm and friendly reception, fresh supplies and perhaps some agreeable socializing ashore. They were to be sadly disappointed.

Approaching in a calm, Cook sent his first lieutenant, Zachary Hicks, ahead in a boat to pick up a pilot, but instead of a pilot the boat returned with a Portuguese subaltern and word that Hicks had been detained until Cook himself went ashore. A dozen soldiers then turned up in a ten-oared vessel and rowed menacingly around, followed shortly by yet another boat containing a Portuguese colonel and a civil servant who interrogated the ship's company about the purpose of the visit. He also said they would have to wait two days before being allowed to take on fresh water.

The following day Cook went ashore to see the Viceroy, Don Antonio Rolim de Moura, and returned with a Portuguese officer who was clearly a member of the Viceroy's security staff, as well as an Englishman, Thomas Forster, a lieutenant in the Portuguese army.

Cook brought bad news to Banks. Neither he nor Solander could live ashore while the *Endeavour* was at Rio, and indeed, only Cook and such sailors as he might need would be allowed ashore. All Banks's plans to make a Brazilian collection were dashed.

But Banks was not to be put off. That evening he and Solander dressed with care and set off across the harbour to the town 'under the pretence of a visit to the Viceroy', but their shore boat was intercepted by a guard boat, and despite all their efforts they were forced back. Cook stormed ashore to complain to the Viceroy who claimed he was acting on the direct orders of the King of Portugal.

With uncharacteristic guile Cook told de Moura that his ship needed repairs and that under the circumstances 'the gentlemen'—Banks and party—could not remain aboard. The Viceroy agreed. They could come ashore and live under house arrest, and that the guards would have orders 'not to let us stir out or anyone come in on any pretence whatever.'

Banks and Cook were furious. For Englishmen on their country's business to be treated in this manner was unendurable. Some idea of the frustration Banks suffered is illustrated in a letter that Solander wrote to Ellis from Rio.

The Viceroy has been so infernally cross and ill-natured, as to forbid us to set our feet on dry land. How mortifying that must be to me and Mr Banks you best can feel, especially if you suppose yourself within a quarter of a mile of a shore covered with palms of several sorts, fine large trees and shrubs, whose very blossoms have such an influence upon us, that we have ventured to bribe people to collect them, and send them on board as greens and salading for our table.

He went on to describe how he and Banks were reduced to foraging through the greenstuff brought on board to feed the sheep and goats.

Solander did manage to get ashore masquerading as the surgeon's mate and was allowed to buy dried plants, seeds and roots from the apothecary's shops, and even snatched the odd growing plant and insect.

Banks and Cook worked off some of their ire in writing memorials to de Moura complaining bitterly at his treatment of them. In his memorial Banks clearly, and in cold, polite terms, set out precisely the role he was playing in the expedition. De Moura did not doubt his explanation, but merely remarked that he should have brought letters of commission from the King of England. To this Banks pointed out that he was sailing under the King. The Viceroy would not be moved.

Whether de Moura really was acting on orders from his monarch or was simply being bloody-minded, is not clear. What is clear, however, is that he did not really believe that the *Endeavour* was a vessel of the Royal Navy. He even accused Cook of being a smuggler, and suggested that the British were great forgers and that that would account for Cook's official papers. Cook commented scathingly to de Moura that it would be hard to forge officers' and marines' uniforms.

Nothing would convince the Viceroy, but neither would Banks be deflected from his determination to get ashore. In his journal he records in the entry for 26 November: 'I myself went ashore this morn before daybreak and stayed till dark night.'

The gateway to the Chelsea Physic Gardens in Chelsea, where the young Joseph Banks studied the exotic plants grown by the great botanist and gardener, Philip Miller, author of the classic 'Gardener's Dictionary' *(Kensington & Chelsea Public Libraries)*

Chelsea was still a village, in 1761, when the 18-year-old Banks moved with his mother, and sister, Sarah Sophia, to Turret House in Paradise Row. Although separated from his beloved Lincolnshire he was able to study botany in the lanes and water-meadows surrounding his new home (*Kensington & Chelsea Public Libraries*)

What in fact happened was that Banks and several of the crew lowered themselves on a rope out of a cabin window into a boat and drifted in the dark until they were out of hearing of the guard boat, and then rowed quietly ashore. They were careful to keep clear of the town, but otherwise they were able to make friendly contact with the farmers and peasants. Banks wrote :

While I was ashore, I met several of the inhabitants who were very civil to me, taking me to their own houses where I bought of them stock for the ship tolerably cheap, a porker middlingly fat for eleven shillings, a muscovy duck something under two shillings, etc.

He worked frantically during the few hours he had ashore collecting plants and insects, shot a bird, had time to examine crops growing in gardens and fields, and even made a hurried survey of the seashore. It must have been the first, and possibly the last, commando raid by a biologist.

Word of the landing reached the Viceroy who sent out search parties to find Banks and his companions, a fruitless task since by then he was safely back on board. But he was fortunate that he was not taken, because he would undoubtedly have been treated as a spy, and at best have been jailed. Some of the *Endeavour* crew had been imprisoned briefly, beaten by the soldiers who took them and 'confined in a loathsome dungeon where their companions were chiefly blacks who were chained.'

But the Viceroy was able to take his revenge for being tricked by arresting Thomas Forster, a number of Englishmen living in Rio and a Portuguese who had helped the *Endeavour* crew who were sent ashore to buy provisions. Forster was accused of smuggling goods ashore from the *Endeavour*—a false charge which was never formally made, but that did not prevent him remaining in prison for a considerable time before he was able to ship back to Portugal.

On 2 December 1768 Banks was able to record :

This morn, thank God, we have got all we want from these illiterate, impolite gentry, so we got up our anchor and sailed to the point of Ilhoa dos Cobras, where we lay and wait for a fair wind which should come every night from the land.

While they were waiting for a fair wind a Spanish brig arrived and the captain, Don Antonio de Monte Negro y Velasco offered to carry letters to Europe, which gave Cook the opportunity to write to the Admiralty a detailed account of the *Endeavour*'s reception at Rio, and for Banks to write an equally aggrieved account to Lord Morton, President of the Royal Society.

Banks described being confined to the ship by the Portuguese while a wealth of material awaited his collection as being like the punishment of Tantalus, who was punished by the gods by being forced to stand in a pool up to his chin, the water of which always receded out of reach when he stooped to drink, and surrounded by fruit always beyond his grasp.

Caught in a calm, Cook ordered boats and crews over the side in an attempt to tow the *Endeavour* out to sea. As they passed the main fortification on the approach to Rio two shots were fired at them, one ball narrowly missing the main mast.

It was not until 7 December that the vessel got under way, and Banks, with relief, was able to record : 'Now we are fairly at sea and have entirely got rid of these troublesome people.'

Despite the incredible difficulties they faced, Banks and Solander were able to collect no less than 315 biological specimens from Rio. And while he was unable to visit the town himself, by cross-questioning Solander and Monkhouse, the ship's surgeon, both of whom got into Rio, he was able to give a remarkably detailed account of the place.

The cruise down the South Atlantic coast of South America towards Tierra del Fuego and the notorious Cape Horn was relatively uneventful. The weather was changeable with heavy swells making work on board difficult. Considerable collections of birds and marine life were made. It was a period of steady and useful work, with a break for Christmas Day, the expedition's first.

Banks wrote :

Christmas Day; all good Christians, that is to say all hands get abominably drunk so that at night there was scarce a sober man in the ship. Wind, thank God, very moderate or the Lord knows what would have become of us.

1769 came in with the ship's company in good spirits and full of confidence. 'New year's day today' Banks wrote, 'made us pass many compliments and talk much of our hopes for success in the year '69.'

Large schools of whales swam majestically around the vessel, and the sea was thick with great rafts of giant seaweed.

Early on the morning of the eighth Tierra del Fuego was sighted,

and the *Endeavour* closed with the coast. Banks was agreeably surprised to see that it was well wooded and not as barren as Lord Anson
had described it in the account of his epic voyage. Smoke was visible,
but otherwise there were no other signs of life. To Banks's satisfaction
Cook announced that he intended to land if a harbour could be found.

'To our great joy', Banks wrote the following day, 'we discovered
an opening into the land and stood in for it in great hopes of finding
a harbour,' but his joy was short-lived. Throughout the twelfth and
thirteenth there was a succession of abortive attempts to land, but on
the fourteenth Banks and Solander were able to take a boat ashore
where in four hours they collected 100 plants.

On the following morning Cook took the *Endeavour* into the Bay of
Good Success and came to anchor; after the midday meal a party of
a dozen, including Banks and Solander, went ashore.

Before we had walked 100 yards many Indians made their appearance on
the other side of the bay at the end of a sandy beach which makes the
bottom of the bay, but seeing our numbers to be ten or twelve they retreated.

Dr Solander and myself then walked forward 100 yards before the rest
and two of the Indians advanced also and set themselves down about 50
yards from their companions. As soon as we came up they rose and each
of them threw a stick he had in his hand away from him and us, a token no
doubt of peace. They then walked briskly towards the other party and
waved to us to follow, which we did and were received with many uncouth
signs of friendship.

This was Banks's first encounter in the wild with primitive people.
The fact that he was able to break the ice and gain the trust and
confidence of people who had had little or no contact with Europeans
was to prove invaluable in the months to come.

Banks and Solander distributed beads and ribbons to the Fuegians,
'at which they seemed mightily pleased, so much so that when we
embarked aboard our boat three of them came with us and went
aboard the ship.'

One of them Banks assumed to be 'a priest or conjuror' because at
every new sight on the *Endeavour*, 'he shouted as loud as he could
for some minutes without directing his speech either to us or to any
one of his countrymen.' Banks concluded that he was exorcising the
vessel for the safety of himself and his companions.

They were given a meal of beef and bread, but only picked at it,
packing up most of the food to take away with them, and turning up

their noses at wine and spirits, which they emptied on the deck after tasting.

After about two hours the Fuegians grew restive and made it clear they wanted to go ashore. Banks accompanied them and spent about half an hour with them and the main group, amazed at the apparent indifference of those who had stayed ashore to the experiences of those who had visited the *Endeavour*.

I cannot say that I observed either the one party curious to ask questions or the other to relate what they had seen or what usage they had met with.

Just after dawn the following morning Banks, Solander, Banks's servants, two seamen to help carry baggage and equipment, Monk-house the ship's surgeon, and Charles Green the astronomer, went ashore for a short expedition into the interior. All seemed set for a pleasant and productive excursion. The weather was good: 'Like a sunshiny day in May' was how Banks described it.

We began to enter the woods at a small sandy beach a little to the westward of the watering place and continued to press through pathless thickets, always going up hill till three o'clock before we gained even a near view of the places we intend to go.

The pleasant spring-like weather and the lack of insects had made the going pleasanter, a great deal pleasanter, Banks remarked, than he had experienced in Newfoundland. But there was disappointment ahead. What had appeared from the sea to be clear grass covered tops to the hills turned out to be waist-high birch scrub.

These were so stubborn that they could not be bent out of the way, but at every step the leg must be lifted over them and on being placed on the ground was almost sure to sink above the ankle in bog.

For over a mile they struggled through the scrub and bog before reaching firm ground, and although the party was showing signs of fatigue they were still in high spirits, particularly Banks who anticipated a rich harvest of alpine plants. Once in the open he thought that the party's troubles were at an end, but they had only just begun.

Alexander Buchan, one of Banks's artists, collapsed, seized by a violent fit. Unknown to anyone he was an epileptic and the tough trek had proved too much for him. 'A fire was immediately lit for him and with him all those who were most tired remained behind.' Banks,

Solander, Charles Green and William Monkhouse pressed on up the hill to collect the alpine plants which they found growing in profusion.

At about this time the fine spring weather gave way to icy winds and sudden squalls of snow. The daylight was going and it was clear that the party, with one sick man and others suffering from exhaustion, would never be able to return to the *Endeavour* before dark.

I had now entirely given over all thoughts of reaching the ship that night and thought of nothing but getting into the thick of the woods and making a fire, which as our road lay all down hill seemed very easy to accomplish, so Monkhouse and Green returned to the people and appointed a hill for our general rendezvous.

Banks's plan was to build a shelter, a 'wigwam' he called it, and hole up for the night.

When he returned to Buchan and the people who had stayed behind he was relieved to find the artist much recovered, and the others well, apart from suffering from the cold. They set off back along their approach route heading towards a small valley beyond the dreaded birch bog, with Banks bringing up the rear to urge on stragglers.

We passed about half way very well when the cold seemed to have an effect infinitely beyond what I have ever experienced.

Surprisingly Solander, a tough, resilient man, was the first to go down.

He said he could not go any further but must lay down, though the ground was covered with snow, and down he laid notwithstanding all I could say to the contrary.

Richmond, one of Banks's black servants, also began to suffer acutely from the effects of exposure. Banks sent Buchan and four men ahead to build a fire in the first sheltered spot they came across, while he stayed behind with four other men to bring Solander and Richmond to safety. 'With much persuasion and entreaty we got through much the largest part of the birch when they both gave out.' Richmond collapsed and even when he was told that he would freeze to death he said that he would lie down and die. Solander said he must sleep and did for fifteen minutes. One of the advance party returned to say that a fire and shelter were only a quarter of a mile ahead. This news roused Solander, but Richmond refused to stir. There was nothing to do but leave the negro servant in the care of two seamen who appeared to be suffering less than most from the cold and get Solander to the relative safety of the camp.

With much difficulty I got the doctor to it and as soon as two people were sufficiently warmed sent them out in hopes that they would bring Richmond and the rest.

Half an hour later the rescue party returned with the grim news that there was no sign of the three men. They had searched and shouted, but found no sign of them.

It was only then that it was discovered that a bottle of rum which had been brought for emergencies was missing, and Banks concluded that the sailors must have drained it and fallen asleep in the snow. About midnight a man was heard shouting in the woods. It was one of the sailors who had woken up and somehow made his way to the camp. Once again Banks turned out into the blizzard with a rescue party, and this time they did find Richmond. He was on his feet, but unable to walk. The second seaman was on the ground 'as insensible as a stone'.

We immediately called all hands from the fire and attempted by all means we could contrive to bring them down, but finding it almost impossible, the road was so bad and the night so dark that we could scarcely ourselves get on nor did we without many falls.

Neither could they light a fire because of the mini-avalanches of snow falling from the trees. As a final desperate measure they built beds of boughs for the two sick men, laid them down and covered them with a thick blanket of boughs, 'and thus we left them hopeless of ever seeing them again alive, which indeed we never did'.

By now the rescue party was suffering severely from exposure. Peter Briscoe, another of Banks's servants, began to fail, and by the time they got back to the camp he was very ill, almost dead from the intense, penetrating cold.

Banks wrote: 'Now our situation could truly be called terrible.' Of the twelve who set out two were beyond help and a third,

. . . so ill that though he was with us I had little hopes of his being able to walk in the morning, and another very likely to relapse into his fits either before we set out or in the course of our journey.

Completely disorientated, they had no idea how far they were from the *Endeavour*. To make matters worse their supplies were exhausted, and all they had to eat, ironically, was a vulture which had been shot during the previous day, and which 'at the shortest allowance could not furnish half a meal'.

The day dawned as squally and bitter as the night, but by about eight the sun broke through and the snow began to thaw. Buchan was far fitter than Banks had imagined, and although Briscoe was still very ill he said he could walk. A party was sent out to where Richmond and the sailor had been left only to return with the news that they were dead.

Now there was nothing left but to attempt to get back to the *Endeavour*. The scrawny vulture was divided into ten pieces, which the men cooked over the fire. It gave them each about three mouthfuls of hot meat, the first meal any of them had had since a cold lunch a day before.

At ten o'clock the bedraggled party set out and after a three hour trek through less difficult country they reached the anchorage. If nothing else, the largely disastrous expedition proved the toughness of Banks. After seeing the survivors fed and into warm beds, he had a boat lowered and hauled a seine net across the bay to collect fish. Sadly this was also a failure.

During the following two days the weather was foul and there were no further excursions ashore, but by 20 January Banks and his party were able to resume collecting. As the number of specimens grew he became increasingly impressed by the abundance and variety of plants in Tierra del Fuego.

Writing enthusiastically in his journal he declared :

Of plants here are many species and those truly the most extraordinary I can imagine. In stature and appearance they agree a good deal with the European ones, only in general are less specious, white flowers being much more common among them than any other colours. But to speak of them botanically, probably no botanist has ever enjoyed more pleasure in the contemplation of his favourite persuit than Dr Solander and myself among these plants; we have not yet examined many of them, but what we have turned out in general so entirely different from any before described that we are never tired with wondering at the infinite variety of Creation, and admiring the infinite care with which providence has multiplied his productions, suiting them no doubt to the various climates for which they were designed.

On the twenty-first the *Endeavour* set sail again, heading towards Cape Horn, which was rounded without incident, indeed it was passed in such a thick fog that there was some doubt as to whether the land they saw was the Horn at all.

During the early part of February Banks, who had so well survived the fatal Tierra del Fuego expedition, was taken ill with a bilious attack, which worried him because Wallis, during his recent voyage, had a similar illness and it remained with him throughout the entire expedition. Clearly Banks must have been feeling a great deal better on 5 February because he made a hearty meal on an albatross that he had shot two days before, and even had the stomach to write the recipe in his journal :

Skin them overnight and soak their carcasses in salt water till morn, then parboil them and throw away the water, then stew them well with very little water and when sufficiently tender serve them with a savoury sauce.

The bird was so good that he declared 'everybody commended and eat heartily of them though there was fresh pork upon the table'.

The *Endeavour* was now heading steadily into the Pacific, and on 24 February Banks woke to find 'studding sails set and the ship going at the rate of seven knots, no very usual thing for Mrs Endeavour'. A month later the weather was becoming warmer and calmer, with large numbers of tropical birds daily about the ship.

After the unpleasant South American experiences the voyage now seemed settled down to a calm, satisfying routine, but on 25 March another tragedy hit the vessel—the suicide of a twenty-one-year-old marine, William Greenslade.

Whether Greenslade killed himself through shame or fear will never be known; it was probably the latter, but the root cause of his death was so trivial as to be absurd.

On the day of his death he was on sentry duty at the door of the great cabin when one of Cook's servants was called away and left a piece of seal's skin in the sentry's care. The servant was planning to make the skin into tobacco pouches, and Greenslade had asked for one, but had been refused. He lost his temper and said that if he was not given a pouch he would steal a piece of skin and make one for himself, and that is what he did.

The owner of the skin was furious but agreed not to report the incident to an officer, but in the meantime the petty crime came to the knowledge of Greenslade's fellow marines. They gave the young marine a very hard time, saying he had dishonoured the corps. The Sergeant of Marines said he would report the theft, which would almost certainly have led to a flogging.

That evening he was called on deck, but in the half light he gave his escort the slip and ran up the deck. The marines thought he had gone to the heads, but so great was his fear that he threw himself overboard. By the time it was realized what had happened it was too late.

Coming so soon after the deaths on Tierra del Fuego, this fresh tragedy might have suggested to the simpler members of the crew that the expedition was in some way damned. But if such feelings were brewing up they were dispelled ten days later when the first of the fabled South Sea islands was sighted.

CHAPTER 4

THE ISLANDS
AND THE ISLANDERS

The first of the Pacific islands was sighted by Peter Briscoe, one of the servants that Banks had brought with him from Revesby. It was the small island of Vahitahi which encompassed a lagoon. A group of armed islanders came down to the shore as the *Endeavour* stood in. 'They appeared to us through our glasses to be tall and to have very large heads or possibly much hair upon them,' Banks observed. He remained on deck exploring the island as best he could with his telescope, and yearning to be walking in the shade of the coconut palms: 'pleasanter groves cannot be imagined' he remarked longingly.

For the next eight days the *Endeavour* made her slow, lumbering progress among the islands, slowed down by recurring thunder storms and violent squalls. But on 11 April, Tahiti—then known variously as George's Land, King George III Island, and Otaheite—came into view, and two days later on a calm, clear morning the *Endeavour* came to anchor in Matavai Bay.

The sight was magnificent. A vast sweep of azure water, bright sand beaches fringed with palm groves, and tall hills rising out of the rich woods and undergrowth. Soon the ship was surrounded by canoes laden with coconuts, breadfruit and fish which were briskly exchanged for beads.

Banks was in his element. Everything he had dreamed about had come alive around him. Not only was a biological treasure house awaiting him, but at last he would be able to meet and study, at leisure, an exotic people.

As soon as the anchors were well down the boats were hoisted out and we all went ashore where we were met by some hundreds of the inhabitants whose faces at least gave signs that we were not unwelcome guests, tho' they at first hardly dare approach us. After a little time they became very familiar. The first who approached us came creeping almost on his hands and knees and gave us a green bough, the token of peace. This we received and immediately each gathered a green bough and carried in our hands.

With palm fronds waving in the air the party moved about half a mile from the landing place. It was a bizarre procession : the Tahitians with their brightly coloured bark cloth cloaks and loin-cloths vivid against their dark skins, with their leaders in even more brilliantly hued robes made from the feathers of gaudy tropical birds, surrounding the explorers, also decked out in their finery—Banks in a fine white coat trimmed with gold lace, Cook and his officers in full dress uniform, and the marine escort pipe-clayed and polished for the occasion.

After walking for about half a mile they came to a patch of ground which the Tahitians stripped of undergrowth before throwing down their palm fronds. The *Endeavour* party did the same, and peace was established.

The marines were drawn up and marching in order dropped each a bough upon those that the Indians had laid down. We all followed their example and thus peace was concluded.

Following the ceremony the procession moved away from the sea into the dense palm groves, with Banks and his companions distributing beads and small gifts to the islanders. For men who had been crammed into a tiny ship for so long it was a blissful experience.

We walked for four or five miles under groves of coconut and breadfruit trees loaded with a profusion of fruit and giving the most grateful shade I had ever experienced. Under these were the habitations of the people, most of them without walls : In short the scene we saw was the truest picture of an arcadia of which we were going to be kings that the imagination can form.

The island's nobles had kept out of sight throughout the first encounter, and although Banks and Cook were pleased to have made such a promising start, they were determined to return the next day to conclude a peace treaty with the 'superior people'.

Early on the morning of the fourteenth a number of canoes came out to the *Endeavour*, two of which carried finely dressed men who were clearly of the 'superior people' that Banks and Cook wanted to meet, and they were invited on board and taken to the great cabin.

Each singled out his friend, one took the captain and the other me. They took off a large part of their clothes and each dressed his friend with them he took off : In return for this we presented them with each a hatchet and some beads.

With the courtesies completed the men indicated that Banks and Cook should follow them.

A boat was lowered and they rowed to a landfall about three miles from the *Endeavour* where they were taken to a long house to meet an old chief. Solemnly Banks and Cook were presented with a cock and a hen, and long lengths of bark cloth. Banks's piece measured eleven yards by two wide, and in return he gave the old man a lace-trimmed silk neck-cloth and a handkerchief.

For the rest of that morning they visited the surrounding houses where the women waited to entertain them. The unabashed advances of the women unnerved the travellers despite the fact that they had been without women for months.

The ladies . . . showed us all kinds of civilities our situation could admit of, but as there were no places of retirement, the houses being entirely without walls, we had not an opportunity of putting their politeness to every test that maybe some of us would not have failed to have done had circumstances been more favourable; indeed we had no reason to doubt any part of their politeness as by their frequently pointing to the mats on the ground and sometimes by force seating themselves and us upon them they plainly showed that they were much less jealous of observation than we were.

Extracting themselves from the affectionate overtures of the native ladies the party was carried off to a feast, where Banks, to his disgust, found himself seated next to the ancient and extremely ugly wife of the chief who was their host.

Our Chief's own wife (ugly enough in conscience) did me the honour with very little invitation to squat on the mats close by me : no sooner had she done so than I espied among the common crowd a very pretty girl with a fire in her eyes that I had not seen before in the country. Unconscious of the dignity of my companion I beckoned to the other, who after some entreaties came and sat on the other side of me. I was then desirous of getting rid of my former companion so I ceased to attend to her and loaded my pretty girl with beads and every present I could think pleasing to her.

The Chief's wife was thoroughly put out, but far from leaving in disgust she stood her ground and plied Banks with fish and coconut milk.

'How this would have ended is hard to say,' Banks reflected. The amorous tussle was brought to an abrupt end, however, by a demonstration of the least attractive aspect of the Tahitian character—theft.

Solander and Monkhouse, who were seated among the ordinary people, discovered that their pockets had been picked. A snuff-box and a spy-glass had been stolen. When told what had happened, Banks leapt dramatically to his feet, striking the butt of his gun. He had discovered earlier in the day that he could persuade the Tahitians to keep their distance by rattling his musket. This time the effect was no less.

'Upon this signal every one of the common sort (among whom was my pretty girl) ran like sheep.' Only the chief, his wives, including Banks's ugly companion, and two or three of the better dressed people remained. The Chief took Banks by the hand and led him to a heap of cloth and offered it in compensation for the stolen property, but Banks made it clear that the snuff-box and spy-glass must be recovered. 'On this he gave me into charge of my faithful companion, his wife, who had never budged an inch from my elbow.' Half an hour later the Chief returned looking extremely pleased with himself, carrying the snuff-box and the empty spy-glass case. Banks was not satisfied and only when he went with the Chief was the glass recovered.

With peace and friendship finally established, Cook took the first steps in setting up a base on the island. On the morning of the fifteenth he took a party ashore and settled on a site on the banks of the River Viapopoo, close to Point Venus, the spot selected for the observation of the Transit of Venus. The river was vital as a source of fresh water.

As usual Banks was in the party. A small tent was pitched which aroused intense curiosity, and before long a large crowd of islanders had gathered to watch the erection of this instant house. When the crowd increased to some hundreds Banks scored a line in the sandy soil with the butt of his musket and indicated that nobody should cross it.

Since all seemed peaceful and cordial, Banks, who by now had become the liaison man between the *Endeavour* party and the islanders, judged it safe to leave to trade for pigs. He took with him an old man who had previously helped the *Dolphin* people. The tent was left in charge of a midshipman, Jonathan Monkhouse, and thirteen marines. As they were returning from the largely unsuccessful trading trip, the peace of the coconut groves was suddenly shattered by the rattle of musket shots. The old guide and three other natives, with palm fronds in their hands, ran towards the camp site, and by the time they and Banks reached it it was deserted by all except Monkhouse and the marines. The only evidence of the islanders were footprints and dark patches of blood soaking into the sandy soil.

Monkhouse, visibly shaken, told Banks that one of the islanders had suddenly run forwards and snatched a musket from an unwary marine. The young midshipman had panicked and ordered the marines to fire into the crowd. Several people were wounded while the thief ran to the shelter of the woods. The marines gave chase and shot him dead.

'Whether any others were killed or hurt no one could tell,' Banks wrote in his journal. Those that had fallen had been carried away by their companions.

No Indian was now to be seen about the tent, but our old man, who with us took all pains to reconcile them again. Before night by his means we got together a few of them and explaining to them that the man who suffered was guilty of a crime deserving of death (for so we were forced to make it). We retired to the ship not well pleased with the day's expedition, guilty, no doubt, in some measure, of the death of a man who the most severe laws of equity would not have condemned to so severe a punishment.

From such a promising start the expedition was now threatened with failure. On the morning following the shooting not a single canoe ventured near the *Endeavour*. Small groups of natives gathered nervously on the shore.

To add to the troubles, Buchan, the figure and landscape painter, collapsed with another epileptic fit, this time even more severe than the near fatal attack on Tierra del Fuego. By the next morning he was dead. Banks was deeply upset, although his grief was not entirely unselfish. He wrote in his journal:

I sincerely regret him as an ingenious and good young man, but his loss to me is irretrevable. My airy dreams of entertaining my friends in England with the scenes I am to see here are vanished. No account of the figures and dresses of men can be satisfactory unless illustrated with figures : had providence spared him a month longer what an advantage would it have been to my undertaking, but I must submit.

Following the necessarily hurried funeral of Buchan, two chiefs approached the *Endeavour* on a peace mission. One was the man who had recovered the stolen spy-glass and snuff-box, whom Banks nick-named Lycurgus 'from the justice he executed on his offending subjects on the fourteenth', and the other, a giant of a man, whom Banks called Hercules. They brought cooked hogs and breadfruit, and were given hatchets and nails in return. Once again peace was established between the expedition and the Tahitians.

Five days after dropping anchor in Matavai Bay, then known as Port Royal, the serious scientific work of the expedition was begun. All hands were ordered ashore to build a fort, and the islanders, not realizing that the strangers were erecting a defence against them, cheerfully helped by hauling timber to the site. When it was completed Fort Venus had high breastworks at each end, with the front and near palisades doubly defended by the River Vaipopoo. Swivel and carriage guns were mounted pointing towards the woods, the most likely direction of attack, and sentries were posted around the clock.

Despite the military character of the fort, the Tahitians seemed to regard it as some kind of eccentric long house and began to settle around it.

Banks's friend, Lycurgus, brought his wife and son and moved in to a shelter nearby. It was an encouraging sign that the chief's confidence had been won. He was a graceful, intelligent man who enjoyed Banks's company and imitated his manners to perfection. When he dined with the visitors he copied them 'in every instance already holding a knife and fork more handily than a Frenchman could learn to do in years.'

Cook quickly recognised Banks's talent for creating trust and confidence among the natives, and made him responsible for trading and diplomacy, a duty that left him little time for collecting. Solander and the remainder of the Banks party had to take on the bulk of the scientific work, which was only hampered by the swarms of flies which settled on Fort Venus. Banks recorded:

The flies have become so troublesome ever since we have been ashore that we can scarce get any business done for them; they eat the painter's colours off the paper as fast as they can be laid on, and if a fish is to be drawn there is more trouble in keeping them off it than the drawing itself.

They tried everything, including baiting a plate with a mixture of molasses and tar, which failed to trap a single fly, but when the plate was put outside a tent to be cleaned,

. . . one of the Indians observing this took an opportunity when he thought that no one observed him to take some of this mixture up into his hand. I saw, and was curious to know for what use it was intended. The gentleman had a large sore upon his backside to which the clammy liniament was applied, but with what success I never took the pains to enquire.

The following days passed quietly enough, although the persistent thieving of the natives created a constant tension. So much was it part of the Tahitian way of life that even when they came on board the *Endeavour* they attempted to take anything that came to hand, including, on one occasion, two porthole lights. However hard he tried, Banks could not impress upon them the fact that theft was a crime.

On the evening of 27 April Lycurgus and a friend came to him in a state of great agitation. Taking him by the hand they hurried to a dwelling where Banks found the ship's butcher. It seemed that the butcher had wanted to buy a stone axe from a woman for a cheap hatchet and a nail. She had refused and the butcher had snatched up the axe, thrown down a nail in payment, and threatened to kill the woman with a reaping hook if she attempted to stop him.

Banks promised that the butcher, Henry Jeffs, would be punished the next day. Lycurgus, and the woman, who was his wife, were mollified, and for Banks it was an opportunity to demonstrate just how seriously the British treated the offence of stealing.

In fact it was not until two days later that Jeffs was punished. There appears to have been an attempt to have him flogged ashore, but in some way this was prevented by the islanders. So two days later, Lycurgus, whose real name, Banks discovered, was Tubourai, and his wife, Tomio, were taken on board the *Endeavour* to witness the punishment.

They stood quietly and saw him stripped and fastened to the rigging, but as soon as the first blow was given interfered with many tears, begging the punishment might cease, a request the captain would not comply with.

During the day before the flogging Banks met a character who was to play a lasting part in his life. She was Oborea (more accurately Purea), a Queen of some consequence, whose relationship with him was to become the inspiration for some wicked lampoons. Major John Scott, a notorious eighteenth-century pamphleteer, who dubbed Banks, 'Voyager, Monster-hunter and Amoroso', wrote two lengthy doggerel poems in which he portrays Banks as an incorrigible lecher, and Oberea as a duped and helpless maiden used by him.

That Banks enjoyed sex is not in doubt, but that Purea was a helpless, wronged maiden is ludicrously inaccurate. She was a tall, heavy, middle-aged woman with an insatiable appetite for sex. After meeting her for the first time Banks wrote:

As a youth, Joseph Banks could hardly have dreamed that the Royal Hospital, founded by Charles II, and designed and built by Sir Christopher Wren, would become the home of the Chelsea Flower Show staged each year by the Royal Horticultural Society, which he helped to form in 1804 (*Kensington & Chelsea Public Libraries*)

It was on the Thames at Chelsea that Banks, and his friend and patron, Lord Sandwich, spent hours at their favourite sport, fishing. Such was their enthusiasm for the pastime that they conceived the wholly illegal plan to drain the Serpentine and study the fish living in it (*Kensington & Chelsea Public Libraries*)

She appeared to be about forty, tall and very lusty, her skin white and her eyes full of meaning. She might have been handsome when young, but now few or no traces of it were left.

George Robertson, Master of the *Dolphin*, in his account of Tahiti, writes with amazement at the extent of Purea's lust.

A member of the powerful Teva clan, she was the daughter of the chief of the Haapape district, which included Matavai Bay, and was married to Tevahitua or Amo, chief of Papara. About 1762 they had a son, Teriirere, who according to custom assumed the title of his father, who in turn became merely his guardian. Indeed, Teriirere was a sacred being, and when Banks met him he was being carried on a man's back so that his feet should not touch the ground, and all the women round about covered their breasts as a mark of respect.

Purea was an ambitious, self-willed woman, but politically unsound, and by the time the *Endeavour* reached Tahiti she had lost most of her political power. She began to lose the support of the lesser chiefs when she imposed a food taboo in favour of her son, and set about building an extravagant and gigantic marea, a cross between a palace and a shrine. Clearly she became too demanding, as there was some kind of uprising which led to a bloody battle. Purea and Amo had to flee for their lives and take refuge in the heavily wooded interior. While Teriirere retained his position as the single most powerful chief on the island, the Teva clan lost its political supremacy.

When the *Endeavour* reached the island, Purea had returned from exile, and had been restored to some position of importance, although (it would seem) on something of a grace-and-favour basis. Her husband had faded from the scene, and in fact the couple had parted. When Banks called on her for the first time he

... was surprised to find her in bed with a handsome lusty young man of about twenty-five, whose name was Obadee. I, however, soon understood that he was her gallant, a circumstance which she made not the least secret of.

Quite unabashed Purea climbed out of bed and dressed herself, and also draped Banks in a length of cloth. He was happily unaware that Purea had put her mark on him and intended wasting no time in hauling him into bed with her.

But any plans she might have made were frustrated when it was discovered that the astronomical quadrant, a bulky piece of equipment vital to the observation of the Transit of Venus, was missing from

Cook's tent. It seemed inconceivable that such a big object could have been stolen by the islanders unobserved, and because it was packed in a large case suspicion fell on the *Endeavour*'s crew, who, Banks and Cook thought, might have mistaken it for a chest of nails, the common currency of the island.

'A large reward was therefore offered to anyone who could find it and all hands sent out to search round the fort.' After an hour of intensive searching there was still no sign of the quadrant.

Banks was now convinced that the islanders had somehow made off with it and he set off into the interior to track down the thieves. While he was crossing the Vaipopoo River he met Tubourai carrying three straws which he formed into a triangle, the shape of a quadrant. He was even able to name the thief.

Accompanied by Green, the astronomer, and a midshipman, Banks and Tubourai took up the chase. Moving eastward, they were told at every house the direction the thief had taken. The temperature climbed steadily into the nineties and the going was heavy.

Sometimes we walked, sometimes we ran, when we imagined (which we sometimes did) that the chase was just before us, till we arrived at the top of a hill about four miles from the tents. From this place Tubourai showed us a point about three miles off and made us to understand that we were not to expect the instrument till we got there.

We now considered our situation; no arms among us but a pair of pocket pistols which I always carried; going at least seven miles from our fort where the Indians might not be quite so submissive as at home, going also to take from them a prize for which they had ventured their lives.

Because of their precarious position, the midshipman was sent back to the fort to ask Cook to follow up with a party of marines.

Banks, Green and Tubourai pressed on to the spot where the return of the quadrant was promised. There they were met by a native with a part of the quadrant in his hand, but he was followed by a large crowd of men—sullen, aggressive and threatening—who surrounded the Englishmen and Tubourai. Banks pulled out a pistol, and the men backed off.

Bit by bit the quadrant was brought back, along with other odds and ends of stolen property, including a pair of reading glasses packed into a pistol case, the latter belonging to Banks. It rather looked as though they had been led to a kind of robber's hide-out.

Mr Green began to overlook the instrument to see if any part or parts were wanting. Several small things were, and people were sent out in search of them, some of which were returned and the others did not; the stand was not there but that we were informed had been left behind by the thief and we should have it on our return, an answer which coming from Tubourai satisfied us very well.

Eventually everything was recovered except a few minor parts which could be replaced, and the quadrant was packed in grass in its case. After about two miles the thief-catchers met Cook and his marines.

Before setting out, Cook, in retaliation, had ordered that no canoes should be allowed to put to sea. Some were launched, including one containing Tuteha, the first senior Chief met by the expedition, but it was intercepted and Tuteha was placed under arrest.

His arrest outraged the islanders, who were already enraged at their canoes being impounded. Cook ordered the release of the Chief, but this failed to ease the tension, and the following morning when Banks and Solander went out to trade there were no sellers. By the end of the day all they could scrape together were a few breadfruit and six coconuts, 'a very disagreeable change from our former situation; we have now no coconuts and not a quarter enough breadfruit for the people.'

Tuteha was allowed to retrieve his canoe, and was little mollified by this; but the incident did produce a bonus that was to prove invaluable to the expedition, in the shape of Tupaia, a priest and Purea's chief adviser. He came to examine Purea's canoe, which had also been seized, and was so satisfied with its condition that he did not even remove it. Instead he stayed at the fort all day, and slept the night in the canoe 'not without a bedfellow, tho' the gentleman cannot be less than forty-five.'

All Banks's efforts to restore good relationships with the islanders seemed doomed to failure. Tuteha, with a fine show of injured dignity, remained aloof and sulky. However, he did send a message saying he wanted to see Cook, and that he would like a shirt and a hatchet, so on 5 May Cook, Banks and Solander set off by boat to Tuteha's house about four miles down the coast. They were met by a large crowd who pressed about the party. A tall, powerfully built man with a heavy stick had to beat a path through the mob to Tuteha, who was seated under a tree with a group of solemn-faced old men. He glowered at his visitors, but mellowed visibly when Cook handed him a hatchet and a gown made of broadcloth trimmed with tape. Banks recorded:

Soon after this Oborea (Purea) joined us and with her I retired to a house adjacent where I could be free from the suffocating heat occasioned by so large a crowd of people as were gathered about us.

Whether or not Purea had planned to force her massive charms on Banks is not clear, but if that was her intention she was once again frustrated by a wrestling match that was staged for the visitors, and preparations for a feast on two roast pigs and huge quantities of bread-fruit. The sight of the food cooking in pit ovens pleased Banks 'very well as my stomach was by this time sufficiently prepared for the repast', but Tuteha was still in an awkward mood. Just as the food was ready he announced that he wanted to go on board the *Endeavour*. One of the roast pigs was loaded into a boat and the party had to row four miles back to the ship 'with the pig growing cold under our noses before he would give it to us'. But once aboard the feast began and the final stage of the reconciliation took place.

After dinner we went ashore. The sight of Dootahah (Tuteha) reconciled to us acted like a charm upon the people and before night breadfruit and coconuts were brought to sell in tolerable plenty.

So once again peace was established, and with it came repeated visits from Purea, who made no pretence of her designs upon Banks. On one of her visits, much to Banks's delight, she was accompanied by her favourite handmaiden, Otheothea, who was none other than his girl with a fire in her eyes, 'my flame' as he called her.

Although Banks makes no direct reference to having an affair with the girl, there is little doubt that she did become his bedmate, for a few days later Purea announced that she did not want her lover, Obadee, admitted to the fort. He, however, hung around the gate looking so dejected that he was let in and stood gazing sorrowfully at the monstrous Queen, who treated him with utter disdain. Banks writes :

She seems to us to act in the character of a Ninon d'Enclos, who satiated with her lover resolves to change him at all events, the more so as I am offered, if I please, to supply his place, but I am at present otherwise engaged; indeed was I free as air her majesty's person is not the most desirable.

Quite how he coped with the situation leaves much to the imagina-tion, particularly since on the night following her offer he had Purea, Obadee and Otheothea sleeping in his tent.

Purea's determination to take Banks as her lover seemed to know no bounds. At the end of May, Banks, Cook and Solander were again summoned by Tuteha. They arrived on the evening of the twenty-eighth. Purea was waiting for Banks and offered him a bed for the night in her canoe. The Tahitians erected awnings over their canoes so that they served both as shelter as well as vessels.

Night came on apace, it was necessary to look out for lodgings; as Dootahah (Tuteha) made no offer of any I repaired to my old friend Oborea (Purea) who readily gave me a bed in her canoe, much to my satisfaction. I acquainted my fellow travellers with my good fortune and wishing them as good took my leave.

We went to bed early as is the custom here : I stripped myself for the greater convenience as the night was hot. Oborea insisted that my clothes should be put into her custody, otherwise, she said, they would certainly be stolen. I readily submitted and laid down to sleep with all imaginable tranquility.

At about eleven o'clock that night Banks woke and wanted to get up. He felt about for his clothes in the place they had been put, but there was no sign of them. Angrily he shook Purea awake and demanded their return. Candles were lit, Tuteha, in a nearby canoe was roused, and he and Purea went off in search of the missing garments.

Banks, naked and in a state of fury, was worried by the fact that his pocket pistols, powder and shot were in his jacket, his best white jacket with the silver frogs. His musket had been left, but as he had failed to load it before going to bed it was of little use if trouble was on the way. And to make matters worse he had no idea where Cook or Solander were spending the night. In fact, at the time Cook was being robbed of his stockings and two midshipmen of their jackets.

Tuteha and Purea returned empty-handed, and there was nothing for it but to return to the canoe, where Purea had him naked and defenceless.

Next morning Banks found Tupaia with his musket, which he had put in the charge of the priest the night before, plus all his clothes with the exception of his jacket. Although pressed neither Tuteha nor Purea made any effort to find the jacket, but Purea did supply a length of bark cloth. So dressed half in European and half in native attire, Banks returned crossly to the fort.

Only a few days remained before the Transit of Venus. Cook was determined to leave nothing to chance. While the main observatory was at Fort Venus, two sub-observatories were set up—one in the eastern part of the island, and the second on a small island, Aimeo, which is now known as Moorea. Banks decided to go to the island, but his party had to wait until the carpenters repaired the long-boat, which was found to have had its bottom almost eaten away by marine worms.

It was the afternoon of 1 June before the party could leave, and they had to row through most of the night to arrive in time to set up the sub-observatory, which was placed on a tiny coral islet just off the shore of Aimeo.

Banks went ashore, wearing, as he did these days, a turban of the native tapa cloth, made from the beaten bark of a fig tree, *Ficus prolixa*, to trade for supplies and to add plants to his now very large collection.

The evening of the second was bright and clear, and confidence ran high for a successful observation of the transit. But during the night the weather became changeable. One or other of the party got up every half hour to report on conditions which varied from hazy to clear. Those fears which might have been raised during the night were laid in the morning, which dawned bright and clear as the previous evening.

Banks again went ashore to collect and trade, and also to meet the local king, Ta'aroa, who presented him with coconuts, breadfruit, a hog and a dog. Banks gave him a shirt, an adze and some beads. Later the king and his sister, Nuna, were taken to the observatory to see the transit through the telescopes. 'To them we showed the planet upon the sun and made them understand that we came on purpose to see it.' What the islanders thought of all this is not recorded. Perhaps they thought the whitemen were simply mad, or else engaged in some strange religious ritual. Whatever their feeling they certainly were not afraid, and at sunset 'three handsome girls' came to the camp.

They had been at the tent in the morning with Tarroa (Ta'aroa), they chatted with us very freely and with very little persuasion agreed to send away their carriage (a canoe) and sleep in the tent, a proof of confidence which I have not met with upon so short an acquaintenance.

In the morning the observatory and camp broke up and headed back to Fort Venus 'in spite of the entreaties of our fair companions who persuaded us much to stay.'

At the fort Banks found Cook and the rest of the company in high spirits. The weather had been perfect for the observation and the exercise had been more successful than anyone could have dared to hope, although the end results proved less valuable to navigation than had been originally thought.

Only one thing marred the occasion and that was the discovery that a large part of the *Endeavour*'s stock of nails had been stolen. Since iron nails were the currency of the island it was the equivalent of a bank robbery. For once the culprits were the ship's crew and not the islanders. One man was caught with seven nails on him, only a fraction of the hundredweight that had been taken, and although he was flogged he refused to name his accomplices. What concerned Banks and Cook was that with so many nails now in circulation their value in trading for fresh supplies would be devalued.

During Banks's absence on Aimeo an old woman of some importance died. Her body was laid close to the fort and surrounded by offerings of food so that the island gods would not eat her body. Nearby was a mourning spot where relatives gathered to weep and slash their heads with shark's teeth. When the melodramatic, noisy mourning ended the tear and blood-stained cloths were scattered by the body. Tubourai promised Banks that he could take part in the final funeral ceremonies.

Tubourai played the leading part, the Heiva, or chief mourner, in a voluminous robe with a towering head-dress. Banks, with two women, was a Neneva—a kind of demonic clown.

I was prepared by stripping off my European clothes and putting me on a small strip of cloth round my waist, the only garment I was allowed to have, but I had no pretensions to be ashamed of my nakedness for neither of the women were a bit more covered than myself. They then began to smut me and themselves with charcoal and water.

A small boy was smeared with the mixture over his entire body, while Banks and the women had only their heads and necks blacked.

After Tubourai had chanted prayers, the weird party made its way to the fort:

. . . to the surprise of our friends and the affright of the Indians who were there, for they everywhere fly before the Heiva like sheep before a wolf.

We soon left it and proceeded along shore towards a place where above 100 indians were collected together. We, the Nenevas, ran towards them, but before we came within 100 yards of them they dispersed every way, running to the first shelter, hiding themselves under grass or whatever else would conceal them. We now crossed the river into the woods and passed several houses, all were deserted. Not another Indian did we see for about half an hour that we spent in walking about. We, the Nenevas then came to the Heiva and said 'imatata' (aima taata), there are no people; after which we repaired home, the Heiva undressed, and we went into the river and scrubbed one another till it was dark before the blacking would come off.

The fact that Banks was allowed to take an active part in such a solemn and important ceremony is evidence of the remarkable bond that he built between himself and the Tahitians. Frequently he spent the night in the woods sleeping among the islanders.

One cannot imagine Cook taking part in such a ritual other than as an observer. Often he seemed more concerned with trying to impress a Western style of morality and order on the natives. Shortly after the funeral a Tahitian stole a coal rake, and Cook again reacted by impounding the islanders' canoes. On this occasion he seized an entire fleet of twenty-five large sailing canoes, which had just returned bringing fish to the island. His move resulted in the speedy return of the coal rake, but he refused to release the canoes until a whole variety of stolen property was returned.

Banks had deep misgivings as to the wisdom of Cook's measure, and while he backed him despite the pleas of the natives for the return of the canoes, he doubted whether any stolen goods would be restored since it was unlikely that the fishermen had stolen them in the first place.

He confided in his journal :

I confess had I taken a step so violent I would have seized either the persons of the people who had stolen from us, most of whom we either know or shrewdly suspected, or their goods at least, instead of those people who are entirely unconcerned in the affair, and have not probably interest enough with their superiors (to whom all valuable things are carried) to procure the restoration demanded.

Cook would have done better to have consulted Banks first before exercising his authority in so draconian a manner. The result was that the islanders hit back in their usual way by withholding all supplies of fresh food.

Three days later the visitors made another clumsy blunder. Ballast was needed for the *Endeavour*. A boat was sent ashore to collect stones. Because none were readily available the officer in charge of the work party ordered them to tear down a burial place. The islanders were outraged and sent for Banks, and the desecration was stopped. There were, as Banks pointed out, plenty of stones to be found in the river.

Although the Tahitians were deeply offended by the insensitiveness of Cook's men it did not prevent them from flocking to the fort in great numbers. When Purea, Otheothea and another companion turned up, the Queen's first visit since Banks's coat was stolen, he had to refuse them shelter for the night because 'my marquee was full of Indians'.

The visitors marched off in a huff to spend the night in their canoes, but returned the next morning bearing gifts, including a very fat dog.

We had lately learnt that these animals were eat by the Indians and esteemed more delicate than pork, now, therefore, was our opportunity of trying the experiment. He was immediately given over to Tupaia, who finding it was a food we were not accustomed to undertook to stand butcher and cook both. He killed him by stopping his breath, holding his hands over his mouth and nose, an operation which took over a quarter of an hour. He then proceeded to dress him much in the same manner as we would a pig, singeing him over the fire which was lighted to roast him, and scraping him clean with a shell. He then opened him with the same instrument and taking out his entrails, pluck, etc., sent them to the sea where they were most carefully washed and then put into coconut shells with what blood he had found in them. The stones were now laid and the dog well covered with leaves laid upon them. In about two hours he was dressed and in another quarter of an hour completely eat. A most excellent dish he made for us who were not much prejudiced against any species of food; I cannot, however, promise that a European dog would eat as well, as these (the Tahitian) scarce in their lives touch animal food, coconut kernel, breadfruit, yams etc., being what their masters can best afford to give them.

Banks's incurable curiosity and remakably strong stomach introduced him to most of the islanders' culinary delicacies. He closely studied their pit ovens in which the food was laid on heated stones and buried. When he returned to England he would entertain guests in Lincolnshire to picnics at which the food was cooked South-Seas style.

He marvelled at the ease with which the Tahitians fed themselves:

Scarcely can it be said that they earn their bread by the sweat of their brow, when the chiefest, breadfruit, is procured with no more trouble than that of climbing a tree and pulling it down. Not that the trees grow here spontaneously, but if a man should in the course of his lifetime, plant ten such trees, which if well done might take the labour of an hour or thereabouts, he would as completely fulfil his duty to his own as well as future generations as we natives of less temperate climates can do by toiling in the cold of winter and in the heat of summer to reap the annual produce of our soil.

Apart from the staple breadfruit, there was no lack of coconuts, fish and shellfish, as well as pork and fowls.

Banks learned to eat, with relish, as an islander, dipping his food into a coconut shell of sea water to season it; eating raw fish, and even growing fond of a sauce made from fermented coconut kernel beaten into a smooth paste with sea water :

The taste of this is very strong and at first was to me most abominably nauseous. A very little use, however, reconciled me entirely to it so much that I almost prefer it to our own sauces with fish.

Before he left the island he even learned to peel a green coconut with his teeth.

He did draw the line at an abominable delicacy, much liked by the island women—rotten jellyfish. Because fresh jellyfish were very tough they were prepared :

. . . by suffering them to stink; custom will make almost any meat palatable and the women especially are very fond of this, tho' after they had eat it I confess I was not extremely fond of their company.

Less than a month before the *Endeavour* sailed from Tahiti to fulfil the mission in Cook's sealed orders, he and Banks, with a small party, circumnavigated the island in the pinnace. The journey, made partly by sea and partly on foot, took a week. It enabled Cook to gather information that proved invaluable for subsequent expeditions, and Banks added substantially to his collections, as well as gathering more data on the culture and customs of the islanders. By the time he left the island he had collected a remarkably comprehensive catalogue of their social, religious and political structure; their dress, food, crafts, and techniques for building boats and houses, as well as a useful vocabulary that would enable any later travellers to communicate intelligibly. Not only was he a botanist and zoologist of considerable ability; he had now added anthropology to his disciplines.

When they set out neither Cook nor Banks thought they would be able to complete a circumnavigation, indeed, so slight was their confidence that they did not even take a change of clothing. After rowing for a few hours on the first day they were approached by a friendly Tahitian who warned them against going any further. He said they were moving out of the area controlled by the fickle chief, Tuteha, and would certainly be killed, but when they did arrive among the supposedly hostile clan they were greeted with great civility, discovering that this was part of the island that had been visited by an earlier European expedition.

On 3 July 1769, a few days after returning from the circumnavigation, Banks and Monkhouse—it is not clear whether it was William Monkhouse, the surgeon, with whom Banks had a short time before had a serious quarrel, almost leading to a duel, over a girl, or the midshipman, Jonathan Monkhouse—set out on an expedition into the interior. As they were trekking inland they met numbers of islanders hauling loads of breadfruit down to the coast, which explained why supplies had remained so plentiful when the trees on the coastal plains had been stripped. It also explained how it was that the *Dolphin*, which had been at the island during the same season, recorded a bountiful supply of the fruit.

But Banks discovered a more disturbing explanation for the ease with which the *Dolphin*'s crew obtained supplies—by threats and violence. Time and again the natives told him how terrified they had been of the *Dolphin*'s guns, and accused the British seamen of killing large numbers of their people.

The trip to the interior gave Banks his first opportunity to search for minerals, a fruitless search; but he did find evidence that the island's rock formations had been subjected to intense heat, and concluded, quite correctly, that they were of volcanic origin.

As the date for departure approached, Banks spent part of his time establishing a garden, which he planted with water melon, lemon, lime and orange seeds he had acquired at Rio. Cook had planted a garden earlier, but clearly he was a better navigator than cultivator. Nothing he planted grew except for mustard.

For some of the sailors the prospect of putting to sea again with all that meant in terms of danger, discomfort and back-breaking work, in exchange for the paradise of Tahiti, was unendurable, and talk of desertion was rife.

While some of the crew were plotting their escape, Banks was busy tying up the loose ends of his research. Eight days before the ship was due to sail, he was making notes on tattooing.

This morn I saw the operation of tattooing the buttock, performed on a girl of about twelve years old. It proved, as I have always suspected, a most painful one.

In fact he knew how painful, having had a discreet tattoo made on his arm. It was a fact that he kept somewhat private, although a few years after his return to England a correspondent in Suffolk asked:

If it is not too much trouble I should be much obliged to you for an exact copy of the characters stained upon your arm.

Describing the operation on the girl, he wrote :

It was done with a large instrument about two inches long containing about thirty teeth; every stroke of this, hundreds of which were made in a minute, drew blood. The patient bore this for about a quarter of an hour with most stoical resolution; by that time, however, the pain began to operate too strongly to be peaceably endured. She began to complain and soon burst out into loud lamentations and would fain have persuaded the operator to cease; she was, however, held down by two women who sometimes scolded, sometimes beat and at others coaxed her.

Banks had already had ample chance to study the ornately decorated charms of the Tahitian women. Shortly after arriving on the island he was treated to a striptease by a young native woman. He had been invited to meet a group of islanders, including a number of women. Pieces of cloth were spread on the ground between him and the women.

The foremost of the women, who seemed to be the principal, then stepped upon them and quickly unveiling all her charms gave me a most convenient opportunity of admiring them by turning herself gradually round.

The performance was repeated and the cloth presented to Banks.

I took her by the hand and led her to the tents accompanied by another woman, her friend. To both of them I made presents but could not prevail upon them to stay more than an hour.

This and another more explicit sexual display were later used in savage lampoons against him.

Banks does not appear to have been present at the latter display, although it was witnessed by some of the *Endeavour*'s officers, and since it involved Purea it was naturally attached to him. An eye-witness account reported :

A young man near six feet high, performed the rights of Venus with a little girl about eleven or twelve years of age before several of our people, and a great number of the natives, without the least sense of it being indecent or improper, but as it appeared, in perfect conformity to the custom of the place. Among the spectators were several women of superior rank, particularly Oborea, who may properly be said to have assisted at the ceremony; for they gave instructions to the girl how to perform her part, which young as she was, did not seem to stand much in need of it.

The uninhibited enjoyment of sex by the islanders was attractive to Banks, who was young and susceptible, and it was no less attractive to most of the *Endeavour*'s company. But it also fascinated him in his role as an anthropologist. He described the dances of the young girls:

. . . singing most indecent words, using most indecent actions, and setting their mouths askew in a most extraordinary manner.

But he was horrified and unbelieving at the discovery of infanticide among the Arioi, an exclusive society largely responsible for ceremonial. They were given almost divine powers, which included the right to kill their infant offspring.

There seemed to be a considerable number of the Arioi, for Banks wrote in his journal:

More than half of the better sort of the inhabitants of the island have, like Comus in Milton, entered into a resolution of enjoying free liberty in love without a possibility of being troubled or disturbed by its consequences; these mix together with the utmost freedom, seldom cohabiting together more than two or three days by which means they have fewer children than they would otherwise have, but those who are so unfortunate as to be thus begot are smothered at the moment of their birth. Some of these people have been pointed out to me and on being asked have not denied the fact.

By 6 July preparations for sailing were well under way. Sails were taken on board and bent, the guns were taken back to the *Endeavour*, and the carpenters set about dismantling the fort and converting the timber into firewood for use during the voyage ahead. The work made the tents harder to protect, particularly the stores and equipment, from the light-fingered islanders.

News that Fort Venus was now easier to crack reached the ears of Monaamia, the man who stole the quadrant. Clearly a master thief who took pride in his vocation, he had been smarting under the disgrace of being caught, and while the *Endeavour* expedition was on Tahiti he had been sulking and plotting in some hideaway. Word reached Banks that Monaamia had landed near the fort and was going to make a final face-saving raid.

The islanders who brought the intelligence volunteered to help Banks frustrate the attempt and at the same time catch the man. The following day the staple and hook was stolen from the main gate.

I, as usual, set out in my ordinary occupation of thief catching. The Indians most readily joined me and away we set full cry, much like a pack of fox hounds. We ran and walked, and walked and ran for, I believe, six miles, with as little delay as possible.

But the thief, cunning as a fox, hid in a reed bed and escaped.

Five days before sailing a fresh hunt became necessary, this time not for islanders but for members of the *Endeavour* company who deserted. Two marines, Clement Webb and Samuel Gibson, took to the hills. When they first went absent without leave Cook decided to do nothing, believing they would come back, but twenty-four hours later the Tahitians said the men had no intention of returning. Banks wrote:

They are, they say, gone up into the mountains where our people cannot get them, and one is already married and become an inhabitant of Otahite.

The deserters were unarmed and a midshipman with a marine and two native guides were sent to find them, despite the islanders' insistence that this would be impossible.

One certain method remained, however, in our power, the seizing of some of their principal people and detaining them, which was immediately resolved upon.

Purea, Tubourai, and even Banks's girl, Otheothea, were arrested. Tuteha was literally kidnapped. Some of the prisoners were taken to the ship while Banks looked after the remainder on shore. The ploy worked, and the deserters were returned, but out of justifiable revenge one of the *Endeavour* party was spirited away by the islanders.

On the morning of 11 July Banks woke to find the remains of the fort virtually surrounded by armed Tahitians.

We were entirely without defences so I made the best I could of it by going out among them. They were very civil and showed much fear as they have done of me upon all occasions, probably because I never showed the least of them.

Gradually the tension was eased, and the British hostage was exchanged for the native prisoners.

After the last of the tents and equipment had been taken on board, Tupaia came to the *Endeavour* insisting that he should be taken to England. Cook refused to accept responsibility for him. His fear was that he would have to support the man in England, because, as Banks pointed out 'the government will never in all human probability take any notice of him.'

However, Banks wanted Tupaia and undertook to look after him:

Thank heaven I have a sufficiency and I do not know why I may not keep him as a curiosity as well as some of my neighbours do lions and tigers at a larger expense than he will probably ever put me to; the amusement I shall have in his future conversation and the benefit he will be to this ship, as well as what he may be if another should be sent into these seas, will I think fully repay me.

Tupaia brought with him a young boy, Tayeto, described by some as his servant, but, judging by the affection he showed towards him, more likely his son.

Tupaia proved to be of enormous value during the months that followed. He knew the islands about Tahiti well, and was to discover when the ship reached New Zealand that he could converse readily with the Maoris.

The last day on Tahiti was spent in feasting with Tuteha in his great Marea, and taking tearful farewells of the islanders who seemed deeply distressed at the departure of the *Endeavour* and its company, despite the bloody clashes they had had.

On the morning of 13 July Purea, Otheothea, and a number of Banks's closest Tahitian friends, were on board for the final parting.

They took their leaves tenderly enough, not without plenty of tears tho' without that clamorous weeping made use of by the other Indians, several boats of whom were about the ship shouting out their lamentations, as vieing with each other not who should cry most, but who should cry loudest—a custom we have often condemned in conversation with our particular friends as savouring more of affected grief than real grief.

Apart from Tupaia, who was moved to genuine grief when he finally had to part from his own people, there were many heavy hearts aboard the *Endeavour* as she gently sailed out of Matavai Bay and away from Tahiti. Ahead lay God knew what dangers and horrors, while on the island remained easy living, and the warm and willing bodies of the island girls.

But the men were fit, rested and well fed, the little Whitby collier was bursting with fresh supplies, and her casks were filled with sweet water. There was also the agreeable knowledge that there were plans to land on some of the other South Sea islands before heading into the unknown.

Four days after leaving Tahiti the *Endeavour* dropped anchor at Fare, a fine sheltered bay at the island of Huahine, having been wafted there by a good breeze, which Tupaia claimed to have obtained by praying to Tane, the Tahitian god of beauty, peace and growing things. In fact Tupaia was quite crafty with his incantations. Banks noticed :

Our Indian often prayed to Tane for a wind and as often boasted to me of the success of his prayers, which I plainly saw he never began till he saw a breeze so near the ship that it generally reached her before his prayer was finished.

As usual, canoes came out to meet the vessel, but unlike the Tahitians the natives of Huahine were shy and even seemed afraid of the strangers, but once reassured by Tupaia, a chief and his wife came aboard. Later, when Banks and a party went ashore there was a long ritual of prayers, led by Tupaia and the presentation of gifts to the island's own god. In return the visitors were given a pig for their god, which, Banks remarked irreverently 'will certainly be our bellies'.

He found the islanders dull and lazy compared with the Tahitians, and when he suggested that some of them should accompany him into the hills they declined, saying they were afraid they would die of fatigue.

For the remainder of July and into the middle of August the *Endeavour* cruised through the Society Islands, with Banks and Solander going ashore at every opportunity. Generally they were well received and it was a productive period of collecting and observing local customs. It was in this latter pursuit that Banks was inclined to become over-enthusiastic. He nearly created a riot by trying to analyse a sacred object.

Wherever they went there was feasting and dancing, and handsome, willing girls, until they reached the island of Rurutu. As the shore boat approached the island a number of natives appeared armed with long lances. They were joined by others until about sixty were assembled. 'The boat standing along shore not intending to land till she got round the next point made them (I believe) think that we were afraid

Hat in hand, Joseph Banks stands with Capt Cook on the historic day in April 1770 when the explorer took possession of New South Wales for the British Crown at Botany Bay. Eighteen years later the territory became a British colony

John Russell's portrait of Dorothea Hugessen, the eldest daughter of a wealthy Kent landowner who married Joseph Banks in 1779. A gentle, rather plain woman, she devoted her life to collecting antique china and helping Banks with his innumerable enterprises (*From the Brabourne Collection, Courtauld Institute of Art*)

Sarah Sophia, Banks's sister, was a tall, angular, and distinctly eccentric woman. An inveterate collector of curios, she never married, but committed her life to helping her brother in his work. The portrait is by John Russell (*From the Brabourne Collection, Courtauld Institute of Art*)

of them.' Certainly the hesitation in landing seemed to give the islanders spirit. While the majority sat on the beach, two armed warriors walked along the strand keeping pace with the boat, and then without warning ran into the sea and began to swim towards the landing party. They were easily outpaced by the oarsmen. Two more men ran forward and tried to swim to the visitors, while a third ran ahead and plunged into the water to cut off the boat, and easily reached it.

Banks tried to persuade John Gore, the officer commanding the boat, to take the islander aboard, because 'it was so fair an opportunity of making friends with a people who certainly looked upon us as their enemies.' Gore refused and the sailors bent to their oars and outran the swimmer and another who had joined him.

When the explorers rounded the point they found another beach equally crowded with armed men. These warriors had a canoe which they launched.

As soon as it approached us we lay upon our oars and called to them that we were friends and would give them nails if they would come to us; they, after a little hesitation came up to the boat's stern and took the nails that were given them, seemingly with great satisfaction, but in less than a minute seemed to have formed a design of boarding our boat and taking her.

Three of the islanders jumped into the boat and began to grapple with the sailors. The first to board landed by Banks:

He instantly snatched my powder horn out of my pocket, which I immediately laid hold of and wrenched out of his hand, not without some difficulty. I then laid my hand on his breast and attempted to shove him overboard, but he was too strong for me and kept his place.

Gore tried to fire his musket over the natives' heads; it misfired, but a volley was discharged and the boarders plunged back into the sea. One of the sailors fired a final shot which grazed the head of one of the men. The wound was not serious, and when he got back to his canoe he stood up shouting defiantly.

By now the crowd on the beach had grown to at least 200, and was becoming increasingly excited and menacing. Suddenly a man with a long lance broke away and began dancing and shaking the weapon, and screaming at the *Endeavour* party. His words, Tupaia said, were a message of hate and defiance. The dancer was joined by another wearing a magnificent head-dress made from the tail feathers of tropic birds, and a costume of red, yellow and brown cloth. He leapt and cavorted with astounding energy, and was dubbed 'Harlequin' by the watching sailors.

Despite the clearly hostile reception that awaited them, the shore party could not land for shoals. They rowed slowly along the coast, always accompanied by the dancers and their followers. Eventually they reached a small coral outcrop where a number of people were gathered. An old man, also armed, hailed them and asked where they came from. 'Tahiti,' Tupaia replied, and then launched into one of his lengthy prayers, which gradually calmed the excited islanders, who unexpectedly began to trade some of their arms and pieces of cloth for nails.

There was a small gap in the coral, but heavy rollers prevented them from landing, and anyway there was no enthusiasm for spending the night on the island. As had been the case so often in the past the shore party was poorly armed. They had a few muskets, but no bayonets.

We left the ship in a hurry taking with us no kinds of arms but our muskets, which without bayonets would have made but a poor resistancse against these people's weapons, all meant to fight hand to hand; but what was worst of all was the difficulty of landing, which we could not do without wetting ourselves and arms.

The islanders themselves, Banks noted, were 'strong and lusty' and were armed with sharpened hardwood lances nearly twenty feet long, and heavy seven-foot clubs. The decision to return to the *Endeavour* was clearly wise, and Banks comforted himself with the knowledge that the island was 'more barren than anything we have seen in these seas'.

The hostile reception at Rurutu, however, brought the South Sea islands expedition to an end on a sour note, though from Banks' point of view it had been an unqualified success. Despite his often time-consuming duties as housekeeper and thief-catcher, he had managed to put together a unique biological and ethnological collection, along with folios of drawings and paintings.

But perhaps most valuable of all is his journal with its detailed descriptions, sharp observations, freshness and wit. Even Cook, with his map-maker's eye for detail, borrowed heavily from it for his own account of the voyage.

CHAPTER 5

ON TO NEW ZEALAND

Two days out from Rurutu there was a short-lived excitement when the hands on deck insisted that they had sighted land. Even Tupaia, who seems to have been a bit of a know-all, gave it a name, but it turned out to be no more than a cloud bank.

Only three days clear of the islands, the fresh fruit and vegetables ran out, most of them having rotted; and by 13 August the hogs and fowls began to die through lack of their familiar diet and the cold winds which were steadily driving the *Endeavour* towards the area of the Great Southern Continent.

The first anniversary of sailing from England was celebrated by Banks and his companions on 25 August with a piece of Cheshire cheese and a tankard of porter which had been reserved for the occasion, 'which proved excellently good, so that we lived like Englishmen and drank the health of our friends in England'. Any opportunity to raise a glass in celebration, or for any other reason, appeared to be welcomed on the *Endeavour*. If Banks is to be believed, drinking was rife on the ship, and there is some evidence to support this. Three days after the first anniversary one of the seamen, a John Reardon, was

. . . found so drunk that he scarce had any signs of life and in about an hour he expired. Where he could have got his liquor is a mystery which, however, nobody seems to enquire into, probably not fairly. I have more than once had occasion to congratulate myself on my prudence in taking wine on board at Madeira, as I believe I may safely say that there is not a cask on board the ship that has not been tapped to the great dissatisfaction of the owners, who in general have had the comfort to find the gentlemen honest enough not to have filled up with salt water; in same cases, however, this was not a consideration of much comfort as many of the casks were two-thirds empty and some quite.

A month out and Banks was ill, vomiting 'a thin acid liquid', and Solander was also unwell. Monkhouse, the ship's surgeon, advised them to take Dr Hulme's concentrated lemon juice, obviously seeing the men's symptoms as the first stages of scurvy. Certainly there was by now a serious shortage of fresh food on board the vessels, although supplies of salted pork and beef, as well as flour and dried peas, were in good condition. The ship's biscuits on the other hand, were alive with weevils. 'I have often seen hundreds, nay thousands shaken out of a single biscuit.' For the officers and Banks and his party the condition of the biscuits was slightly improved by baking them in an oven

. . . not too hot, which makes them (the weevils) all walk off, but this cannot be allowed to the private people who must find the taste of the animals very disagreeable as they every one taste as strong as mustard or rather spirits of hartshorn.

Always the naturalist, Banks identified five varieties of weevil, some feeding on the biscuit and others preying on the eggs of the others. It is a wonder there was any biscuit left at all.

Banks, who had to provision his own party, complained that he and his people were on shorter rations than the crew. His private stores, however, did not seem to be all that bad—seventeen sheep, four or five fowls, about as many Tahitian hogs, and muscovy ducks, an English boar, and a sow with a litter. 'In the use of these we were rather sparing as the time of our getting a supply is rather precarious. Salt stock we have nothing worth mentioning.'

Although the threat of scurvy was never absent when ships were at sea for any length of time, Cook kept it at bay by feeding his crew on a regular ration of sauerkraut. But one problem which did make its ugly appearance after leaving Tahiti was venereal disease. When the *Endeavour* left England a few men were found to be infected, though they were to all appearances clear by the time they reached Cape Horn; but within two weeks of arriving at Tahiti venereal disease reappeared among the crew. When they left the island, twenty-four sailors and nine of the eleven marines were diseased.

During the latter part of the eighteenth century there was a running, and often acrimonious, argument concerning which nation took venereal disease to Tahiti. The British blamed de Bourgainville and his expedition, de Bourgainville blamed Wallis and the *Dolphin* crew. The Tahitians further confused the situation by calling the disease Apa no Pretane (the English disease), but despite this they blamed de Bourgainville, who visited the island with his two ships between the British landings.

Apart from some illness and concern about the state of the ship's stores, the voyage was reasonably uneventful, and on 6 October 1769 land was sighted by one of the boys, Nicholas Young.

I was luckily upon deck and well I was entertained. Within a few minutes the cry circulated and up came all hands; this land could then not be seen even from the tops, yet few were there who did not plainly see it from the deck till it appeared that they looked at least five points wrong.

But land there was, and the *Endeavour*, rolling on the swell, slowly closed with it.

At first Banks thought that the jagged profile on the horizon might be two large islands. On the morning of 7 October it was clearly to be seen as a large body of land. Smoke was spotted rising from several points among ranges of hills which were dominated by mountains, 'some of which appear enormously high'. 'All hands', Banks wrote, 'seem to agree that this is certainly the Continent we are in search of.' Although it was New Zealand they were approaching, Banks hung grimly to his belief in the Great Southern Continent.

The following day the *Endeavour* sailed into Poverty Bay. A few canoes came towards the ship, but turned away before reaching hailing distance, and seemed to deliberately ignore the visitors, although a group of natives did gather and sit on the beach, presumably keeping the aliens under observation.

Possibly because it was a large land, Banks and his companions seemed to assume that it and its people would be more developed than the Tahitians. From the number of fires smoking on shore he concluded that it was heavily populated, and when the stockade of a fortified village was spotted on a hilltop most were 'of the opinion that it must or shall be a park of deer, or a field of oxen and sheep.'

At four o'clock on the eighth the *Endeavour* came to anchor, and in the evening Banks went ashore with a party of sailors and marines. They marched along the coast in search of good water, and the few natives they saw took fright and ran away. But while the main group was away, a small war-party attacked the shore boat, which had been left in the care of four of the ship's boys. The boys managed to get the boat into a river, but were still being threatened when the pinnace came to their rescue, opening fire on the attackers and killing one.

The sound of gunfire brought Banks and his people hurrying back. On the shore they found the body of a man shot through the heart. It was Banks's first sight of a Maori at close quarters, and needless to say he described him :

He was a middle-sized man tattooed in the face on one cheek only in spiral lines very regularly formed; he was covered with a fine cloth of a manufacture totally new to us; his hair was tied in a knot on the top of his head; his complexion brown, but not very dark.

That night they could hear the Maoris having some kind of council of war, their voices ringing angrily out across the water. At daybreak Cook decided to attempt another landing to make contact with the Maoris, although he and the ship's company were uneasy at the hostile reception they had received, especially having become accustomed to the indolent, almost over-generous charm of the Tahitians. A show of force was decided on and three boats manned with sailors and marines headed towards the shore, where a high surf did not make landing easy. But when it was seen that a group of about fifty Maoris had retreated to the farther side of the river Cook concluded that they had been sufficiently cowed to be manageable.

So landing with the little boat only the Captain, Dr Solander, Tupaia and myself went to the river side to speak to them. As soon almost as we appeared they rose up and every man produced either a long pike or a small weapon of well polished stone about a foot long and thick enough to weigh four or five pounds, (the latter was a Patu, a kind of stone knife more useful for clubbing than cutting) with these they threatened us and signalled us to depart. A musket was then fired wide of them, the ball of which struck the water. They saw the effect and immediately ceased their threats.

Despite the effect of the shot, the four men decided to retreat and wait for the marines to come up. As at the landing on Tahiti the marines were expected to make a show of strength. The only difference was that instead of being greeted with palm fronds of peace they now faced a tough, determined people, but they still made a brave show as they marched in close formation

. . . with a Jack carried before them to a little bank about fifty yards from the river . . . here they were drawn up in order and again we advanced to the river side with Tupaia, who now found that the language of the people was so like his own that he could tolerably well understand them and they him.

Tupaia explained that the British expedition wanted provisions and water and was prepared to pay with iron. He also asked the Maoris to lay down their arms. Having seen the power of a musket they understandably refused to do so, but they were prepared to trade. Tupaia was not happy. He sensed treachery and warned Banks to be on his guard.

The negotiations dragged on until finally one of the Maoris stripped off his clothes and swam across the river. He was followed by two more and was eventually joined by the remainder, all still bearing their arms. Banks, Cook and their companions handed out beads and nails which hardly impressed the warriors who merely gave a few feathers in exchange, a far cry from the pigs, fruit and vegetables that the *Endeavour* so badly needed. The Maories were, however, demonstrably eager to exchange their weapons for muskets.

They made several attempts to snatch the guns from the visitors. 'We were on our guard so much that their attempts failed and they were made to understand that we must kill them if they snatched anything from us.' But the threat had little effect. When Charles Green, the astronomer, turned to talk to someone, a Maori leapt forward and whipped his hanger from its sheath, and calmly walked away waving it triumphantly over his head and yelling with glee.

It now appeared necessary for our safety that so daring an act should be instantly punished.

Banks, who had often used threats, but rarely violence, on Tahiti, was the first to demand action, and Cook agreed with him.

I fired my musket which was loaded with small shot, levelling it between his shoulders who was not fifteen yards from me. On the shot striking him he ceased his cry, but continued to wave it over his head, retreating as gently as before. The surgeon who was nearer him seeing this fired a ball at him, at which he dropped.

Two Maoris ran forwards, one grabbing the felled man's patu, and the other trying to take the hanger, which the surgeon retrieved just in time.

But even the shooting failed to intimidate the Maoris, and any hope of making peaceful contact was at an end. There was nothing for it but to return to the boats and search for a fresh anchorage for the *Endeavour* in a bay which seemed 'more fruitful'. It was while they were surveying the bay that two canoes appeared, one sailing and the other being paddled.

The Captain now resolved to take one of these, which in all probability might be done without the least resistance, as we had three boats full of men and the canoes seemed to be fishermen, who probably were without arms.

The boats were positioned in such a way that it would be hard for the natives to escape.

The paddling canoe first saw us and made immediately for the nearest land, the other sailed on till she was in the midst of us before she saw us. As soon as she did she struck her sail and began to paddle so briskly that she outran our boat. On a musket being fired over her she, however, immediately ceased paddling and the people in her, seven in all, made all possible haste to strip, as we thought to leap into the water, but no sooner did our boat come up with her than they began with stones and paddles to make so brisk a resistance that we were obliged to fire into her, by which four were killed. The other three, who were boys, leaped overboard. One of them swam with great agility, and when taken made every effort in his power to prevent being taken into the boat; the other two were more easily prevailed upon.

As soon as they were in the boat they squatted down, expecting, no doubt, instant death, but on finding themselves well used, and that clothes were given them, they recovered their spirits in a very short time and before we got to the ship, appeared almost totally insensible of the loss of their fellows.

Once on board the *Endeavour* they were given bread, which they wolfed down, and more clothes.

This good usage had such an effect that they seemed to have entirely forgot everything that had happened, put on a cheerful and lively countenance, and asked and answered questions with a great deal of curiosity.

In the evening the Maori boys ate a vast quantity of salt pork and bread, and settled peacefully to sleep on the deck. Once again from the shore came the sound of loud angry voices, while on the *Endeavour* there was a feeling of guilt and remorse for the explorers' trip ashore had left five natives dead and three wounded.

Banks, who had urged the use of firearms in the first place, sat down and in anguish wrote in his journal :

Thus ended the most disagreeable day my life has yet seen. Black be the mark for it, and heaven send that such may never return to embitter future recollection.

What happened that day was shocking and savage, but in mitigation it may be remembered that the *Endeavour* expedition was entirely on its own in an unknown land where the inhabitants were clearly hostile. It was a simple, harsh case of 'kill or be killed'.

The next morning, Banks, Cook and an armed party went ashore resolved to make another attempt at establishing peaceful relations with the Maoris by using the three boys as the link between them and the natives. But the peace bid only led to further confrontation, although a man claiming to be the boy's uncle did approach the party and talked at length.

Four days after arriving the *Endeavour* sailed from Poverty Bay, so named by Cook because nothing that his ship wanted could be obtained. Banks complained that he had gathered only forty species of plants, which, in the circumstances, seems to have been quite an achievement.

Despite the mayhem of the brief stay in Poverty Bay, as soon as the *Endeavour* began to pull out, seven canoes containing about fifty men paddled out to her and engaged in brisk trading, even to the extent of parting with their clothes and paddles.

Banks and Cook were anxious to discover what had become of the three boys they had set ashore. They persuaded four men to come aboard, one of whom Banks recognised from a war party that had threatened him. From these men they discovered that the boys were well and unharmed, and indeed, that it was because of their account of their treatment that the canoes had ventured so near the ship.

Banks wrote of the men :

Their behaviour, while on board showed every sign of friendship. They invited us very cordially to come back to our old bay or to a small cove which they had showed us nearer to it. I could not help wishing that we had done so, but the Captain chose rather to stand on in search of a better harbour than any we had yet seen. God send that we may not there have the same tragedy to act over again as we so lately perpetrated.

Once again Banks was stricken by the wasteful killings of 9 October, and in his choice of words admitted that he and the *Endeavour* party carried the blame.

Shortly before sunset the little fleet of canoes left for the shore, but three Maoris elected to remain on board. They enjoyed their dinner and entertained the crew with singing and dancing, but the following morning when they woke to discover they had been carried a considerable distance from their homes, they became distraught, and 'began to lament and weep very much'. Early in the morning, however, a number of canoes came up to the ship. One contained a chief, who was splendidly clothed and carried a fine whalebone patu. He came on board and when he left he took the three men with him.

Any hopes that the *Endeavour* expedition had made a lasting peace with the Maoris were swiftly dashed when the ship ran into dangerous reefs and shoals and had to twist and weave her way to safety. The odd manoeuvres attracted the attention of the Maoris, and five canoes filled with armed men sped across the water towards her.

They came so near us shouting and threatening that at last we were in some pain lest they should seize our small boat which had been lowered down to sound and now towed alongside. A musket was therefore fired over them. The effect of this was rather to encourage them than otherwise, so a great gun was ordered to be prepared and fired wide of them loaded with grape. On this they all rose in their boats and shouted, but instead of continuing the chase drew all together and after a short consultation went quietly away.

Round one to the *Endeavour*, but the following day, 13 October, nine canoes appeared, but whether to fight or trade was never discovered, because with a good breeze the normally slow vessel was easily able to outrun the canoes. Later that day a single large canoe with about twenty men aboard approached the ship: 'although they could not get within a mile of us, they shouted and threatened most prodigiously.'

Next morning about one hundred and fifty heavily armed men paddled towards the explorers, chanting war songs and brandishing their spears, clearly intent on attack. When they got within a hundred yards a charge of grape shot was fired just ahead of them. It had the desired effect and the attackers withdrew, only to return with six war canoes in the evening. This time Tupaia was able to get the warriors into conversation. He said that if they would lay down their arms they would all be friends. To everyone's surprise and relief the Maoris loaded their weapons into one canoe, which stood off, while the others came alongside and received gifts. At last it looked as if the explorers were making some progress without bloodshed.

On 15 October in Hawke Bay on North Island, fishermen came alongside and traded their catch for Tahitian bark cloth, which was held in high value by the Maoris. Trading went smoothly until 'little

Tayeto, Tupias boy', who was over the side handing up fish, was suddenly snatched into one of the canoes, which was immediately paddled away. The marines opened fire, killing one of the captors and wounding others. In the confusion Tayeto broke away and swam back to the *Endeavour*, pursued by a large canoe,

. . . but on some muskets and a great gun being fired at them (it) left off the chase. Our boat was lowered down and took up the boy, frightened enough, but not at all hurt. What number were killed in the boats we cannot tell, probably not many as the people who fired at the boat in which the boy was, were obliged to fire wide of her least they should strike him, and the other boats had only a few shots fired at them. When they attempted to return some of the gentlemen who looked through glasses said, however, that they saw three carried up the beach when the boats landed who were either dead or much wounded. From this daring attempt the point was called Cape Kidnappers.

During the nine days or so during which the *Endeavour* had been cruising down the New Zealand coast, the land had appeared barren and uninviting, so on 16 October Cook put the vessel about. Further contacts were made with the Maoris who now seemed distinctly subdued. They came to the ship in small groups, traded freely, and led the explorers to Anaura Bay and fresh water. They even provided Banks and Solander with a canoe to take them back to the ship when the shore boats were busy freighting fresh water. However, Banks and his party were so clumsy that they overturned the canoe in the breakers 'and were very well soused'.

Despite the alarms and fears of the previous days, Banks was developing a liking and respect for the Maoris. He found them cleaner and neater than the Tahitians, and was impressed that every three or four houses had a communal 'necessary house' (lavatory) 'and consequently the neighbourhood is kept clean, which was by no means the case at Tahiti'.

The new and refreshing friendliness of the natives continued. They traded peacefully and honestly, and even guided the *Endeavour* to a safe anchorage and landing place in Tolaga Bay where Cook was able to complete the job of watering and fuelling the ship. Banks and Solander went ashore for a long and fruitful botanising expedition, during which they came across a natural curiosity in a valley, which enchanted Banks.

In pursuing a valley bounded on each side by steep hills we, on a sudden, saw a most noble arch or cavern through the face of a rock leading directly to the sea, so that through it we had not only a view of the bay and hills on the other side, but an opportunity of imagining a ship or any other grand object opposite to it. It was certainly the most magnificent surprise I have ever met with, so much is pure nature superior to art in these cases.

The two naturalists were also treated to a display of Maori martial arts. As they were making their way back to the bay they were stopped by an old man who

. . . detained us some time showing the exercise of this country's arms, lance and patu, as they are called. The lance is made of hardwood from ten to fourteen feet long, very sharp at the ends. The patu is made of stone or bone, about a foot long. A stick was given him for an enemy. To this he advanced with most furious aspect brandishing his lance which he held with vast firmness; after some time he ran at the stick and supposing it a man run through the body he immediately fell upon the upper end of it, laying on most unmerciful blows with his patu, any one of which would probably have split most skulls. From hence I should be led to conclude that they give no quarter.

A few days later they were invited to a war dance, which involved both men and women.

They distorted their faces most hideously, rolling their eyes and putting out their tongues, but kept a very good time, often heaving most loud and deep sighs.

If all these demonstrations did not convince the explorers that they were dealing with a most determined and warlike people, Tupaia confirmed, through converation with the Maori priests, that it was the common habit to eat the bodies of their slain enemies.

On 31 October, having rounded the East Cape, a group of canoes approached

. . . and threatened us at a distance, which gave us much uneasiness as we hoped that an account of us and what we could and had done had spread farther than this.

One canoe came close to the ship, and at the same time a huge war canoe was launched,

. . . full of people, all armed with long lances .They came near and received signals from the boat that was near us. We judged there could not be less than sixty people in her, sixteen paddles of a side, besides some who did not paddle, and a long row of people in the middle from stem to stern, crowded as close as possible. On a signal from the small canoe they paddled briskly up towards the ship as if to attack. It was judged right to let them see what we could do, least should they come to extremeties we might be obliged to fire at them in which case numbers must be killed out of such a crowd. A gun loaded with grape was therefore fired ahead of them : they stopped paddling, but did not retreat : a round shot was fired over them : they saw it fall and immediately took to their paddles rowing ashore with more haste than I ever saw men, without so much as stopping to breathe till they got out of sight.

The repulse caused Cook to name the cape they stood opposite Cape Runaway.

The belief that the display of fire-power had put an end to attacks was dashed the following day when an even heavier attack was mounted. More canoes than before came out and the Maoris at first only seemed interested in trading. Relationships seemed friendly enough until a native snatched a bundle of linen that was hanging over the side. The thief stood up in his canoe and jeered at the seamen.

A musket was fired over him which did not at all spoil his mirth. A small shot was then fired at him, which struck him upon the back; heated, I suppose he was, for he regarded it less than most men would do a stripe, just shrinking his body without ceasing to bundle up the very linen he had stolen.

Only another volley of musket and round shot drove off the canoes, but at nightfall a double canoe came out with its crew hurling stones at the *Endeavour*. The attack was repeated at dawn.

The harrassment of the expedition continued with canoes coming out day and night, their occupants chanting war songs and promising to kill the visitors. Warning shots seemed to have little lasting effect.

On 4 November it became necessary to find an anchorage and a land base from which to carry out an observation of the Transit of Mercury. A spot was found where the River Purangi drained into the sea, and was named Mercury Bay.

Despite relationships with the Maoris being very strained and uneasy, a camp was set up and trading undertaken. Large quantities of wild celery were found, providing much-needed fresh vegetables.

On the ninth a successful observation of the Transit was made, and

Banks and Solander were able to devote some time to botanising. But at noon on the day of the observation the shore party was alarmed by the roar of one of the *Endeavour*'s heavy guns. Once again a Maori had been caught stealing and had been shot. A great gun had to be fired to scare away canoes so that a shore boat could make land without being attacked.

Surprisingly the Maoris later said that they thought their companion deserved to die, a view which was not shared by either Cook or Banks.

With trading producing little in the way of supplies, the lack of fresh food was proving a problem. During a short expedition inland about twenty shags were shot; not, one would imagine, the most agreeable food, but, wrote Banks, everyone declared

. . . that they were excellent food, as indeed I think they were. Hunger is certainly most excellent sauce, but since our fowls and ducks have been gone we find ourselves able to eat any kind of birds (for indeed we throw away none) without even that kind of seasoning. Fresh provision to a seaman must always be acceptable if he can get over the small prejudices which once affected several in this ship, most or all of whom are now, by virtue of good example, completely cured.

On 14 November it was decided to make ready to sail, and all hands were sent ashore to collect oysters (which abounded), wild celery, and lobsters, which Banks described as 'the largest and best I have ever met'. He and Solander gathered a huge number of fresh botanical specimens for Parkinson to draw and paint.

The following day the ship sailed, and only three days later she was again under attack, but fortunately it was mainly verbal. 'Come ashore and we will kill you all,' the Maoris yelled repeatedly. 'Well,' said Tupaia, 'but while we are at sea you have no manner of business with us. The sea is our property as much as yours.' Banks was impressed by the argument.

Such reasoning from an Indian, who had not the smallest hint from any of us, surprised me much, and the more as these were sentiments I never had before heard him give a hint about in his own case.

Despite the threat to their lives the expedition went ashore to explore a river that emptied into the Hauraki Gulf, which so reminded them of the Thames that Cook named it after London's river. Here, at least, they were warmly welcomed, and Banks had the leisure to examine the trees that grew thickly on the banks, and which he thought the 'finest timber my eyes ever beheld. Every tree as straight as a pine and of immense size'. Years later he recommended New Zealand as an ideal place to cut masts for the eastern shipping fleet.

Towards evening the shore party headed back to the *Endeavour*, but they had completely misjudged the distance, and although they rowed until midnight a freshening wind and heavy showers finally defeated them. Exhausted and wet through, they found a sheltered harbour in which to spend an uncomfortable night. Before daybreak they set out again, this time in fog and drizzling rain, and it was not before an hour after daylight that they sighted the ship.

We made shift to get on board by seven, tired enough, and lucky it was for us we did, for before nine it blew a fresh gale so that our boat could not have rowed ahead.

More trouble broke out the day after the expedition returned when a young Maori, one of a number trading on board, stole a half-minute glass, part of the equipment for measuring the speed of the vessel. He was caught, and the first lieutenant, in the absence of Cook, decided that he should be flogged. As the sailors were trying to tie him down his companions attempted to rescue him. The Maoris thought that the youth was about to be killed, but when Tupaia 'assured them that their friend would not be killed, he would only be whipped', they, according to Banks who was on deck at the time, were 'well satisfied'.

He endured the discipline and as soon as he was let go an old man, who perhaps was his father, beat him very soundly and sent him down into the canoes.

At the end of November the anchor was set in the Bay of Islands, one of the most beautiful parts of the coast of North Island, where again they had to face what now seemed to be the inevitable confrontation, only in this case the danger proved to be greater than before.

Following a clash with a large number of canoes, which were dispersed with a warning shot, it was thought to be safe to make a landing on the island of Motu Arohia.

At our parting from the ship not a canoe stirred, which we judged a good sign, but no sooner had we set a foot on the shore about three-quarters of a mile from the ship, but every canoe put off in a moment and pulled towards us. We were in a sandy cove behind the two heads of which the most of them landed, one or two only in sight; out of these they came running with every man his arms, others appeared on the tops of the hills and numbers from behind each head of the cove, so that we were in a moment surrounded.

The officers left on the *Endeavour*, who watched what was happening with growing alarm, estimated that the shore party was surrounded by five or six hundred warriors. Banks thought this an over-estimation, and put the numbers at no more than two hundred. Either way the small party was heavily outnumbered.

Banks and Cook showed extraordinary courage and coolness.

We now every man expected to be attacked but did not choose to begin the hostilities, so the Captain and myself marched up to meet them. They crowded a good deal but did not offer to meddle with us, tho' every man had his arms lifted up to strike. We brought them towards the party and made a line signing to them that they were not to pass it : they did not at first, but by this time a party from the other side had come up and mixed with our people.

The situation was crucial. In a hand to hand fight the explorers would have stood little chance. The only hope was to hold off a full attack long enough to give the *Endeavour* time to manoeuvre into a position that would enable her to discharge a broadside. So the party stood its ground while the warriors broke into a war chant, swaying and chanting, and twisting their faces into horrible grimaces. But when six natives broke away and attempted to haul the *Endeavour*'s boats up on the beach, the shore party had to act.

It was now time to fire. We, whose guns were loaded with small shot did so which drove them back. One man attempted to rally them; he, who was not twenty yards from us, came down towards us waving his patu and calling to his companions. Dr Solander, whose gun was not discharged, fired at him, on which he too ran.

The Maoris retreated to high ground, but were dislodged by muskets loaded with ball, 'none of which took effect farther than frightening them'.

For over a quarter of an hour the marines, sailors and scientists held off the attack, by which time the *Endeavour* was in her firing station and

Joseph Banks was only thirty-five when he was elected President of the Royal Society, a position he held for 42 years. When, after fierce opposition, he was elected, he arrived breathless in the Council Chamber, and announced: 'I believe never did a President of the Royal Society run so fast'. The portrait is by John Russell (*From the Brabourne Collection, Courtauld Institute of Art*)

Thomas Phillips's portrait of Sir Joseph Banks. Although crippled by gout in later life, Banks retained an iron grip on the affairs of The Royal Society, earning himself a reputation for autocracy from those Fellows who wished to see him voted out of office (*National Portrait Gallery*)

. . . fired at the Indians who were on the tops of the hills. The balls went quite over them, notwithstanding which they went off and at last left us our cove quite to ourselves, so that the muskets were laid down and all hands employed in gathering celery, which was here very plentiful.

The coolness of these eighteenth-century travellers was amazing. They seemed hardly to regard the constant danger around them. True, they were armed with firearms, but in the long run there was little that they could do to overwhelm the sheer weight of numbers opposed to them, as indeed was to be proved with the murder of Captain Cook on Hawaii ten years later in February 1779.

Banks observed that on the day following an attack the natives would invariably reappear in a peaceful, almost cowed frame of mind.

One general observation I here set down, that they always after one night's consideration have acknowledged our superiority, but hardly before. I have often seen a man whose next neighbour was wounded or killed by our shot not give himself the trouble to enquire how or by what means he was hurt, so that at the time of their attacks they, I believe, work themselves up into a kind of artificial courage which does not allow them time to think.

A sudden fair wind on 5 December brought the order to sail, but before the ship could get under way the wind turned foul, and finally sank away altogether leaving the vessel becalmed. Another attempt was made to leave the Bay of Islands that night and again the *Endeavour* was becalmed,

. . . so that the ship would neither wear nor stay : in a moment an eddy tide took hold of us and hustled so fast towards the land that before the officers resolved what was best to be done the ship was within a cable's length of the breakers. We had thirteen fathom water but the ground was so foul that they dared not drop an anchor. The eddy now took another turn and set her along the shore opening another bay, but we were too near the rocks to trust to that. The pinnace was ordered to be hoisted out in an instant to take the ship in tow. Every man in her was, I believe, sensible of the danger we were in so no-one spared to do his best to get her out fast. The event, however, showed how liable such situations must be to confusion. They lowered down too soon and she stuck upon a gun : from this she must be thrust by main force, in doing which they had almost overset her which would have tumbled out her oars. No man thought of running in the gun. At last that was done and she was afloat, her crew was soon in her and she went to her duty.

By this time the Endeavour was almost in the breakers, and the shore was lined with Maoris jeering and threatening to kill the entire ship's company when the vessel foundered. But providence was at hand. A small off-shore wind sprang up 'and with that and towing she, to our great joy, got head way again'.

Relief spread through the ship. 'We were all happy in our breeze and clear moonlight.' But the pleasure was short-lived. Banks was sitting on his cot undressing when the *Endeavour* struck a rock. 'Before I could get upon my legs she struck again.' However, the luck held. She freed herself without damage and sailed into a clear channel 'much to our satisfaction', Banks remarked drily, 'as the almost certainty of being eat as soon as you come ashore adds not a little to the terrors of shipwreck.'

During the following day the wind proved foul and troublesome. On some days the stocky little collier tacked to and fro for hours without making any progress at all. On Christmas Eve, 1769, the ship was becalmed and Banks went out shooting in a small boat. 'I had good success, killing chiefly several gannets or Solan Geese, so like European ones that they are hardly distinguishable from them.' They were the New Zealand Gannet (*Sula bassana serrator*).

As it was the humour of the ship to keep Christmas in the old-fashioned way it was decided to produce a goose pie for the festivities. It was 'eat with great approbation and in the evening all hands were as drunk as our forefathers used to be upon the like occasion'. Clearly it was a good party because on Boxing Day Banks noted, 'this morn all heads ached with yesterday's debauch'.

The wind continued foul as 1770 dawned, but with sufficient periods of calm for Banks to take out his boat, shooting sea birds and observing and collecting marine life.

By the middle of the month the *Endeavour* was abreast of Mount Egmont, which reared its snowcapped peak over 8,000 feet above the surrounding Taranaki district. Here they again made contact with the Maoris, a meeting that followed the now familiar pattern of threats from the armed warriors and warning shots from the explorers.

They went ashore which was botanically disappointing, although while fishing for fresh supplies in one haul of the seine alone a dozen different species of fish were caught.

The *Endeavour* was now in Queen Charlotte Sound, and it was here that Banks confirmed what he had long suspected, that the Maoris were habitual cannibals. On the evening of 16 January he was ashore with

Solander, Tupaia and a small party of seamen. They came on a native family preparing their evening meal which consisted mainly of a dog which was being broiled in an earth oven. Nearby were some baskets. In one Banks spotted two bones

. . . pretty clean picked, which as appeared upon examination were undoubtedly human bones. Tho' we had from the first of our arrival upon the coast constantly heard the Indians acknowledge the custom of eating their enemies we had never before had proof of it, but this amounted almost to a demonstration. The bones were clearly human, upon them were evident marks of their having been dressed on the fire. The meat was not entirely picked off from them and on the grisly ends which were gnawed were evident marks of teeth, and these were accidently found in a provision basket.

On asking the people what bones are these? they answered, The bones of a man. And have you eat the flesh? Yes. Have you none of it left? No.

As they were coming ashore the party had spotted the body of a woman floating in the water. She turned out to be a relative of the cannibal family, who explained that they disposed of their dead by burial at sea, and that she must have broken free from the rock used to sink her body.

'Why did not you eat the woman?' Banks asked.

'She was our relative.'

'Who then is it that you do eat?'

'Those who are killed in war.'

Questioning revealed that five days before an enemy war party came into the bay. Seven warriors were killed, and Banks's little family had eaten at least one of them. Although hardened to most things the seamen were nauseated.

The horror that appeared in the countenances of the seamen on hearing this discourse, which was immediately translated for the good of the company, is better conceived than described. For ourselves, and myself in particular, we were before too well convinced of the existence of such a custom to be surprised, tho' we were pleased at having so strong a proof of a custom which human nature holds in too great abhorance to give easy credit to.

But all was not horror in Queen Charlotte's Sound. The morning after meeting the cannibals Banks woke to the sound of hundreds of bell-birds singing.

Their voices were certainly the most melodious wild music I have ever heard, almost imitating small bells, but with most tuneable silver sound imaginable.

Because there was a plentiful supply of fresh food, the *Endeavour* stayed several days in the Sound. It was there, from the top of a hill, that Cook saw the Pacific Ocean and was convinced there was a passage through to it—as indeed there was, a passage that was for ever to bear his name—Cook Strait—dividing the two islands of New Zealand.

Evidence of cannibalism continued to intrude. The astute Maoris soon recognised the morbid curiosity of the English sailors and carried on a brisk trade in human bones 'the flesh of which they had eat'.

It seems that the Maoris' sexual habits also came under suspicion, judging by an account of one of the crew who returned to the ship in a towering rage. He had tried to buy a girl for a piece of cloth.

One was chose, as he thought, who willingly retired with him, but on examination proved to be a boy; that on his returning and complaining of this another was sent who turned out to be a boy likewise.

The more furious he became the more the Maoris laughed at him. Whether or not the natives were homosexual seems open to doubt. It is more likely that the Maoris were offended at the trade and were merely making a fool of the man.

Throughout February and March the *Endeavour* sailed steadily round South Island, with Banks and a few others still arguing that this was, indeed, part of the Great Southern Continent—not a belief shared by Cook.

On 24 February he wrote:

We are now on board two parties, one who wished that the land in sight might, and the other that it might not, be a continent; myself have always been the most firm for the former, tho' sorry I am to say that in the ship my party is so small that I firmly believe that there are no more heartily for it than myself and one poor midshipman. The rest begin to sigh for roast beef.

His belief in the continent was boosted on 5 March, when

. . . a point of land seen this morn which inclined much to the westward was supposed by the no continents the end of the land; towards even, however, it cleared up and we Continents had the pleasure to see more land to the Southward.

On the sixth he continued:

Land seen as far as south so our unbelievers are almost inclined to think that Continental measures will at last prevail

But four days later Banks had to admit defeat. The *Endeavour* rounded the South Cape and headed into the Tasman Sea.

March 10 : Blew fresh all day, but carried us round the Point to the total demolition of our aerial fabric called Continent.

On 29 March Banks was taken ill with violent headaches and sickness, a malady which had affected others of the company and led to a fever. In fact he recovered in twenty-four hours, but it did mean that it left him no time for last-minute collecting.

Although he had had relatively few opportunites of going ashore as the *Endeavour* sailed round the two islands (and when he and his fellow travellers did so they were more involved in dealing with the Maoris than engaging in scientific research), he was able to produce a remarkably detailed impression of New Zealand. With his trained farmer's eyes, he assessed its potential for settlers.

He wrote :

The soil is in general light, and consequently admirably adapted to the uses for which the natives cultivate it, whose crops consist entirely of roots.

He saw

. . . very large tracks of ground . . . and an immense quantity of woodland, which was yet uncleared, but promised great returns to the people who would take the trouble of clearing it.

There were swamps, which like his native Lincolnshire fens, could be drained and turned into farmland. But it was the natural timber that most impressed him.

The straightest, cleanest, and I may say the largest I have ever seen—at least speaking of them in the gross; I may have seen several times single trees larger than any I observed among them, but it was not one but all these trees which were enormous, and doubtless had we had time and opportunity to search we might have found much larger ones than any we saw, as we were never but once ashore among them, and that but for a short time on the banks of the River Thames, where we rowed for many miles between woods of these trees, to which we could see no bounds.

Indeed it was the River Thames that he pinpointed as an ideal place to establish a colony.

A ship as large as ours might be carried several miles up the river, where she would be moored to the trees as safe as alongside a wharf in London river, a safe and sure retreat in case of an attack from the natives, as she might even be laid on the mud and a bridge built to her.

The noble timber, of which there is such abundance, would furnish plenty of materials either for the building of defences, houses or vessels. The river would furnish plenty of fish, and the soil make ample returns of any European vegetable sown in it.

Hardly could a more encouraging presentation have been made, particularly to a country like Great Britain, whose American colonies were threatened, and who was looking for room to expand.

On top of this Banks also produced copious observations of native habits and customs; their houses, weapons and tools, and with the help of Tupaia, assembled a useful Maori vocabulary. He noted local food, and such food as could be obtained by foraging.

So while he had not been able to botanise and collect as much as he would have chosen, he was content when, on 31 March, the *Endeavour* turned her stern on New Zealand with the purpose of finding Van Dieman's Land.

CHAPTER 6

THE 'ENDEAVOUR'
IN AUSTRALIA

The *Endeavour* voyagers had been away from home for nearly two years. They had wallowed in the joys of Tahiti, had met cannibals in New Zealand, and had gone a long way towards proving that the fabled Terra Australis Incognita—the Unknown Southern Land—did not exist. Brilliant navigation and sheer hard work had caused to fade, if not disappear altogether, a dream that had haunted men for years, for not only was this undiscovered land regarded as the mass that balanced the world, but it was thought that it must also be a continent containing unimaginable riches.

It was perhaps the realisation that it almost certainly did not exist that bred a restlessness among the *Endeavour*'s people. That and the fact that the ship's supplies were low and stale.

Only a few days out from New Zealand it was found that the course was too far to the north. Banks, who was only too keen to continue the voyage, remarked caustically in his entry in his journal for 3 April

. . . the compass showed that the hearts of our people hanging that way caused a considerable north variation, which was sensibly felt by our navigators, who called it a current, as they usually do everything which makes their reckonings and observations disagree.

As far as Banks was concerned the sailors were deliberately altering course so that there would be no alternative but to return home. If this was their design, they were frustrated.

Sailing into calm, hot weather, Banks spent much of his time working around the ship in a small boat, shooting birds and netting marine life. He was able to make a detailed study of the stinging mechanism of the Portuguese man-of-war (*Holothuria obtusata*).

Early on the morning of 19 April the east coast of Australia (New South Wales) was sighted—'sloping hills, covered in part with trees or bushes, but interspersed with large tracts of sand.'

The following day Banks was more enthusiastic about the passing terrain, and observed :

The country this morn rose in gentle sloping hills which had the appearance of the highest fertility, every hill seemed to be clothed with trees of no mean size.

Columns of smoke rising further inland were the first evidence of inhabitants, which they sighted two days later. The Aborigines were gathered along the shoreline and 'appeared through our glasses to be enormously black'.

As the *Endeavour* cruised gently along the coast, Banks's view of the passing country varied from the enthusiastic to the disparaging.

The country, tho' in general well clothed, appeared in some places bare. It resembled in my imagination the back of a lean cow, covered in general with long hair, but nevertheless where her scraggy hip bones have stuck out farther than they ought, accidental rubs and knocks have entirely bared them of their share of covering.

On the twenty-seventh the *Endeavour* stood in close to the shore and Cook decided to attempt a landing; on being launched the pinnace was found to be too leaky, but the yawl was sound although it would carry only three passengers—in this case, Cook, Banks, Solander and four oarsmen. As they approached the beach four Aborigines squatted on a rock, but they ran away before the boat was within a quarter of a mile of the landing place. The high surf, however, made a landing impossible.

The following day a landing was effected, but not before the Aborigines had threatened them with spears, throwing sticks and boomerangs. Forearmed with their Maori experiences the explorers fired warning shots from which the natives fled into the surrounding countryside, leaving their small children hidden under pieces of bark in their rough shelters. Banks and his party left the children where they were, and also left gifts of beads, ribbons and pieces of cloth, but they did seize all the fishbone-pointed spears they could find, which amounted to about fifty. So long as the party was ashore the Aborigines remained hidden in the bush. But later in the evening when all were back aboard the ship the natives returned to their homes.

It was quickly noted that when the Aborigines put on a display of aggression they did so from a safe distance, but for most of the time they appeared to be completely indifferent to the presence of the visitors, barely raising their eyes from any task they were employed upon. Such a situation made it possible for Banks and Solander to make collecting trips deep into the country, and while they hardly saw any natives they did find many hitherto unknown plants.

The spot that provided such an abundance of new plants was to feature large in Australia's history and folk law—Botany Bay. It was a place that was to live with Banks for the rest of his life.

On 1 May 1770 Banks, Cook, Solander and an escort set out on a serious penetration into the country. It was remarkably lush, richly covered with plants and trees. When heavy rain called a temporary halt to excursions, Banks remarked:

We who had already got so many plants were well contented to find an excuse for staying on board to examine them a little at least.

With the exception of Tierra del Fuego, at no other landfall in the entire expedition had Banks and Solander been so free from interference to engage in their favourite pursuit. Wherever they went the Aborigines fled before them, and there was no question of thieving or serious threats to life.

By 3 May Banks was able to record:

Our collection of plants was now grown so immensely large that it was necessary that some extraordinary care should be taken of them least they should spoil in the books.

To avoid such a danger, two hundred quires of paper were taken ashore and spread in the sun to make sure they would be dried beyond reasonable danger of spoiling.

While the work was being undertaken a small group of Aborigines in canoes came quite close to the naturalists, but were so intent on their fishing that they barely seemed to notice the intruders. One, somewhat bolder than his companions, did come ashore and spied on some of the *Endeavour* people who were shooting game, but he prudently kept himself out of sight.

In the evening Cook and Solander were exploring the bay. Whenever they saw a fire they approached it, but the natives fled. So terrified were they that they even left their meals of shellfish still cooking. Rather unkindly Cook and his party ate the fish, although they did leave beads and ribbons in exchange.

As was so often his fancy, Banks spent a good deal of time botanising on his own. On 4 May he noted:

Myself in the woods botanizing as usual, now quite void of fear as our neighbours have turned out such rank cowards.

If the natives were unwilling to make contact or trade in any way, at least the *Endeavour* company was able to live well off the land and, indeed, from the sea. Some gigantic sting-rays were caught in the bay, weighing up to 336lbs, which were eaten with relish with a kind of native spinach (*Tetragonia expansa*), which Banks introduced into England.

On the sixth, the ship continued on her voyage passing fertile and well-wooded country, and ample evidence of a reasonably flourishing population. But still the Aborigines demonstrated their extraordinary lack of interest in the explorers. Perhaps they were working on the theory that if they ignored the strangers they would simply fade away. During one morning they watched a group of about twenty natives carrying loads:

Not one was observed to stop and look towards the ship. They pursued their way in all appearance entirely unmoved by the neighbourhood of so remarkable an object as a ship must necessarily be to people who have never seen one.

Seventeen days later the *Endeavour* was riding at anchor in Bustard Bay, where Banks went ashore and was rewarded with the discovery of a great number of plants. He also experienced the doubtful pleasure of trekking through a mangrove swamp. In the branches of the trees

. . . were many nests of ants, one sort of which were quite green. These, when the branches were disturbed came out in large numbers and revenged themselves very sufficiently upon their disturbers, biting sharper than any I have felt in Europe. The mangroves also had another trap which most of us fell into, a small kind of caterpillar, green and beset with many hairs: these sat upon the leaves many together ranged by the side of each other like soldiers drawn up, twenty or thirty perhaps upon one leaf; if these wonderful militia were touched but ever so gently they did not fail to make the person offending them sensible of their anger, every hair of them stinging much as nettles do, but with a more acute tho lasting smart.

Banks also discovered eucalypti, and noted that one in particular, *Eucalyptus crebra*, produced the gum-like *sanguis draconis* (dragon's blood), a substance used in the manufacture of shellac.

It was while the explorers were at Bustard Bay that there occurred quite one of the nastiest incidents of the voyage, and one that for some reason Banks does not mention in his journal. On the night of 22 May the ship's clerk, Orton, clearly not over-popular, went to bed very drunk and collapsed into a deep alcoholic sleep. While he snored and grunted in boozy oblivion all his clothes were cut off his back, and not content with that his tormentors cut off part of his ears.

Cook was outraged by this crude and savage practical joke (or was it revenge?). Suspicion at first fell upon a young American midshipman, James Mario Matra, who is also sometimes known as Magra. He was eventually cleared, and later cropped up in Banks's life when he asked for support for a plan to found a colony in Australia for loyalist refugees from the American rebellion.

Subsequent events suggested that the ear-cropping was the work of another midshipman, Patrick Saunders, who deserted at Batavia after Cook offered a reward for information that would lead to the naming of the culprit.

Apart from the richness of plants, the area supported large numbers of pelicans, but they were so shy that Banks was unable to shoot a specimen; though he did bag a fine bustard, which was consumed a day later. Writing on a well-filled stomach on 24 May, he said:

At dinner we eat the bustard we had shot yesterday. It turned out an excellent bird, far the best we all agreed that we have eat since we left England, and as it weighed fifteen pounds our dinner was not only good, but plentiful.

Added to which, their menu included oysters which were found in great numbers in the mud of the mangrove swamps.

By the end of the month they were going ashore again when the ship anchored in Thirsty Sound, named for the obvious fact that the anchorage failed to produce any fresh water. Banks lost no time in going in search of plants, and quickly found some new species.

Despite sand burrs, whose wicked hooked seeds worked their way through clothes and into the flesh, and clouds of mosquitoes, the naturalists pushed into the country, and were rewarded with a profusion of butterflies.

The air was for the space of three or four acres crowded with them to a wonderful degree : the eye could not be turned in any direction without seeing millions and yet every branch and twig was almost covered with those that sat still.

On a tree they found a chrysallis 'as bright as if it had been silvered over with the most burnished silver'. It was taken back to the ship and hatched the following day :

. . . into a butterfly of a velvet black changeable to blue, his wings both upper and under marked near the edges with many light brimstone coloured spots, those of his underwings being indented deeply at each end.

And not only was Banks rewarded with butterflies, he also made the first observation of that curious little fish the mud-skipper.

It was about the size of a minnow in England, and had two breast fins, very strong. We often found him in places quite dry where he may have been left by the tide : upon seeing us he immediately fled from us leaping as nimbly as a frog by the help of his breast fins : nor did he seem to prefer water to land for if seen in the water he often leaped out and proceeded upon dry land, and where the water was filled with small stones standing above its surface, would leap from stone to stone rather than go into the water.

By the beginning of June the explorers were heading steadily into the Great Barrier Reef, and the going became increasingly dangerous and treacherous.

On 1 June Banks wrote :

In the night it rained and at times blew strong but not much to our satisfaction who were in a situation not very desirable, as if our anchor should come home or cable break we had nothing to expect but going ashore on some or other of the shoals that lay around us.

On the second he recorded : 'at noon the irregularity of the soundings made it necessary to send the boat ahead again.' To add to Banks's worries Tupaia complained of swollen gums, a sure sign of scurvy.

For the next week the vessel tip-toed through the maze of islands and reefs. Just as dark was falling on the night of the tenth, rocks and shoals were seen ahead, towards which the *Endeavour* was driven by an off-shore wind.

While we were at supper she went over a bank of seven or eight fathom water which she came upon very suddenly; this we concluded to be the tail of the shoals we had seen at sunset and therefore went to bed in perfect security, but scarce were we warm in our beds when we were called up with the alarming news of the ship being fast upon a rock, which she in a few moments convinced us of by beating very violently against the rocks. Our situation became now greatly alarming : We had stood off shore three hours and a half with a pleasant breeze so knew we could not be very near it : we were little less than certain that we were upon sunken coral rocks, the most dreadful of all others on account of their sharp points and grinding quality which cut through a ships bottom almost immediately.

The officers, however, behaved with inimitable coolness void of all hurry and confusion; a boat was got out in which the master went and after sounding round the ship found that she had run over a rock and consequently had shoal water all round her. All this time she continued to beat very much so that we could hardly keep our legs upon the quarter deck; by the light of the moon we could see her sheating boards etc., floating thick round her; about twelve her false keel came away.

By the time boats and anchors had been put overboard so that an an attempt could be made to haul her off, the tide had ebbed, and they had to wait until it rose again 'if she would hold together so long'. Added to this was the fact that she had struck at the top of the tide, so there would not be that much water on which to float her off.

For our comfort, however, the ship, as the tide ebbed, settled to the rocks and did not beat near so much as she had done; a rock, however, under her starboard bow kept grating her bottom, making a noise very plainly to be heard in the fore store rooms; this we doubted but would make a hole in her bottom, we only hoped that it might not let in more water than we could clear with our pumps.

When daylight came the explorers saw they were about twenty-four miles from the shore and with no islands nearby. But the dawn did bring a slackening of the wind which died down into a flat calm. Anchors were laid to haul the ship off, water and ballast were jettisoned and the six heavy guns on the deck were tossed overboard.

All this time the seamen worked with surprising cheerfulness and alacrity; no grumbling or growling was to be heard throughout the ship, no not even an oath (tho' the ship in general was as well furnished with them as most in His Majesty's service).

As the tide rose the ship once again began to work violently against the coral rock, and she began to make water, indeed, she made water so fast that despite desperate pumping with three pumps (a fourth would not work), she only just kept clear.

Now in my own opinion I entirely gave up the ship and packing up what I might save, prepared myself for the worst.

The most critical part of our distress now approached : the ship was almost afloat and everything ready to get her into deep water, but she leaked so fast that with all our pumps we could just keep her free : if (as was probable) she should make more water when hauled off she must sink and we well knew that our boats were not capable of carrying us all ashore, so that some, probably the most of us, must be drowned : a better fate maybe than those would have who should get ashore without arms to defend themselves from the Indians or provide themselves with food, on a country where we had not the least reason to hope for subsistance had they even every convenience to take it as nets etc., so barren had we always found it; and had they even met with good usage from the natives and food to support them, debarred from any hope of ever again seeing their native country or conversing with any but the most uncivilised savages, perhaps in the world.

The dreadful time now approached and the anxiety in everybody's countenance was visible enough : the capstan and windless were manned and they began to heave : fear of death now stared us in the face; hopes we had none of being able to keep the ship afloat till we could run her ashore on some part of the main where out of her materials we might build a vessel large enough to carry us to the East Indies. At ten o'clock she floated and was in a few minutes hauled into deep water where to our great satisfaction she made no more water than she had done, which, indeed, was full as much as we could manage tho' no one there was in the ship but who willingly exerted his utmost strength.

By 'everyone' Banks meant just that. All, including himself, took shifts on the pumps. Two days after striking the reef he wrote :

The people who had been twenty-four at exceeding hard work now began to flag; myself, unused to labour, was much fatigued and had laid down to take a little rest, was awakened about twelve with the alarming news of the ships having gained so much upon the pumps that she had four feet of water in her hold : add to this that the wind blew off the land a regular land breeze so that all hopes of running her ashore were totally cut off. This, however, acted upon everybody like a charm : rest was no more thought of but the pumps went with unwearied vigour till the water was all out, which was done in a much shorter time than was expected, and on examination it was found that she never had half so much water in her as was thought, the carpenter having made a mistake in sounding the pumps.

As one man handed over his place at the pumps to another the relieved man would collapse in the water flowing over the deck to revive.

With the good news that the leak was being contained the anchors were got up—one had to be cut free—for another attempt to make the shore. Jonathan Monkhouse then suggested fothering the leak.

Fothering was a little-used technique whereby a piece of sailcloth, studded with fist-sized bundles of wool and oakum, was lowered over the side, and by suction formed a seal over the leak.

About half an hour after the fother was in place:

To our great surprise the ship was pumped dry and upon letting the pumps stand she was found to make very little water, so much beyond our most sanguine expectations had this singular expedient succeeded.

That night they anchored with only the slightest leak invading the vessel, and an almost light-headed sense of relief running through the ship.

We were in an instant raised from almost despondency to the greatest hopes: we were now almost too sanguine, talking of nothing but getting her into some harbour where we might lay her ashore and repair her, or if we could not find such a place, we little doubted to the East Indies.

Throughout 13 June the *Endeavour* cautiously followed the ship's boats through a maze of reefs and shoals, searching unsuccessfully for a place to beach the vessel for repairs, because, as Banks remarked, there was 'nothing but a lock of wool between us and destruction'. Long after dark the pinnace returned to the crippled mother ship with news of a perfect harbour.

The following morning Banks and Cook went ashore and found that the harbour answered perfectly for their purposes. 'It was the mouth of a river, the entrance of which was to be sure narrow enough and shallow', but once in it would be an easy matter to unload the *Endeavour* and lay her down. Because of fresh winds it took three days to bring the ship to safety.

Only the day before docking, Tupaia developed advanced symptoms of scurvy, failing to respond to any treatment and becoming extremely ill. Green, the astronomer, was also in a bad way. But once ashore Tupaia at least appeared to cure himself with a fish diet. Banks noted on the eighteenth:

Tupaia, who had employed himself since we were here in angling and had lived entirely on what he had caught, was surprisingly recovered. Poor Mr Green still very ill.

The weather, which had been squally on their arrival, cleared and Banks and Solander were able to get out and botanise, which proved fruitful.

By the twenty-second the *Endeavour* was hauled down and Banks saw the hole in her bottom for the first time.

In the middle was a hole large enough to have sunk a ship with twice our pumps, but here providence had most visibly worked in our favour for it was in great measure plugged up by a stone which was as big as a man's fist.

In the gap left round the stone was the fothering. Banks marvelled at the way in which the coral had cut and gashed the ship's planking and timbers 'so that the whole might easily be imagined to be cut with an axe'.

It was while the expedition was confined to the river, fittingly called the Endeavour River, that kangaroos were first spotted. Some seamen who had been sent into the country to shoot pigeons reported 'an animal as large as a greyhound, of a mouse colour, and very swift'. A day or so later a seaman returned from the woods speaking of another strange creature 'about as large and much like a one gallon keg, as black as the devil and had two horns on its head'. It had moved slowly but the sailor did not dare touch it. From the description it was probably a fruit bat.

With the liberty to ramble through the woods and across the open countryside, or even wading through mangrove swamps, Banks was in his element. His pleasure was marred only by the discovery that when the *Endeavour* was hauled ashore the water still in her ran into the stern where he had stored plant specimens in the bread room. 'Nobody had warned me of this danger', he grumbled, 'which had never entered into my head.' By working through every daylight hour, however, the plants were retrieved and 'many were saved, but some entirely lost and spoiled'.

By the beginning of July the repairs on the *Endeavour* had been completed, and now the explorers faced the problem of getting out to the open sea again.

(left) Of all the honours that Sir Joseph Banks earned throughout his long career, none meant more to him than the Presidency of The Royal Society, which he fiercely protected from the intrusion of new learned societies

(below) Number 32, Soho Square was Sir Joseph Banks's London home for most of his life. It became the centre for men of science from all over the world, and an inspiration for young men starting out on careers as explorer-scientists *(John Freeman Group)*

Whipcord del.

The FLY CATCHING MACARONI! 1772

I rove from Pole to Pole, you ask me why.
I tell you Truth, to catch a _____ Fly!

Pub. by Marly acor to act July 12. 1772/30/Strand

Sir Jos. Banks

In common with most distinguished men of the 18th century, Sir Joseph Banks became the butt for cartoonists and lampoonists. In this cartoon of 1772 he is characterised as a butterfly-chasing buffoon (*John Freeman Group*)

We went upon a high hill to see what passage to the sea might be open. When we came there the prospect was indeed melancholy : the sea every-where full of innumerable shoals, some above and some under water, and no prospect of any straight passage out. To return as we came was impos-sible, the trade wind blew directly in our teeth; most dangerous then our navigation must be among unknown dangers. How soon might we again be reduced to the misfortune we had so lately escaped ! Escaped indeed we had not till we were again in an open sea.

So it was filled with these gloomy reflections that the men waited for suitable conditions for refloating the ship. Banks kept his mind occupied with drying and preserving his plant collection, which was now enormous.

The pinnace was sent out to find a passage through the reefs, which she discovered, but an off-shore wind was needed to carry the *Endeavour* through, and there had not been a breath of such a wind since they had been in the river. The pinnace did return, however, loaded with giant clams, 'one of which was more than two men could eat'.

When the *Endeavour* was refloated it was found that she had been strained by being pulled ashore and had sprung fresh leaks. So once again she was hauled up for inspection and repairs. It meant further delays, and, for Banks and his companions, more time for exploring and collecting.

They travelled some way up the river, finding the country rich in plants, including a strikingly beautiful hibiscus (*Hibiscus tiliaceus*). They saw flying foxes and more kangaroos, observing for the first time that the animals hopped rather than ran.

Meanwhile the pinnace had again been out looking for a more suitable passage, but without success; although once more it had returned with fresh food, this time turtles. It was heartening to know that if the expedition was going to be holed up in the Endeavour River for months at least there was a ready source of fresh food available.

The promise of such plenty of good provisions made our situation appear much less dreadful; were we obliged to wait here for another season of the year when the winds might alter we could do it without fear of wanting provisions : this thought alone put everybody in vast spirits.

On 10 July the first really satisfactory contact was made with the Aborigines. They were still very shy, but two in a canoe came to the visitors, while another two hovered in the background. They were

armed, but their belligerence was confined to noise and threats rather
than any real action. They were given the usual gifts which they
accepted without any obvious signs of pleasure. The only gift that
excited them was a small fish, which so delighted them that they
shoved off with signs that they would bring their companions. Still
armed, the four returned and stood in a row with their spears poised
for throwing. Tupaia approached them and persuaded them to lay
down their arms. More presents were handed out and it looked as if
progress was being made. Indeed the next day another group appeared
—one with a bone through his nose, the first such ornament the
travellers had seen—bearing a gift of a fish. Banks refers to the
Aborigines as a tribe, but they were probably a band of no more than
thirty or so. Although living by the sea and a sizeable river they were
probably more settled than many Aborigine bands that had to keep
on the move to survive. They also seemed to be somewhat more
sophisticated than those whom the explorers had met before. Their
canoes were better constructed and their weaponry more fearsome.

Their lances were much like those we had seen in Botany Bay, only they
were all of them single pointed with the stings of sting rays and bearded
with two or three beards of the same, which made them a most terrible
weapon; the board or stick with which they flung them was also made in a
neater way.

On the fourteenth there was another success when the first kangaroo
was shot and brought back for examination: 'to compare it to any
European animal would be impossible as it has not the least resemblance
to any one I have seen', Banks exclaimed, and then went on to give
his usual accurate description, after which 'the beast was dressed for
our dinners and proved excellent meat'. This exotic diet was supple-
mented with turtles 'far preferable to any I have eat in England'.

Two days later the *Endeavour* was ready to sail, and Banks and
Solander were busy, as Banks quaintly put it, 'winding up our botanical
bottoms', which meant completing last-minute jobs.

Although the ship was ready to sail there seemed to be a general
reluctance to leave. On the eighteenth Cook and Banks again climbed
the hill and looked out over the Great Barrier Reef,

. . . which afforded a melancholy prospect of the difficulties we were to encounter when we came out of our present harbour : in whichever direction we turned our eyes shoals innumerable were to be seen and no such thing as any passage to the sea but through the winding channels between them, dangerous to the last degree.

Next day, no less than ten Aborigines came on board. They were more heavily armed than before, although they left their spears in a tree. The purpose of the visit was quickly evident; they wanted one of the turtles lying on the deck, which were to be carried away as a source of fresh meat when the ship resumed her voyage. When they were refused, the natives became angry and attempted to drag one turtle to the side of the vessel. When they were restrained they jumped into their canoes and made for the shore,

. . . where I had got before them just ready to set out plant gathering. They seized their arms in an instant and taking fire from under a pitch kettle which was boiling they began to set fire to the grass to windward of the few things we had left ashore with surprising dexterity and quickness; the grass, which was four or five feet tall and as dry as stubble, burnt with vast fury. A tent of mine which had been put up for Tupaia when he was sick was the only thing of any consequence in the way of it so I leaped into a boat to fetch some people from the ship in order to save it, and quickly returning hauled it down to the beach just time enough.

Cook and some men gave chase to the Aborigines to prevent them destroying some linen and a seine net which had been laid out to dry. He and his party were unarmed and unable to frighten the natives, and were forced to return for weapons.

Mine was ashore and another loaded with shot, so we ran as fast as possible towards them and came just time enough to save the seine by firing at an Indian who had already fired the grass in two places just to windward of it. On the shot striking him, tho' he was full forty yards from the Captain who fired, he dropped his fire and ran nimbly to his comrades who all ran off pretty fast.

The Aborigines were hastened on their way by a musket ball fired ahead of them by Cook 'to shew them they were not yet out of our reach'. But this display of fire power did not totally deter the natives who were heard heading towards another party of *Endeavour* men who were washing in the river. The sight of muskets turned the would-be attackers away. Had the fire attack taken place a week before, the situation could have been very serious, because then all the ship's powder was stored ashore.

July ended and August came in and still the *Endeavour* was tied up in the river, and Banks was becoming ever more edgy and anxious to be away. He had exhausted the botanical resources of the area and as far as he was concerned had carried out a very satisfactory survey of the local natural history. He began to suspect that the sailors were deliberately stalling rather than face the coral again. This was unfair since the delays were the result of minor mishaps and adverse winds. Even so, few relished the coming voyage through uncharted and hideously dangerous waters.

On 4 August the ship did finally leave the river. Almost immediately a fresh wind got up which developed into a gale, and despite the anchors being set the vessel was gradually driven towards a shoal. At the last minute the anchors held and another disaster was averted.

Three days passed before it was safe to get under way again. By early afternoon on the tenth the *Endeavour* seemed to have sailed into a kind of natural trap of reefs and islands.

The people at the masthead saw, as they thought, land all round us, on which we immediately came to an anchor, resolved to go ashore and from the hills examine whether it was so or not.

In fact the land all round turned out to be a series of islands, one of which, about fifteen miles away, was higher than the rest. The following day Banks and Cook took a party to the island. From its highest point they had a clear view of the outer reef and to their relief and delight saw several openings. It was decided to camp on the island, now called Lizard Island from the numbers of the reptiles that Banks found in a small wood, and send a boat next morning to examine the openings in the reef.

While the survey party was away Banks, as usual, botanised, collected and noted, and later shared in the high spirits when the boat returned with the news that

. . . the sea broke vastly high upon the reef and the swell was so great in the opening that he could not go into it to sound. This was sufficient to assure us of a safe passage out.

At two o'clock on 13 August the *Endeavour* passed through the reef, using the opening which was named Cook's Passage.

It was about half a mile wide. As soon as the ship was well without it we had no ground with one hundred fathom of line so became in an instant quite easy, being once more in the main ocean and consequently freed from all our fears and shoals.

By the following day the explorers were, for the first time in three months, out of sight of land. But this was not part of Cook's plan. He wanted to prove whether the charted passage between New Holland and New Guinea really existed, so the ship was steered back towards the land.

On the sixteenth the reef was once more visible and it was not an encouraging sight. Banks wrote :

The large waves of the vast ocean meeting with so sudden a resistance make here a most terrible surf, breaking mountain high.

To make matters worse, when the *Endeavour* was only between twelve and fifteen miles from the reef the wind dropped and the swell drove the tiny vessel towards the wall of surf and coral. The hundred-fathom line failed to touch the bottom so there was no chance of anchoring, and attempts to launch boats to tow the ship to safety were frustrated by the pinnace having had a plank stripped off for repair, and the long boat being so firmly secured that it took some time to free it. By the evening they were within a cable length of the reef. 'Two large oars or sweeps were got out at the stern ports to pull the ship's head round the other way.' Before this could be achieved they were within forty yards of the reef.

The same sea that washed the side of the ship rose in a breaker enormously high the very next time it did rise, so between us and it was only a dismal valley the breadth of one wave; even now the lead was hove, three or four lines fastened together, but no ground could be felt with above 150 fathom.

Now was our case truly desperate, no man, I believe, but who gave himself entirely over. A speedy death was all we had to hope for and that from the vastness of the breakers which must quickly dash the ship all to pieces was scarce to be doubted. Other hopes we had none : the boats were in the ship, and must be dashed in pieces with her, and the nearest dry land was eight or ten leagues distant.

Despite these apparently hopeless odds the explorers struggled to free the long boat.

At this critical juncture, at this, I must say, terrible moment, when all assistance seemed too little to save even our miserable lives, a small air of wind sprang up, so small that at any other time in a calm we should not have observed it. We, however, plainly saw that it instantly checked our progress; every sail was therefore put in a proper direction to catch it and we just observed the ship to move in a slanting direction off from the breakers.

What they did not realise at the time was that they had arrived at the reef just before the tide ebbed. It turned at the same time as the breeze sprang up.

Being snatched away from certain death gave the seamen fresh strength. They freed the long boat, launched it and took the *Endeavour* in tow. The breeze died but it returned a second and third time allowing the ship to manoeuvre towards a narrow opening in the reef. But by this time the tide was running out with such force that instead of getting through the reef the ship was driven out to sea. With the pinnace now repaired and over the side, the *Endeavour* was pushed and pulled about two miles off the reef before the tide again turned 'and our suspense began again'.

As they were waiting, not knowing whether they would be drawn on the reef and this time smashed into oblivion, another opening was spotted. An officer was sent in a small boat to inspect it. He returned to report that it was very narrow but led to a safe anchorage and a passage free from shoals.

The ship's head was immediately put towards it and with the tide she towed so fast that . . . we entered and were hurried in by a stream almost like a mill race, which kept us from even a fear of the sides tho' it was not above a quarter of a mile in breadth.

By late afternoon on that heart-stopping, eventful day they were safely at anchor within the Great Barrier Reef once again, with Banks pondering on the curious fact that only a few days before, little more than hours really, all they had wished for was to escape from it.

Next day, now riding easily at anchor, parties were sent out searching for turtles and clams. Banks caught two water snakes, but was only to take a cursory look at the wealth of coral and marine life.

On the eighteenth the sails were set, and while their route was still littered with shoals, the expedition sailed uneventfully through them, and on 26 August 1770 once more they broke out of the reef and sailed towards the coast of New Guinea.

CHAPTER 7

HOMEWARD BOUND

As the *Endeavour* was heading back towards civilisation—her course was set for the Dutch East Indies. In England there was growing anxiety for her safety. Nothing had been heard of the expedition since the ship had put into Rio de Janeiro, and those letters and reports that did arrive from that unfriendly port can hardly have set people's minds at rest. In the late summer and autumn of 1770 rumours of disaster began to spread in London and then further afield. One report suggested that the *Endeavour* and her company had perished in some skirmish at sea, possibly with a Portuguese vessel. After all, there had been all the trouble at Rio, and no word of the explorers had come from the Falkland Islands, even then under British protection. This, of course, was easily explained by the fact that the ship did not touch at the islands, but the people at home were not to know that.

Thomas Pennant, referring to a newspaper report, wrote to his friend, the Rev George Ashby, in October 1770, saying:

I do not know what to say about Mr Banks. The account shocked me greatly. What makes me uneasy is that I do not hear anybody had a line from him from the Falkland Islands, which were long in our possession after he touched at them. I have wrote to his family and hope to find the newspapers contradicted.

How Banks's mother and his sister, Sarah Sophia, responded to the gloomy and alarmist reports can only be imagined. Both were religious women, which perhaps comforted them, and Sarah Sophia, who was given to composing appropriate prayers for various occasions, doubtless penned one for her brother's safety. No doubt well-meaning friends weighed in reminding all that they had warned the foolish young man against so hazardous an undertaking. As for poor Miss Blosset, closeted in the country with her tedious younger sister, she must have been too distraught to stitch her lover's fancy waistcoats.

Two hundred years ago it was all too easy to speculate on the most spectacular disasters for expeditions which had been away for many months without word reaching home, let alone tidal waves and water-spouts, whirlpools and great black storms that seemed to tear the very oceans apart. Let these alone, for were there not also grotesquely sadistic pirates; savages who fed on human flesh, and many-limbed sea-monsters that could draw a ship under the waves and consume the crew as easily as a man would eat a fistful of raisins at his own table? And of course the French and Spanish were never above suspicion. The one fact known to all was that the *Endeavour* was small, slow and lightly armed, no match for a well-equipped fighting vessel.

While such lurid and gloomy speculation was growing in the news-papers and salons of London, the *Endeavour* was sailing gently along the coast of New Guinea, from which Banks remarked, came 'a very fragrant smell . . . it resembled much the smell of gum Benjamin (gum benzoin)'.

On 3 September Banks, Cook, Solander and a small party went ashore with the pinnace, having to wade for the last two hundred yards because the water was so shallow. There were clear signs of habitation—a rough shelter containing freshly picked coconuts and the prints of naked feet in the sand. Although there were coconuts on the trees the visitors were unable to get them, and Cook refused to fell trees to pick fruit, knowing that he would be responsible for destroying the local people's food supply. One breadfruit tree was discovered, but it was bare, and plantains equally were without fruit.

The search for fresh food was interrupted by a sudden attack by three natives who 'rushed out of the woods with a hideous shout'. They were armed with darts and fire containers which they made flash almost exactly like a discharged musket, which the devices were taken for by the people watching the action from the ship.

Cook and his party discharged a volley of small shot which had little effect, but a second volley, with ball, set the attackers to flight.

There seemed little that New Guinea could offer. Banks listed only twenty-three species of plant, most of which he knew, and it was obvious that if they foraged further inland for food it would lead to more clashes with the local tribes and inevitable bloodshed and death. The decision not to linger had a pleasing effect on the crew who were weary of the voyage and only wanted to set a course for England.

As soon as ever the boat was hoisted in we made sail and steered away from this land to the no small satisfaction of, I believe, three-fourths of our company. The sick became well and the melancholy looked gay. The greatest part of them were now pretty far gone with the longing for home, which the physicians have gone so far as to esteem a disease under the name of nostalgia. Indeed, I can find hardly anybody in the ship clear of its effects but the Captain, Dr Solander and myself, indeed we three have pretty constant employment for our minds, which I believe to be the best if not the only remedy for it.

Even Banks was not immune to pangs of homesickness, or nostalgia, as he would have it. When they sighted land which they thought was Timor he thought of 'our countryman Dampier; this thought made home recur to my mind stronger than it had done throughout the whole voyage'.

Contrary winds which made progress slow and tedious fanned the flames of discontent among the grumblers, 'croakers' Banks called them, who predicted the onset of the monsoon, which, they said, would prevent the ship reaching a safe harbour and fresh provisions. Certainly fresh food was in very short supply, and when two sharks were caught and served up there was not a single complaint from 'the captain to the swabber'.

Banks kept up his spirits by observing such passing land as there was, and the bird and fish life about the ship. On the night of 16 September he observed a remarkable phenomenon, the Aurora Australis.

About ten o'clock a phenomenon appeared in the heavens in many things resembling the Aurora Borealis, but differing materially in others; it consisted of a dull reddish light reaching in height about twenty degrees above the horizon : its extent was very different at different times, but never less than eight or ten points of the compass. Through and out of this passed rays of a brighter coloured light tending directly upwards.

It was still lighting up the night sky when Banks went to bed at midnight.

The next day a landing was made on Savu (Sawu), where the visitors were well received and given a few coconuts, and the following day a formal trading agreement was reached with the Rajah of Savu. Indeed the explorers were assured of an abundance of buffaloes, sheep, pigs and fowls. There were endless hold-ups and interference, however, probably because the bribes for the local Dutch East India Company official were not readily forthcoming. It was not until 20 September that stock was brought down to the beach and traded—eight buffaloes, thirty dozen fowls, six sheep, three pigs, limes, coconuts, garlic, syrup and a great many eggs, half of which proved to be rotten.

On the night of 1 October the *Endeavour* passed Java Head in a thunderstorm, and the following night in brilliant moonlight she sailed past Krakatau, the dramatic volcanic island which one hundred and thirteen years later blew itself into oblivion.

The second found them close to two East Indiamen from whom they were to learn some news of Europe, the first for nearly two years. It would probably have been as well left unheard. They were told

... that the Government in England were in the utmost disorder, the people crying up and down the streets 'Down with King George, King Wilkes for ever'; that the Americans had refused to pay taxes of any kind in consequence of which a large force was being sent there both of sea and land forces.

Elsewhere in Europe there was unrest, with Poland in revolt against Russia, and Russia at war with Turkey.

If this were not enough to dampen the spirits of the adventurers now longing for home, the dour Dutch seamen

... told us that our passage to Batavia (Jakarta) was likely to be very tedious, as we should have a strong current constantly against us and at this time of year calms and light breezes were the only weather we had to expect.

The information proved correct and the remainder of the voyage to Batavia tried the company's patience to the extreme, but the port was eventually reached on 9 October.

Batavia had a world-wide reputation as one of the unhealthiest places on the face of the earth. Banks had early evidence of this when a patrol boat came alongside to identify the *Endeavour*. He wrote of the officer in command and his men:

Both himself and his people were almost as spectres, no good omen of the healthiness of the country we were arrived at.

Banks and his party moved into a hotel, which, far from providing a spot of well deserved luxury, was shabby and expensive and produced very poor food.

Our dinners and suppers consisted of one course each, the one of fifteen, the other of thirteen dishes, of which when you came to examine, seldom less than nine or ten were of bad poultry, roasted, boiled, fried, stewed, etc., and so little conscience had they in serving up dishes over and over again that I have seen the same identical roasted duck appear upon table three times as roasted duck before he found his way into the fricassee, from whence he was again to pass into forcemeat.

Through constant complaints an improvement was brought about, as a result of which he rented a small house next to the hotel for his collections and books so that work could continue while the *Endeavour* underwent essential repairs, the only reason for coming to Batavia. But there was little peace to be had.

Every Dutchman almost that came by running in and asking what we had to sell, for it seems that hardly any individual had ever been at Batavia before who had not something or other to sell.

By the time he had hired two carriages Banks felt sufficiently settled to send for Tupaia and Tayeto. Tupaia had been suffering for some time from some kind of stomach disorder for which he stubbornly refused to take any medication.

On his arrival his spirits, which had long been very low, were instantly raised by the sights which he saw, and his boy, Tayeto, who had always been perfectly well, was almost ready to run mad.

The sight of the town and port must have been a truly amazing spectacle for the Tahitians brought up in flimsy dwellings scattered through coconut and breadfruit groves.

Houses, carriages, streets, in short everything were to him sights which he had often heard described, but never well understood, so he looked upon them all with more than wonder, almost mad with the numberless novelties which diverted his attention. From one to the other he danced about the streets, examining everything to the best of his abilities.

Tupaia was fascinated by the innumerable national dresses to be seen in this cosmopolitan place, and insisted on wearing his native robes. This, and the fact that Banks was able to buy food similar to the Tahitian diet, gradually improved Tupaia's health.

Although they were warned that as newcomers they would be vulnerable to the fever and disease endemic to Batavia, Banks and his party treated the warnings lightly. Before the end of the month they regretted their attitude. Tupaia, who had shown signs of improvement, was the first to go down, weakened as he was by his illness at sea, and he deteriorated rapidly, Tayeto caught a cold and developed inflammation of the lungs. Two of Banks's servants, Peter Briscoe and James Roberts, Solander and Banks himself, began to suffer from attacks of fever. Indeed, most of the ship's company was affected to a greater or lesser degree. It was, of course, malaria, and Batavia, with its numerous stinking canals, was a prime breeding ground for the mosquitoes which transmitted the disease.

The situation was not helped by the lengthy delays in obtaining permission for the ship to go into the repair docks.

We now began sensibly to feel the ill-effects of the unwholesome climate we were in: our appetites and spirits were gone, but none were yet really sick except for poor Tupaia and Tayeto, both of which grew worse and worse daily, so that I began once more to despair of poor Tupaia's life. At last he desired to be removed to the ship where he said he should breathe a freer air clear of the numerous houses which he believed to be the cause of his disease by stopping the free draught.

He was taken to the inlet in Batavia road where the *Endeavour* was undergoing an overhaul:

. . . and on his liking the shore had a tent pitched for him in a place he chose where both sea breeze and land breeze blew right over him, a situation in which he expressed great satisfaction.

The seamen began to go down with malaria so fast that the tents pitched ashore for them were constantly full. Banks stayed with Tupaia until he was satisfied that he was at least happy, before returning to the town, where he was seized with fever 'so violent as to deprive me entirely of my senses and leave me so weak as scarcely to be able to crawl down stairs'.

William Monkhouse, the ship's surgeon, was among the most severely striken, and on 5 November 1770 he died.

The Malay slaves, 'naturally the worst attendants in nature', were of little help to the sick men, so that Banks and Solander decided:

. . . to buy each of us a Malay woman to nurse us, hoping that the tenderness of the sex would prevail even here, which indeed we found it to do for they turned out by no means bad nurses.

By the middle of the month Solander was so ill that Banks, who sat up all night with him, feared that his friend would die. On the suggestion of a local doctor they took a house in the country about two miles out of the town, where they were joined by Herman Sporing, Banks's scientific clerk, a seaman, and Cook's own servant, John Charlton, who were sent to lend a hand. In fact Banks and Solander had quite a considerable entourage of nurses and attendants about them—ten Malays and two white servants.

When, on 14 November, news came that the repairs to the *Endeavour* had been completed, the sick were given new hope. That the ship needed repairs was not in doubt.

When examined she had proved much worse than anybody expected, her main plank being in many places so cut by the rocks that not more than one-eighth of an inch in thickness remained, and here the worm had got in and made terrible havoc; her false keel entirely gone, and her main keel much wounded.

All that now held up the departure was re-loading the stores and equipment that had been removed to the safety of a warehouse, but the seamen were so ill 'that not above thirteen or fourteen were able to stand to their works'.

Cook was laid low with fever, Solander improved by slow degrees, and Banks was wracked with ague. Tragically, little Tayeto, who was always so full of fun and the favourite of the seamen, died. This was too much for Tupaia to bear. For three days, almost insane with grief, he cried out the child's name. Then he too died. Banks wrote:

We received the news of Tupaia's death. I had given him quite over ever since his boy died, whom I well knew he sincerely loved, tho' he used to find much fault with him during his life time.

Just to add to the general misery there was a violent storm at the end of November, heralding the rainy season. Banks's country house leaked like a sieve 'and through the lower part of it ran a stream almost capable of turning a mill'.

It was with considerable relief that on Christmas Eve the ship's company, and the gentlemen naturalists, boarded the *Endeavour* to leave Batavia. Banks was not impressed with the capital of the 'Dutch dominions in India'. It was, he said, a filthy town, with canals stinking with human ordure 'as there is not a necessary house in the whole town'. Dead horses, pigs and buffaloes were left to putrefy in the canals until they were carried away by a flood.

He had the lowest opinion of the local merchants who:

. . . have joined all the art of trade that a Dutchman is famous for to the deceit of an Indian. Cheating by false weights and measures, false samples etc., are looked upon only as arts of trade.

Most of the labour in the colony was provided by slaves who were treated with extreme harshness. The common punishment was flogging with 'rods made of split rattans which fetch blood at every stroke', although the slaves were to some extent protected from excessively brutal masters, who could face murder charges and execution if they caused the death of a slave. But by and large the justice administered by the Dutch authorities was dispensed with a massive prejudice in favour of Europeans.

In civil matters I know nothing of their proceedings, but in criminal they are rather severe to the natives, and too lenient to their own countrymen. . . . the poor Indians are flogged, hanged, broke upon the wheel, and even impaled, without mercy.

Couple all this with the vileness of the place and it is hardly surprising that on Christmas Day 1770

. . . there was not . . . a man in the ship but gave his utmost aid in getting up the anchor, so completely tired was everyone of the unwholesome air of this place.

The departure was delayed by the desertion of Patrick Saunders, the man accused of the ear-cropping incident.

The real tragedy of the stay at Batavia was that having arrived with a largely healthy company, the *Endeavour* sailed leaving six dead and carrying others who would certainly die before reaching England.

Winds were either light or contrary and it took over ten days to reach Princes Island, just clear of the Sunda Strait, where they were able to stock up with fresh provisions, including turtles.

Banks's fever returned, but he was cheered by the sight of the retreating shore when the ship stood out to sea on 15 January 1771.

On the sixteenth he wrote with genuine pleasure: 'This morn waked in the open ocean, nothing in sight but sea and sky.' Fresh sea air, the fever-ridden explorers believed, would restore them to health, but they were cruelly disappointed. Almost all the crew went down with dysentery. Sporing became very ill, as did the gentle, industrious Sydney Parkinson, one of the finest botanical and zoological artists of his time.

On the twenty-third a seaman died, and on the same day Banks went down with dysentery, accompanied by excruciating pains in his bowels. Next day Sporing died, and another seaman the following day. During the evening of the twenty-sixth Parkinson and yet another sailor died. Still in great pain Banks wrote on the twenty-eighth :

This day Mr Green, our astronomer and two of the people died, all of the very same complaint as I laboured under, no very encouraging circumstances.

Three more died the next day and on the thirtieth he wrote :

One person only died today, but so weak were the people in general, officers and men included, not more than eight or nine could keep the deck so that four in a watch was all they had.

It was not until 7 February that there was real signs that the disease aboard the ship had spent its force, but by the time the voyage was completed thirty-eight men had died, most of them as a result of the stay in Batavia.

The fourth of March found the *Endeavour* a few miles off the coast of Natal, somewhere about the port of St John, north of East London. The appearance of land caused some alarm as it was not expected and an on-shore wind seemed to be carrying the ship towards the rock coast where the sea 'broke mountains high'. In fact the danger was not as great as Banks imagined, and the vessel was sailed out of harm's way, coming, on the fourteenth into Table Bay.

Solander, who had been ill on and off for some time now, was taken violently ill with fever and bowel pains, and for two weeks was confined to bed. Normally a well-built, not to say tubby man, he was, Banks recorded, 'very much emaciated by his tedious illness'.

The expedition stayed for about a month in Table Bay, and Banks, now largely restored to good health, surveyed the scene with his usual thoroughness, and what he saw he liked. At the time the Governor of the Cape was Ryk Tulbagh, a man of the highest principles, who virtually stamped out the corruption which was rife in the colony.

Banks was attracted to the South African women. He observed:

In general, they are handsome with clear skins and high complexions and when married (no reflections upon my countrywomen) are the best housekeepers imaginable and great child bearers; had I been inclined for a wife I think this is the place of all others I have seen where I could have best suited myself.

Clearly, by now, Miss Blosset was far from his mind.

He studied the products of the country—the crops grown and the stock raised; admired the animals kept in the Dutch East India Company's garden, and was extremely uncomplimentary about the Hottentots

. . . whom . . . are generally represented as the outcasts of the human species, a race whose intellectual faculties are so little superior to those of beasts that some have been inclined to suppose them more nearly related to baboons than men.

In pursuit of what he called the 'Grand Quaere of natural history' he investigated reports that the Hottentot women had much enlarged labia, in some cases 'equal to a garment for all purposes of decency', but concluded the reports were exaggerated.

There was a brief stop at Robben Island, even then a penal settlement, to obtain fresh vegetables, but the armed guards refused to allow them to land.

On 1 May the *Endeavour* reached St Helena where a convoy of Indiamen was found poised to leave with an armed escort because of the likelihood of a breach with Spain, and it was decided to join them. Their stay was brief, which was just as well as Banks thought it a wretched place, and was sharply critical of the English inhabitants and their treatment of their slaves.

I am sorry to say that it appeared to me that far more frequent and more wanton cruelty was exercised by my countrymen over these unfortunate people than even by their neighbours, the Dutch, famed for inhumanity, are guilty of.

After dinner on the fourth the party sailed with the convoy, keeping up with some difficulty until the morning of the twenty-seventh when

. . . in the morn to our great surprise we had no sight of the fleet, even from our mast head, so were obliged to jog on by ourselves.

So, indeed, they did jog along through the remainder of May and all of June, until 12 July when 'at three o'clock we landed at Deal'.

The great South Sea Caterpillar, transform'd into a Bath Butterfly.

Description of the New Bath Butterfly taken from the Philosophical Transactions for 1795.—"This Insect first crawl'd into notice from among the Weeds & Mud on the Banks of the South Sea; & being afterwards placed in a Warm Situation by the Royal Society, was changed by the heat of the Sun into its present form—it is noticed & Valued Solely on account of the beautiful Red which encircles its Body, & the Shining Spot on its Breast: a Distinction which never fails to render Caterpillars valuable.—

When Sir Joseph Banks was awarded the Order of the Bath by King George III, the cartoonists rewarded him with scorn and ridicule. The great South Sea Caterpillar, they said, had become a Bath Butterfly (*John Freeman Group*)

The **SIMPLING MACARONI.**

Like Soland-Goose from frozen Zone I wander,
On shallow Banks grows fat, Sol . . . . .

Pub accor to Act by MDarly Strand July 13. 1772

Dr Daniel Solander, recognised as the most brilliant and distinguished botanist working in England, could not escape the cartoonist who depicted him growing fat on the patronage of Sir Joseph Banks (*John Freeman Group*)

CHAPTER 8

MISS BLOSSET
AND MISS B . . . N

Banks wasted no time. As soon as he was able he hurried, with Solander, to London where his family and a wide circle of adoring and admiring friends were waiting for them. Society threw open its doors to the daring explorers, and Banks in particular was hugely lionised. Tall, good-looking, young, rich, and bronzed by sun and wind, he was the most prized guest at every social event of consequence. There was not an ambitious hostess who did not attempt to get him to her table to divert her guests with tales of adventure, of savages, of strange lands and beasts. Only twenty-eight, this was the splendid young man who had eschewed the delights of gaming and wenching (the latter not entirely true) to mingle with primitive people and deliciously terrifying cannibals. His stories held the elegant soirées spellbound, and his huge collection of plants, animals and birds, insects, shells, minerals and native artifacts was the season's great attraction.

Less than a month after the travellers' return, Sir John Pringle, President of the Royal Society, introduced Banks and Solander to King George III. The first meeting at court was followed by a second at Richmond where they spent some time describing the voyage to the monarch. And later still Banks displayed a selection of the most prized and curious items from his collections to the royal family.

The result of these meetings was a close and lasting friendship between Banks and the King. They had much in common—a great interest in agriculture and in plants, particularly those plants which could benefit society as food or as raw material for manufacturing.

Dr Samuel Johnson, a man not easily given to praising other men, enjoyed the company of the two explorers, although in conversation with Boswell said that such an expedition as the two men had completed held little attraction for him because 'there is very little of intellectual in the course'. But after an evening with them he wrote to Banks:

Sir,

I return thanks to you and Dr Solander for the pleasure which I received in yesterday's conversation. I could not recollect a motto for your goat, but have given her one. You, Sir, may perhaps have an epick poem from some happier pen than mine.

Johnson's distich on the goat which had kept Banks and his companions in fresh milk during the voyage, read:

Perpetui, ambita bis terra, praemia lactis
Haec habet altrici Capra secunda Jovis.

> In fame scarce second to the nurse of Jove
> This goat, who twice the world has traversed round
> Deserving both her master's care and love
> Ease and perpetual pasture now has found.

Lady Mary Coke, one of the most untiring observers of the eighteenth-century scene, followed Banks's and Solander's progress with interest in her journals.

On 9 August 1771 she recorded:

But the people who are most talked of at present are Mr Banks and Doctor Solander: I saw them at court and afterwards at Lady Hertford's, but did not hear them give any account of their voyage round the world, which I am told is very amusing.

In a rather sick reference to Green, the astronomer who died during the passage home from Batavia, Lady Mary wrote:

. . . laughed very much at Lord Strafford's idea of Mr Banks and Dr Solander's having eat their companion. I did not hear that they had been in any distress for provisions, and cannot suppose that choice would have led them to such a meal.

While London society clawed Banks into its arms, one person was left with empty arms; none other than poor Harriet Blosset. Still in her country retreat, she waited in vain for him to come for her.

Banks ignored her, and Banks played the coward in this case. Quite obviously he had long abandoned the idea of marriage. After all in South Africa was he not contemplating a South African wife, had he been in the marrying mood? In the end the hapless Miss Blosset had to come to London, where the couple met. There were distressing scenes, tears and fainting. At one point Banks did weaken and say that he would go through with the marriage, but swiftly reversed the decision. Finally he had to extricate himself with an out of court breach of promise payment.

Naturally the affair was at the centre of gossip. After a visit to the heir of Sir William Morrice, Lady Mary Coke wrote:

I saw Mr Morrice this morning: he has had a confinement of two months with the gout, and has now taken a house at Richmond for the air, intending to escape going this summer to his fine place in Devonshire. He was excessively droll according to custom, and said he hoped Mr Banks, who since his return has desired Miss Blosset will excuse his marrying her, will pay her for the materials of all the worked waistcoats she made for him during the time he was sailing round the world. Everybody agrees she passed these three years in retirement, but whether she employed herself in working waistcoats for Mr Banks I can't tell you, but if she loved him I pity her disappointment.

Only ten years before he died Banks again came under attack for the Blosset affair in the fourth edition of James Lee's *Botany*. The book included a brief life of James Lee by Robert John Thornton, and it was in this that Banks was scathingly criticised.

James Lee was a Scotsman who came to London and at Hammersmith developed a famous nursery garden, which at the time ranked with Kew as the most important repository of rare and exotic plants. As a young man Banks was a regular visitor at the nursery, and obviously liked and admired James Lee.

Giving a list of the leading naturalists who courted Lee's company, Thornton says:

. . . and we would willingly add Sir Joseph Banks: but Lee had a virtuous bluntness in his nature, and could not sacrifice his love of truth, for what, with him, was the paltry consideration of gain. Mr Banks when in the prime of life, quitted (although possessing every means for enjoying the same), the pleasures of a gay metropolis, the seductive paths of politics, the soft blandishments of polite intercourse; not to visit the sumptuous palaces of continental courts; not to see the finished labours of human skill; not to compare the manners of this country with those of others; but to view the stupendous scenes of uncultivated climates; to behold nations never before gazed on by European eye; and birds, and animals, and plants unknown to former naturalists; to bring home with the rich discoveries of Captain Cook, treasures for a cabinet of natural productions, which stands unrivalled.

Mr Lee was guardian to a young lady, Miss Blosset, who possessed extraordinary beauty, and every accomplishment, with a fortune of ten thousand pounds. Mr Banks had often seen her, when visiting the rare plants at Lee's and thought her the fairest amongst the flowers. In short, he was smitten with her charms, and she merited indeed a gentleman like Mr Banks. On his going abroad with Captain Cook, like other lovers, he made many solemn vows and protestations, and even left a ring for his marriage upon his return, with Mr Lee. Some people are ill-natured enough to say, that, vitiated in his taste by seeing the elegant women Otaheite (Tahiti), who must have something very peculiar in their natures to captivate such a man, upon his return, Mr Banks came, indeed to see the young lady, and the plants; but she found her lover now preferred a flower, or even a butterfly to her superior charms; and her three years of anxiety and expectation ended in a most mortifying disappointment; for Mr Banks paid down a sum of money rather than marry; and his present choice, for whom he entered into the bands of wedlock fifteen years afterwards, shows his peculiar taste; but this weighty lady had instead of ten, sixty thousand pounds; and double that sum might not have procured her any other husband. The reader of sensibility will be happy to hear that the disappointed elegant young lady has been since extremely well married to a virtuous clergyman, Dr Dessalis, and has been blessed by a numerous and lovely family, whereas Sir Joseph can boast of no heir to his immense fortune.

While Banks did, perhaps, deserve a measure of criticism for his treatment of the wretched Miss Blosset, what does seem unnecessarily unkind is the unsolicited attack on the plainness and figure of Lady Banks.

It was obvious that Banks no longer considered himself ready for marriage. He had plans for further travelling which would take up all his time and efforts for the foreseeable future. There was an additional reason, possibly the most significant, and that was another woman in his life; a pretty, well-born, but impoverished girl whom he took as his mistress, and whom he undoubtedly loved. She has come down in history simply as Miss B . . . n.

The fullest account of the affair was printed in 1775 in *The Town and Country Magazine: or Universal Repository of Knowledge, Instruction and Entertainment.* This was a popular publication filled with news, gossip, poetry, comment, births, deaths and marriages, an agony column, letters and moral tales. In the case of the latter the magazine's lofty, censorious style was merely a device used to justify the most scurrilous details of prominent people's private lives. It was as a moral tale that the story of Banks and his mistress was told.

Illustrated with portraits of Miss B . . . n, a delicately pretty girl, and a suntanned Banks, referred to as the Circumnavigator, the article describes him as :

A man of extensive fortune, whose prevailing passion was sailing round the world in search of undiscovered countries, in order to have occular demonstration of the manners, customs, habits, dispositions, appearances, notions, vices and caprices of the inhabitants of these unknown regions; and at the same time to collect plants and other natural curiosities of which the European virtuosi were completely ignorant. In these pursuits our hero stands confessedly the most conspicuous and the most successful man now living.

The article then goes on to poke fun at Banks. It recalls the highwayman story, and adds :

. . . and he has been so eager in the pursuit of the butterfly of a peculiar species as to fall into a river and narrowly escape being drowned.

It then gets down to the real point :

As nature has been his constant study, it cannot be supposed that the most engaging part of it, the fair sex, have escaped his notice and if we may be suffered to conclude from his most amorous descriptions, the females of most countries that he has visited have undergone every critical inspection by him. The queens and women of the first class we find constantly soliciting his company, or rather forcing their's upon him : at other times we find him visiting them in their bed-chambers, nay in their beds.

The author refers to his sexual adventures whilst an undergraduate at Oxford, and then goes on to describe Miss B . . . n as the daughter of a gentleman who died penniless as a result of gambling and dissipation. Banks met her when she was still a young girl at boarding school. He was attracted by her beauty and visited her regularly until she was seventeen and left school, and he left on the *Endeavour*.

When he returned, 'his first inquiry was for Miss B'. He discovered that she had been left destitute and was the companion of an old woman. He persuaded her to leave and put her with a family. He at that time harboured no designs against her virtue, but was, nevertheless a constant visitor and organised parties and jaunts into the country. On all these trips Miss B was accompanied by another young woman who lodged in the same house, until one day :

A jaunt to Hampton Court being fixed, and this young lady being in the intermediate time taken ill, Mr B . . . unwilling that Miss B . . . n should be disappointed, proposed a tete-a-tete party.

According to the magazine the young couple set off with the purest of motives to spend the day in the fresh air and sunshine.

But alas! Opportunity and nature proved too powerful for reason to oppose. From this moment a connexion of a more familar kind began, and a few months later testified it to the world.

Banks moved her out of her lodgings into

. . . a genteel house in the New Buildings; here she soon became a mother, and this pledge of the natural fondness, still further increased their affection and regard.

It seems that the arrangement was one of domestic bliss, because, says the magazine :

The great decorum with which this correspondence is conducted, induces her neighbours and servants to believe her a married woman; and indeed in everything except the ceremony there is scarce the most trivial distinction.

Even allowing for the excesses of *The Town and Country Magazine*'s author, there is no doubt at all that Miss B . . . n bore Banks a child. John Christian Fabricius, a Scandinavian naturalist who specialised in insects, and produced a system for classifying them, was a close friend of Banks and worked on the collections from the *Endeavour* voyage. In a letter to Banks he enquires about life at New Buildings in Orchard Street.

My best compliments and wishes in Orchard Street; what has she brought you? Well, it is all the same, if a boy, he will be clever and strong like his father, if a girl, she will be pretty and genteel like her mother.

Why Banks did not marry the girl is a secret he carried with him to the grave. Perhaps Miss B . . . n was just not well enough born to take her place as the mistress of Revesby, or maybe, as Dr A. M. Lysaght has suggested in her sketch of Banks in her book on the Newfoundland and Labrador expedition, she died in childbirth. Certainly, shortly after Fabricius wrote his charming little inquiry, Banks was with Lord Sandwich, Lord Mulgrave and two or three women of pleasure at an inn in Berkshire, where they were staying during a trout-fishing holiday, possibly a distraction for a grief-stricken young man.

And there is an even more curious incident which is reported by Captain Cook at the start of his second voyage round the world, a voyage that Banks was to have joined.

When the *Resolution* reached Madeira, Cook heard that

. . . three days before we arrived a person left the island who went by the name of Burnett. He had been waiting for Mr Banks arrival about three months, at first he said he came here for the recovery of his health, but afterwards said his intention was to go out with Mr Banks, to some he said he was unknown to this gentleman, to others he said it was by his appointment he came here as he could not be received on board in England, at last when he heard that Mr Banks did not go, he took the very first opportunity to get off the island. He was about thirty years of age and rather ordinary than otherwise and employed his time in botanising etc.,—Every part of Mr Burnett's behaviour and every action tended to prove that he was a woman. I have not met with a person that entertains a doubt of a contrary nature. He brought letters of recommendation to an English house where he was accommodated during his stay. It must be observed that Mrs Burnett must have left London about the time we were ready to sail.

Extraordinary as this story is, it does have the ring of truth by being told by Cook, who was a man who dealt in hard facts and was not given either to gossip or romancing.

Also there was a precedent. The French naturalist, Philibert de Commerson, who sailed to the South Seas with de Bougainville, took with him a valet called Baré, who turned out to be a woman.

Despite the Blosset affair, and rumour and gossip about Miss B . . . n, Society continued to pamper Banks. But not all was plain sailing, and not everyone loved him. One man who had no liking for the young explorer was Stanfield Parkinson, the brother of Sydney.

Stanfield Parkinson was an upholsterer, but unlike his talented brother, was illiterate, ill-natured, and, as events were to prove, unbalanced.

Quite properly on his return, Banks handed over to Stanfield a will that Sydney had written. But Stanfield was convinced that Banks was holding back documents and collections belonging to his brother. In fact Banks did part with some curiosities after the Parkinson family refused to sell them to him. But he did keep some loose papers which appeared to be a rough draft of a journal of the voyage. The reason for this was that one of Sydney Parkinson's dying wishes was that his papers should be given to James Lee to read.

Stanfield also claimed ownership of all Sydney's drawings and paintings, a completely false claim since Sydney had been employed by Banks as a draughtsman. What he failed to make public was the fact that Banks gave the Parkinson family £500 instead of the £160 that was still outstanding on Sydney's salary.

The dispute dragged on tediously and even went to court after Stanfield obtained the draft of the journal, and with the aid of a hack writer produced a book—*A Journal of a Voyage to the South Seas in HMS Endeavour*. Dr John Hawkesworth, who was commissioned to write the official account of the voyage, took the issue to law in an attempt to prevent publication. He failed, and Stanfield Parkinson used the preface of the journal as a vehicle to attack Banks. He detailed his complaints and added:

The persons of whom I complain are men from whose superior talents and situation in life, better things might be expected; however, they have in this instance been misemployed in striving to baffle a plain unlettered man.

The voyage of the *Endeavour* had been so successful that very soon after the return of the expedition a second was proposed.

Although Cook had proved pretty conclusively that Terra Australis Incognita was a myth, further proof was needed finally to lay the ghost, quite apart from the fact that there were clearly more discoveries to be made in the South Seas. A follow-up expedition had the support of the Admiralty, not least Banks's friend Lord Sandwich, the King, and the leading men of science.

That Cook should lead it was never in doubt, but there was also widespread approval for the plan to put the scientific side in Banks's hands.

Once again Cook chose Whitby colliers—the *Resolution* and the *Adventurer*—while Banks made his plans on a lavish scale. His party consisted of no less than sixteen people. There was, of course, Dr Solander, plus John Zoffany, the distinguished painter, three draughtsmen, two secretaries, nine servants, among whom were two horn players. The bulk of the party was to travel with Banks in the *Resolution*, the remainder with the *Adventure*. Also attached to the scientific party were three astronomers, William Wales and William

Bayly, and the distinguished Dr James Lind, the Edinburgh astronomer and physician, who was to be paid the handsome sum of £4,000 for his services.

From the beginning Banks seemed set on taking over the expedition, and he was quick to complain when he first visited the ships. The *Resolution*, he declared, was too small for his purposes. He pressured the Admiralty to make alterations to the *Resolution* when they refused to provide larger vessels. The alterations were such that they made the ship top-heavy and totally unsafe, and she had to be restored to her original state. At this point Banks refused to take part in the expedition. He claimed that his plans for alterations had been ignored by the Admiralty which had deliberately rendered the *Resolution* unseaworthy in order to exclude him from the voyage.

After the heat and fury of the row that broke out had died down, Banks put his side of the story in the introduction to his journal of his expedition to the Western Isles and Iceland.

Soon after my return from my voyages round the world I was solicited by Lord Sandwich, the First Lord of the Admiralty, to undertake another voyage of the same nature. His solicitation was couched in the following words viz : 'if you will go we will send other ships.' So strong a solicitation agreeing exactly with my own desires was not to be neglected. I accordingly answered I was ready and willing. The Navy Board was then ordered to provide two ships proper for the service. This they did and gave me notice when it was done. I immediately went on board the principal ship and found her most improper for our purpose. Instead of having provided a ship in which an extraordinary number of people might be accommodated, they had chose one with a low and small cabin, and remarkably low between decks. This I objected to.

Banks was told that nothing could be done to meet his objections, whereupon he wrote direct to Lord Sandwich, who ordered alterations to raise the ceiling height of the cabin by three inches and to lay a spar deck :

. . . the whole length of the ship for the accommodation of the people. This order, I suppose, must have hurt the Navy Board for from that time they never ceased to pursue me with every obstacle they could throw in my way and at last overthrew my designs.

First to the proposed alterations they added a round house for the Captain to be built over all this and all other alterations they made with timber so heavy and strong that the top of the roundhouse was literally thicker than the gundeck of the ship. This, tho' I saw, I could not remedy.

The ship was made so crank by it that she could not go to sea.

Some of the oldest sea officers, who, I believe, were jealous that discovery should go out of their line, procurred an order that the ship might be reduced to her original state. In this situation then, I was offered the alternative to go or let it alone, with a great deal of coolness, however, for I now had inadvertantly opened to them every idea of discovery which my last voyage had suggested to me and these they thought themselves able to follow without my assistance now they had once got possession of them.

As the alterations which they had made rendered it impossible for my people to be lodged or to do their respective duties, I resolved to refuse to go and wrote a letter to Lord Sandwich . . . stating my reasons.

The air of outraged innocence is not entirely convincing, but Banks's theory that the crusty old gentlemen of the Admiralty objected to a civilian playing a major organisational role in what was essentially a naval exercise certainly does have the ring of truth. On the other hand it does seem a little unlikely that they would have ordered expensive alterations to the *Resolution* knowing they would render her unseaworthy, merely to frustrate a civilian, particularly one who was a close friend of the First Lord. The more plausible explanation is that they followed Banks's ideas, but without the materials of technology to make them work.

That the revamped *Resolution* was quite unfit to sail in, is in no doubt. Charles Clerke, a young naval officer who had sailed in the *Endeavour*, and who was a close friend of Banks, wrote to him describing the proving run of the enlarged vessel.

We weighed anchor at Gravesend this morning about ten o'clock, with a fine breeze from the eastward. The wind from that quarter laid us under the necessity of working down the reaches : which work, I am sorry to tell you, we found the *Resolution* very unequal to. She is so bad that the pilot declares he will not run the risk of his character so far as to take charge of her further than the Nore without a fair wind; that he cannot, with safety to himself, attempt working her to the Downs. Hope you know me too well to impute my giving this intelligence to any ridiculous apprehensions for myself. By God, I'll go to sea in a grog-tub, if required, or in the *Resolution* as soon as you please; but must say I think her by far the most unsafe ship I ever saw or heard of. However, if you think proper to embark for the South Pole in a ship which a pilot will not undertake to carry down the river all I can say is you shall be cheerfully attended as long as we can keep above water.

Clearly Banks was not without friends, or at least loyalty, when he fell out with the Admiralty. All of his own party stood by him and refused to sail in the reduced ship. They were

. . . to a man so well convinced of the impropriety of our going out in the state the ship was now reduced to that they all to a man refused with me and so well were they satisfied with my conduct that tho' I believe everyone but Dr Solander, were separately tampered with to embark without me, not one would at all listen to any proposals which could be offered to them.

But Banks's long relationship with Lord Sandwich was severely strained, although Sandwich behaved with commendable restraint.

In his letter to Lord Sandwich explaining why he would not sail with the *Resolution*, Banks appears to be under the impression that the entire expedition was being mounted for the furtherance of his purposes, and he accuses, with some arrogance, the Navy Board not only of inefficiency, but also of a disregard for the safety and health of all those taking part in the journey.

His view of his role is clearly expressed when he declared that he had pledged himself :

. . . to all Europe, not only to go the voyage, but to take with me as many able artists as the income of my fortune would allow me to pay, by whose means the learned world in general might reap as much benefit as possible from those discoveries which my good fortune or industry might enable me to make.

He had made it clear from the start, he said, that he regarded the two ships bought by the navy 'as improper for the voyage', in particular the *Resolution* in which he would have sailed.

Alterations were made to provide Banks and his party with extra space, but these came in for Banksian criticism, which enraged the Navy men. One paragraph, especially, was more than they could stand.

In expeditions of this nature the health and accommodation of the people are essential to success; when sickness and discontent are once introduced it will be absolutely impossible to continue the discovery. By the alterations already made the accommodations of the people are very much reduced, for the spar deck being cut away thirty of the crew are to be removed under the gun deck before sufficiently crowded, which being very low and confined, without a free air, must infallibly in so long a voyage produce putrid distempers and scurvy, and, what my Lord, ought more to be dreaded by a discoverer than such calamities, which must soon oblige him to quit his discovery and very probably even put it out of his power to bring home any account of what he has done previous to its fatal influence?

Here was a clear accusation that the Navy had little regard for the health and welfare of its seamen.

He doubts that the public could blame him for refusing to sail

. . . in a ship in which my people have not the room necessary for performing the different duties of their professions, a ship apparently unhealthy and probably unsafe.

The fact was that Banks wanted a larger ship.

He also sent Sandwich the draft of a letter, again highly critical, which he had prepared for publication. Sandwich replied with a short, cool, restrained letter, which pointed out the danger of making public such damaging charges against the Navy Board. He regretted that Banks was dissatisfied with the alterations to the *Resolution*, and sorrier still that he intended to publish such

. . . a heavy charge against this Board to suppose that they mean to send a number of men to sea in an unhealthy ship. In this point, and in most of the reasoning of the above mentioned letter, I differ greatly with you in opinion, and shall therefore be sorry if anything is printed on either side; but I am sure if you will give yourself time to think coolly, you will at once see the impropriety of publishing to the world an opinion of your own, that one of the King's ships is unfit for a voyage she is going to be employed in, and that the crew will be in danger of losing their lives if they go to sea in her.

You are certainly your own master and have a thorough right to determine for yourself and your attendants, but when this is done, I cannot think you should endeavour to make those who remain on board uneasy with their situation. It can answer no purpose to you, and I am positive the probability that this will be an unhealthy ship is not founded, and that if called upon we shall be able to bring the fullest proof to the contrary.

A memorandum from the Navy Board, commenting on Banks's letter to Lord Sandwich, was less gentle. It pointed out that his objections were confined only to 'the conveniences for himself'.

As for the proper kind of ship, and her fitness and sufficiency for the voyage, his opinion was never asked, nor could he have been asked with any propriety, he being in no degree qualified to form a right judgement in such a matter; and for the same reason his opinion now thereon is not to be attended to.

The memorandum went on to point out that even after being restored to her former condition, the *Resolution* offered Banks and his party better accommodation than had been available on the *Endeavour*. Scathingly the Admiralty men remarked :

Mr Banks seems throughout to consider the ships are fitted out wholly for his use; the whole undertaking to depend on him and his people; and himself as Director and Conductor of the whole; for which he is not qualified, and if granted to him, would have been the greatest disgrace that could be put on His Majesty's Naval Officers.

Banks had asked for two frigates—the *Emerald* and the *Stag*. To that request the Navy Board pointed out :

Had either of those ships been in the *Endeavour*'s place on the coast of New Holland, they would never have been heard of again; even if they had got off the rocks they could not have been hauled up to repair damages, as was done by the *Endeavour*.

As a result of Lord Sandwich's warning letter, Banks did not publish his condemnation of the Navy Board, but there was no going back on his decision to quit the enterprise. He was a bitter and disappointed man. Not only had he lost face, he had also invested a small fortune in the exercise.

Now all he wanted to do was get away, partly because he had set his heart on another voyage, but also because he was not anxious to stay in London as the target for malicious gossip and jibes.

For a short while he toyed with what seemed to be an offer by the East India Company to send him on a similar voyage to that of the *Resolution* and *Adventure*, but it came to nothing, even supposing it was a serious proposition in the first place. He records :

My People, all remain faithful to me. Even Mr Zoffany, tho' he was, the moment I refused to proceed, sent by the King to copy some pictures for him in the Florentine, engaged to leave that business and return to meet me at a fortnight's warning.

The rest were all left upon my hands and as they were a considerable running expense I thought it prudent to employ them in some way or other to the advancement of science. A voyage of some kind or other I wished to undertake and saw no place within the compass of my time so likely to furnish me with an opportunity as Iceland, a country which, from its being in some measure the property of a Danish trading company, has been visited but seldom and never at all by any good naturalist to my knowledge. The whole face of the country new to the botanist and zoologist, as well as the many volcanoes with which it is said to abound, made it very desirable to explore it, and tho' the season was far advanced, yet something might be done, at least hints might be gathered which might promote the further examination of it by some others.

CHAPTER 9

ACTION IN ICELAND

For £100 a month Banks took a four-month charter on a 190-ton brig, the *Sir Lawrence*, with her captain, Captain Hunter, and a crew of twelve. To his own party he added a gardener and a cook.

Although Moreland, the gardener, who was hired to tend any living plants collected, and also look after seeds, and Anthony Donez, the cook, were new to Banks's travels, there were some familiar names among the Iceland party—his loyal servants, James Roberts and Peter Briscoe, and John Gore, who had been Third Lieutenant on the *Endeavour*. Banks also took along Alexander, the Malay servant he had brought back from Batavia.

Late at night on 12 July 1772 the *Sir Lawrence* slipped her mooring and sailed down the Thames. The following morning there was a brief encounter with Lord Sandwich, who was on board his yacht, the *Augusta*, returning from a visitation to the southern dockyards, but there was no meeting between the old friends. That evening they went ashore at Dover and walked to the castle to admire 'the great brass cannon which lies on the cliff'. Bad weather kept them at Dover until the fifteenth, but Banks filled in the time botanising.

On the fifteenth they continued their journey, but were caught off Beachy Head in a stiff wind and rough sea. Once again Banks was afflicted by his old travelling enemy, sea-sickness. Five days later he wrote :

The wind has been in our teeth ever since the sixteenth, and myself too sick to write. Now for the first time the weather is rather more moderate and we hope to anchor within the Isle of Wight tonight.

Indeed they did, sampling the then simple delights of Cowes 'a pleasant town', and walking in the country botanising and inspecting the local salt works. In fact they arrived early enough in the day to be on their way again in the afternoon.

At three o'clock, the tide of ebb making, we got under way and proceeded, the wind being contrary and our people very much tired, we agreed to go no further than Yarmouth, at which place we arrived about six, and as I and my servants, almost all landsmen seemed desirous of landing I resolved to carry everyone ashore while the crew of the ship slept. Accordingly we landed with the French horns to the no small surprise of the people, who little expected to see such a motley crew appear from so small a vessel.

After more sightseeing and botanising the party pressed on to Plymouth, where Banks renewed his acquaintanceship with Mount Edgecumbe.

On 24 July they sailed into a fresh wind which made Banks 'sicker than I have been since we sailed'. In fact during the following days as they beat around Land's End, he was constantly ill. By 30 July they were just off Dublin, but did not go ashore in Ireland, pushing on, instead, for the Scottish Isles.

In the eighteenth century the Highlands and Islands were remote and relatively little visited, and for a man of Banks's inquisitive character they held an inevitable fascination.

The expedition's first stop was the Isle of Islay. Their arrival coincided with the annual receiving of the sacraments, and the main town was packed with the faithful, so much so that the party were unable to get rooms in the two inns and had to pitch tents. Despite the crowds and heavy rain they contrived to 'amuse' themselves with 'a plentiful Highland dinner composed of various legs of mutton and puddings'.

Although the rain continued to fall relentlessly, the expedition searched the island for the curious and rare. The artists were put to work sketching the wretched hovels of the Highland peasants, and the ruins of a religious foundation at Killarn. They went to a cave 'of which we had heard a very pompous account, but found it a dirty nasty hollow in a rock'.

During the days that followed they explored Jura and Oronsay, everywhere being met 'with all the marks of hospitality which tho' not to be met with in England are yet so common in these unpolished countries'.

On 11 August they continued their voyage through the islands, with Banks becoming lyrical at the sight of Morven, the wooded 'land of heroes'.

I could not even sail past it without a touch of enthusiasm, sweet affection of the mind which can gather pleasure from the empty elements and realise substantial pleasure which three-fourths of mankind are ignorant of. I lamented the busy bustle of the ship and had I dared to venture the censure of my companions would certainly have brought her to anchor. To have read ten pages of Osian under the shade of those woods would have been a luxury above the reach of kings.

Later they did go ashore to watch the rather mundane operation of kelp burning, and it was while they were on the island that Banks was told of the remarkable rock formations of Staffa. Without delay he and eight of his companions set out for the island.

On arrival it was realised that the tent they had brought with them was too small for all to sleep in, so Solander and four others agreed to pass the night in a crofter's cottage after being assured that there were no lice in the bedding. In fact the assurance was less than truthful and they were eaten alive. When they complained to the man of the house, he coolly remarked:

Lice, indeed if they have any lice they certainly brought them here for I am sure there were none upon the island when they came.

Before daybreak on 13 August they set out for the rocks 'a scene of magnificence which exceeded our expectations'. The towering basalt columns moved Banks to write:

Compared to this what are the cathedrals or the palaces built by man; mere models or playthings, imitations as diminutive as his works will always be when compared with those of nature. Where is now the boast of the architect? Regularity, the only part in which he fancied himself to exceed his mistress nature is here found in her proportion and here it has been for ages uncounted. Is not this the school where the art was originally studied and what had been added to this by the whole Grecian school? A capital to ornament the column of nature of which they could execute only a model and for that capital they were obliged to a bush of acanthus!

If the fantastic wonders of the rocks of Staffa and the splendour of Fingal's Cave had not been 'counted' before, Banks rectified that omission.

With our minds full of such reflections we invaded along the shore treading upon another Giant's Causeway . . . till in a short time we arrived at the mouth of a cave, the most magnificent, I suppose, that has ever been described by travellers.

Astelia nervosa (Bush Flax), with its dramatic scarlet flowers and elegant foliage, was one of the hundreds of new plants collected by Banks and Daniel Solander during the historic voyage round the world in The Endeavour, commanded by CaptJames Cook, between 1768 and 1771 *(British Museum, Natural History)*

Phormium tenax (New Zealand Flax), which was first recorded by Banks and Solander during the voyage of The Endeavour, became an important source of cordage for The Royal Navy and the British merchant fleet *(British Museum, Natural History)*

The accounting soon began with the most detailed measurements and drawings of the rock columns and the cave itself.

From Staffa they made their way to Iona for the ruins of St Columba's great religious house. Here the people were clearly more accustomed to tourists.

Banks wrote :

We were received by a number of people who told us they had heard of our coming and proferred us every convenience the town could afford, but we soon found the difference between these and the simple people we had had to do with before. Few strangers as these people had seen, those few had corrupted the hospitality of this country. One of the first questions asked us after we had agreed to accept their offers was how much we would give, a question which had not been put to us since we were came into the Highlands till this time.

As it is a much easier matter to deal with people for a favour before it is received than after, we rejoiced that they had not arrived at the next step of civilization, that of bestowing and after the receipt requiring an enormous recompense. Our bargain was soon made; we were furnished with an empty house, plenty of clean straw, sour curds and cream, and a good fire, which we could well have dispensed with as money could not purchase a chimney to let out the smoke. We therefore put it out and having eat our sour supper, retired to rest.

Late on the afternoon of 14 August the party set off for St Columba's house, which they found a total ruin inhabited only by chough, crows and jackdaws. But at the 'Chapel of Oran, a fellow saint', the party was entertained by their guide with a story about the hapless saint. In obedience to a vision Oran was

. . . buried alive in this place . . . the next day he was dug up and found alive. No sooner was he uncovered than he began to blaspheme, crying out 'you are all deceived, Hell is a trifle and the Devil a mere illusion invented to deceive you'. Columba, on hearing this, with great presence of mind, cried out 'earth on the head of Oran'. He was instantly obeyed and poor Oran was buried again, never more to arise till the last trump shall awake him.

From Iona they joined the *Sir Lawrence* at Tobermory 'prodigious fine harbour . . . capable of containing in safety a large fleet', and on the fifteenth went to Oronsay to shoot deer.

With moderate weather to help them the party set sail on the sixteenth and cruised among the islands, with the intention of landing on St Kilda, but on the eighteenth,

... the weather being dirty, a great swell and foul wind, so turned our heads towards Iceland. In a short time sea sickness reigned among us as much as ever.

All next day the rough weather persisted and all Banks could bring himself to write in his journal is one spidery line 'dirty rough weather. Everybody sick'.

After ten days, during which the sea-sickness subsided enough for the study of the sea-birds which swarmed about the ship, land was sighted, and two days later, after a fisherman agreed to act as a pilot, they reached 'Bessestedr'.

Helped no doubt by Solander's ability to communicate freely with the shy Icelanders, and that of another Swedish companion, a young clergyman, Dr Uno von Troil, later to become Archbishop of Uppsala, Banks rapidly established a close relationship with the Icelanders he met, and for many years later he was remembered with fondness and respect.

Banks found the Icelanders of

... a good honest disposition; but they are, at the same time, so serious and sullen, that I hardly remember to have seen any one of them laugh.

Serious and sullen they may have been, but nevertheless the visitors seem to have enjoyed a full social life. In a contemporary account of the visit, Jon Steingrimsson described an evening at the home of a Mr Muller, who, seated at the head of his table

... took a musical instrument and played it, but eight Englishmen sat down on the bench opposite to me and joined in the music, bending sideways and playing the same tune with their hands and feet, stamping on the floor hard and soft according as the music rose and fell, so that it seemed to me that the house was taking part in the playing.

One evening a doctor, Bjarni Palsson, entertained them to a typical Icelandic dinner. It started with a glass of brandy. In the middle of the table was a dish of sliced dried fish. This was followed by roast mutton, broth, salmon-trout, sour butter, cheese, biscuits and corn-brandy. It was not an unqualified success with the visitors shying somewhat at the sour butter and dried fish, as well as the large helping of boiled and dried shark and whale meat.

But science, not entertainment, was the purpose of the trip and during the month they were on the island they explored Havnefiord,

Langarvatn, Skard, and Reykjavik. At Langarvatn they cooked trout, mutton and even a ptarmigan in the hot springs.

Naturally they botanised as they went, but in addition to collecting plants, Banks also bought a fine collection of Icelandic manuscripts, which he later presented to the British Museum.

The high point, in every sense, however, was the expedition to Mount Hekla, to see the volcano. They pitched their tents at the foot of the mountain, and made the first part of the ascent on horseback, but for the final assault they had to abandon the horses and complete the climb on foot.

Although Banks's account of Iceland is sparse in the extreme, he did spare time to write an account of the climb.

We ascended Mount Hekla with the wind blowing against us so violently that we could with difficulty proceed. The frost, too, was lying upon the ground, and the cold extremely severe. We were covered with ice in such a manner that our clothes resembled buckram. On reaching the summit of the first peak, we here and there remarked places where the snow had melted, and a little heat was arising from them; and it was by one of these that we rested to observe the barometer, which was 24°.838. Thermometer 27 degrees. The water we had with us was all frozen. Dr Lind filled his wind machine with warm water; it rose to 1.6 degs, and then froze into spicule, so that we could not make observations any longer. We thought that we had arrived at the highest peak, but soon saw one above us, to which we hastened. Dr Solander remained with an Icelander in the intermediate valley; the rest of us continued our route to the summit of the peak, which we found intensely cold; but on the highest point was a spot of three yards breadth, where there proceeded so much heat and steam that we could not bear to sit down upon it.

During the following days Banks and his party explored the island, studying the natural phenomena, collecting plants and examining the antiquities. When they sailed away he left behind Icelanders who were to remain his friends for life.

In London there is a memorial to Banks's Iceland expedition in the form of blocks of lava rock in the Chelsea Physic Garden which were brought back as ballast in the *Sir Lawrence*.

Years later during the conflict with France, Banks helped Icelanders who found themselves stranded in Britain, usually as a result of Icelandic vessels being seized by the Royal Navy.

When Denmark was blockaded, and Iceland was virtually cut off from the rest of the world, Banks raised the question whether Britain should assume hegemony over the island. He produced a detailed plan to take over and rule under a federal system, and described how trade could be restored under naval protection. An eleven-page letter to Lord Hawkesbury, who as Lord Liverpool was later to become Prime Minister, dated 30 December 1807, gives the details—size of Iceland, its geological make-up, population, products and constitution. He even argued that the island was properly part of Great Britain.

It is scarcely possible, even for an unthinking observer who casts his eyes over the chart of Europe with a view of examining what relation the respective Kingdoms into which it has been divided bear to each other, not to be struck with the evident propriety of Iceland being considered as a part of the group of islands called by the Ancients, Brittanica. Great Britain, Ireland, Orkney, Shetland, Ferroe and Iceland form together an archipelego naturally offering to the mind a section eminently fitted for the establishment of a naval empire incomplete if the whole are not united under one monarch; but capable when joined together, of furnishing inhabitants sufficient by the manifold advantages deriveable from maritime strength to keep the whole world in awe, and if necessary, in subjection.

In the final paragraph he agrees that his idea might be 'Utopian and visionary' but should it become reality he made himself available and

. . . most ready to communicate to your Lordship every part of the detail, which in thinking a considerable time on the subject, has occurred to me.

Hawkesbury was impressed and having consulted 'the King's servants' he asked Banks to discover how 'Iceland could be secured to His Majesty, at least during the continuance of the present war'. To assist in any negotiations the Government declared itself ready to release some Icelandic ships being held at Leith.

Apart from his wish to see Iceland under the wing of Britain, Banks was deeply concerned about the plight of the people of the island, who were suffering dreadfully as a result of the war. The Danes had put a stop to any kind of trade, except with Denmark itself, and as a consequence the Icelanders had been brought to the verge of starvation.

It was against this background that a colourful swashbuckling figure appeared on the scene, one Jorgen Jorgensen, an Anglicised Dane, who was in London on parole after being captured in command of a Danish privateer off Flamborough Head. Jorgenson was a man of ability, but also an incurable romantic and opportunist. He started life as a ship's boy on a British collier. He had joined the Royal Navy, served under Matthew Flinders, and rose to the rank of midshipman. He was a first-rate seaman and a brilliant navigator.

At one point in his career he had met Banks, and, hearing of the plans to take Iceland under British protection, and of Banks's anxiety over the plight of the Icelanders, he lost no time in renewing the acquaintanceship. Always the most plausible of men, Jorgensen convinced Banks that, with his Danish background, he had obtained trading concessions with the island and could land a cargo of essential supplies. With Banks's backing he had no problem in persuading a rich London soap merchant, a Mr Phelps, to finance the venture. In exchange for his backing he would get a cargo of tallow, which at the time was in short supply.

Needless to say Jorgenson had absolutely no contacts in Iceland, and instead of taking vital supplies in Phelp's charter, the *Clarence*, he loaded it with expensive luxury goods.

Arriving at Reykjavik, Jorgenson was refused permission by the Danish authorities to land his cargo, so he turned privateer again, seized a Danish vessel which was lying at anchor and said he would release her only when he was allowed to off-load his luxury cargo. Permission was speedily granted, but since all trade on the island was controlled by Danish merchants, no-one would buy, and neither could he obtain an ounce of tallow to take home. In the end frustrated on every hand, he sailed home with an empty ship and an empty purse.

It would not have been unreasonable had Jorgensen now ended up in prison or on a convict transport, or even at the end of a rope— but not at all. Golden-tongued as ever, he talked the gullible Phelps into financing a second trip to Iceland. This time, however, the soap merchant decided to join the expedition to protect his investment.

With a crew scratched up from the dockside pubs of Gravesend, and this time carrying a more practical cargo, a new charter, the *Margaret and Anne*, set sail for Iceland. Among her company was a brilliant young botanist, William Hooker, later to become one of the most distinguished directors ever to run Kew Gardens. He had come under the patronage of Banks, who had urged him to make the trip in order to put together a thorough collection of the island's flora.

Shortly before the ship reached Reykjavik an agreement had been made between the Danish Governor of Iceland, Count Trampe, and the commander of a British man-of-war, for the resumption of trade between Britain and the island. This did not fit in with the empire-building plan that Jorgensen had privately formed in his mind. He required a hostile environment so that Phelps and the master of the *Margaret and Anne* would fall in with his scheme, so he persuaded the Icelandic pilot who came aboard to spread the rumour that Count Trampe had threatened death to any pilot attempting to bring a British vessel into harbour, and that an armed escort was waiting to arrest Phelps and his party.

On 20 June 1809, in order to avoid 'arrest', Phelps, the ship's captain, Liston, Jorgensen and Hooker, were put ashore on a remote beach and taken to a friendly house. Jorgensen's fabrication was given substance when it was discovered that Count Trampe, despite the agreement he had made, was doing all he could to make trading with Iceland difficult, if not impossible. Six days after the secret landing Phelps agreed to send Liston and twelve armed men to arrest the Governor.

What happened was witnessed by the gentle William Hooker, with a mixture of horror and amusement. He was returning from a trip to some hot springs when he saw the outraged Counte Trampe being hustled out of his residence by the party of armed sailors, led by Liston brandishing a drawn cutless. The wretched Governor was confined on the *Margaret and Anne*, and the British colours were run up on his own vessel, the *Orion*.

Jorgensen's plan had worked perfectly. In no time he established himself in the Governor's residence, now flying the Union Jack in place of the Danish flag, and had dubbed himself 'Governor and Protector of the whole island of Iceland and chief Commander by sea and land'. He recruited a bodyguard of Icelanders and carried out a house-to-house search for arms. The total haul amounted to 'twenty wretched muskets, most of them in a quite useless state and a few rusty cutlasses'. Danish citizens were confined to their houses on pain of death, but not one shot was fired or one blow exchanged in this extraordinary toy-town coup.

While taking a somewhat childish pleasure in his newly won status and titles, Jorgensen proved to be a resourceful and enlightened ruler. He built a fort to protect Reykjavik from attack by the Danes, and put in hand a whole series of reforms. Six hundred pounds was granted to the island's main school so that it could be cleaned and white-washed, and the scholars provided with decent clothing, bedding and food. He increased teachers' and clergymen's salaries, and cut the crippling Danish taxes by half, making up the shortfall with a small duty on imports and exports. In addition he released the Icelanders from debt due to the Danish Crown, and provided the investment to improve the island's vital fishing industry.

His reforms were welcomed by the Icelanders, and most of the island's officials who had served under the Danes willingly switched allegience to him. Jorgensen's weakness was his failure to seek British approval before embarking on the venture—no doubt because he knew it would not have been granted, since he was not only a foreigner by birth, but also a prisoner-of-war on parole. But he did believe that having pulled off the invasion he would receive the thanks of a grateful British Government, and had he had more time to consolidate his position this might have been so.

Unfortunately for Jorgenson, word of the exploit reached the ears of the Hon Alexander Jones, commander of the British sloop-of-war, the Talbot, then cruising off the Icelandic coast. To Jones it sounded dangerous and revolutionary. He altered course for Reykjavik, where he was confronted with the outrageous spectacle of Jorgensen coming aboard the *Talbot* in the uniform of a post-captain of the Royal Navy, a rank to which he had no claim.

He was immediately seized and placed under close arrest. Count Trampe was released, and the fort that Jorgenson had built was destroyed.

Jones decided that the self-styled Governor should be returned to England in the *Orion*, which was taken as a prize, while Count Trampe would be taken to London in the *Margaret and Anne* as a prisoner of honour in order to register his complaint.

The *Margaret and Anne*, laden with a valuable cargo of tallow, and also carrying William Hooker and his plant collection, left first by a slow but safer route through the dangerous approach to Reykjavik. About sixty miles off the coast a fire broke out in the tallow in the hold. It quickly got out of control, and it seemed as though the ship and her company must perish. Indeed they would have done so but for Jorgensen, who brought the *Orion* through the rock-strewn fast route. Although the *Margaret and Anne* and her cargo were lost, not a single seaman or passenger died.

There is no doubt that Jorgensen displayed great courage and skill in this rescue at sea, and it helped to ease his situation when he arrived in England. Hooker spoke up for him, and Jorgensen lost no time in trying to restore himself in Banks's favour.

In his own account of his venture, Jorgensen wrote of his meeting with Banks:

On my arrival in London I immediately drove to Sir Joseph Banks and acquainted him with my arrival and dined with Lady and Miss Banks the same day. He (Sir Joseph) was of the opinion that Captain Jones had done wrong in destroying the fort, and enjoyed much of what I told him concerning our proceedings.

At first it seemed that he had been forgiven. He was lodged at the Spread Eagle in Gracechurch Street, and was allowed complete freedom of movement. But three weeks after his return he was arrested for breaking his parole and sent to the convict hulks at Chatham for twelve months. But it is significant that he was never brought to trial for his escapade in Iceland.

In the end, however, he did lose Banks's patronage. Almost exactly a year after the Iceland incident Banks set down his view of Jorgensen, Phelps and Count Trampe in a letter to Hooker.

My mind is that Jorgensen is a bad man, Phelps as bad and that Count Trampe is a good man, as good a man I mean as Danes are when they are good, which is by no means as good as a good Englishman.

As for Jorgensen, he went from bad to worse. He became a compulsive gambler, was imprisoned for debt, and finally transported to Tasmania for robbing his landlady.

But some good did come from the invasion of Iceland. An agreement was reached between Britain and Denmark which gave the island immunity during the remainder of the Napoleonic Wars, and the freedom to trade with Britain.

For Banks, Iceland always remained a magical place, rich in excitement for the natural historian and the antiquary, a view that he also attached to the Highlands and Islands of Scotland.

On his return journey from Iceland he stopped at Orkney to examine the Stones of Stannis and the Skail burial grounds, and to make detailed measurements and drawings.

He wound up his trip in Edinburgh, finally returning to London in November 1772.

CHAPTER 10

COLLECTING FOR KEW

The return from Iceland effectively marked the end of Banks's career as a voyager and explorer. There was a brief visit to Holland with the Hon Charles Greville, where they attended a meeting of the Batavian Society in the spring of 1773. He also considered a Mediterranean expedition with the object of making an extensive plant collection. As for the East India Company project, nothing more was heard of that. But there was another foray into Wales, which included the ascent of Snowdon.

But roles more important even than discovery lay before him. Ever since their first meeting the friendship between Banks and George III had steadily developed. The King was only five years his senior, and the two men had much in common. Both were intensely interested in natural history and agriculture, and they shared a scientific approach to the subjects. They both recognised that with the world rapidly opening up there were natural products being discovered which would play a vital part, not only in the home economy, but in the economies of the colonies.

Up to the second half of the eighteenth century interest in natural history had largely been a pleasant pastime for the wealthy who enjoyed assembling cabinets of curiosities to exhibit to their friends, or collected exotics in their gardens and stove houses in much the same way as they caged wild animals in their menageries.

Banks and the King were practical men. For them there was as much excitement in development as there was in discovery, and Banks had a unique quality which especially appealed to the King—he was politically non-aligned, with the declared intention never to become involved in political manoeuvring. Banks believed that he could achieve nothing if he was tied down by partisan loyalties. For the King, surrounded by political puppeteers, such an attitude was beautifully refreshing, and when such a man also shared his private interests it was inevitable that the friendship should flourish.

One of the major interests of the Royal Family was the gardens at

Kew. Originated by Sir Henry Capel shortly after the Restoration, the gardens came under royal care in 1730 when Frederick, Prince of Wales, took a lease on Kew House from the Capel family. Twenty-one years later, Augusta, Dowager Princess of Wales, directed all her energies towards developing the gardens. She was helped by the politically unpopular Earl of Bute, who was a skilled horticulturist, and responsible for the gardens at Mount Stuart on the Isle of Bute, the Gardens at Luton Hoo, and at his property at Christchurch in Hampshire.

Bute's misfortune was that George III loathed him, and when the Dowager Princess died in 1772 the Earl was given his marching orders. His departure left a vacuum at Kew which had to be filled. Under the care of Augusta and Bute the gardens had flourished and grown in importance, superseding the place long occupied by the Chelsea Physic Garden, which was no longer large enough to receive the increasing flow of new species.

The King wanted the gardens at Kew to be developed on scientific lines to serve a scientific purpose, as well as a purely ornamental one. The obvious man for the job was Joseph Banks, who not only had first-hand experience of exotic plants, but was a qualified botanist and a skilled plantsman.

Early in 1773 he was appointed as special adviser and director of the Royal Gardens. While the everyday running was left to the Royal Gardener, William Aiton, the broad design and development of Kew was in the hands of Banks, a task which was to occupy much of his time for the remainder of his long life.

Banks was a convinced colonialist. He had no doubt that British settlers would spread the British influence throughout the world and that this would result in a mighty network of trade, and perhaps more importantly the hitherto largely untapped resources of nature would be developed to the advantage of man. In Kew Gardens he saw the opportunity of establishing an international clearing house for plants and seeds.

Throughout his career as a collector he had made a special study of techniques for bringing living plants and viable seeds and bulbs back to Britain over long distances and under the most unfavourable conditions. Until his time the introduction of plants had been a most haphazard business. Even when he took over Kew it was still a hit-and-miss affair.

If Kew was to flourish he realised that collecting would have to be placed on a much more business-like basis. Before he took on the Directorship he had already established a wide correspondence with naturalists throughout the world and was receiving a steady flow of botanical specimens from his correspondents for his private collections. Kew was an extension, on a grand scale, of his private activities. It would, he determined, become a great seed and plant exchange.

But obviously he could not depend solely on the goodwill of fellow enthusiasts, and therefore he conceived the notion of professional collectors—men as dedicated as himself, prepared to face every kind of hazard and privation; disease, violent extremes of climate, hostile natives, dangerous wild animals, accident and starvation—who would scour the world for new plants. They had to be keen since they were rarely paid more than £100 a year for their pains.

Surprisingly he found such men prepared to go where he bade them and to carry out his instructions, which were minutely detailed. Mainly they were simple men from humble backgrounds, gardeners who had become entranced by the plants they tended.

It was perhaps because he had himself worked in the field, and experienced (and survived) great hardships, that his collectors were so remarkably loyal and resilient. It was hard for them to advance excuses to a man who could quote personal experience back at them. They were dealing with no armchair traveller.

The first of Banks Kew collectors, although he left on his travels a year before Banks took over the direction of Kew, was Francis Masson.

Banks had told the King that the Cape of South Africa would prove a rich area for botanical exploration and collection.

Masson, a tough, enterprising Scot, who had been trained as a gardener at Kew, was taken to the Cape by Cook on the outward leg of his second voyage round the world. He landed at Cape Town at the end of 1772 and made a preliminary excursion to Swellendam. He also explored the mountains between Cape Town and False Bay.

Later, in the company of the Swedish botanist, Carl Peter Thunberg, a pupil of Linnaeus, he travelled as far north as the Karroo, then little known to Europeans. His industry was prodigious and Kew benefited by his introduction of hundreds of new species, including heaths, pelargoniums, mesembryanthemums, lobelias and oxalis, many of which have become popular garden and pot plants.

During a long collecting career Masson remained faithful to Kew and Banks. He collected tirelessly in North America, Spain, Madeira, the Canaries, the Azores and the West Indies.

Archibald Menzies, a naval surgeon who was commissioned by Banks, made two distinguished introductions, the Giant Redwood (*Sequoia sempervirens*), and the Monkey Puzzle tree (*Araucaria araucana*). The latter he discovered whilst dining with the Viceroy of Chile. He noticed some curious 'nuts' in dishes on the table and slipped a few into his pocket. Later he planted them and was able to bring young plants back to England, one of which was planted in the garden of Banks's home, Spring Grove at Heston.

John Ledyard, an adventurer from Connecticut, was sent to Kamchatka in Russia, and later to Africa, where he died.

William Hooker, as has already been told, went to Iceland, but was prevented by his family from going to Java to collect plants for Banks, who, although annoyed by this apparent feebleness, nevertheless remained a close friend and adviser. Hooker's son, Joseph, became a most distinguished plant collector, particularly of rhododendrons from the Himalayas, before, like his father, becoming Director of Kew.

China was a country that had long fascinated Banks, not least for its wealth of plants. In the eighteenth century the country remained a mystery with its aloof and secretive attitude towards the rest of the world, but it was known to possess superb gardens and skilled gardeners. Banks's first more or less direct contact with the flora of China was through Sir George Staunton, who was attached to Lord Macartney's Embassy to Peking and was a spare-time botanist.

Banks had to wait until 1806 before he was able to get a professional collector into the rich China field. He sent William Kerr, another Scotsman, who faced great difficulties not just in collecting, but in getting the plants and seeds back to England; but he did introduce some fine and now well-loved plants – the Tiger Lily (*Lilium tigrinum*), the Banksian Rose (*Rosa Banksiae*), *Lilium japonica*, *Pieris japonica*, and *Begonia evansiana*.

Dr Clarke Abel, the British Embassy physician, collected for Kew, and Banks supplied him with collecting equipment and a Kew-trained gardener to tend plants awaiting shipment home. In a letter dated 10 February 1816 he urged Abel to collect roses and lilies, and any elegant plants growing in Chinese gardens.

Among those which are most wanted are the many varieties of the Azalea indica, and those of the Moutan or Peonie arborea, different from those known in Europe. We are told of yellow and blue Moutans, and have seen drawings of them; but whether these are fictitious or realities is not quite certain. All plants that produce oils are interesting to our manufacturers.

To this he added a note asking for varieties of tea plants.

Whenever he sent out a collector Banks always set out the most explicit and detailed instructions on what to look for, and how to collect and transport living plants, and how to package and preserve seeds. Considering the long journey involved, the problems of transport and the difficulties involved in keeping sea water off the plants, it is quite astonishing that so many survived to flourish at Kew and produce stock for the botanical gardens that were being developed throughout the Empire.

Clarke Abel was not the most successful plant collector. His collections, including a fine pink azalea, doubtless of the indica class, were destroyed through the combination of shipwreck and piracy. But the most spectacular collecting disaster of all in which Banks had a hand was the *Bounty* expedition to collect breadfruit plants from Tahiti.

The main purpose of the exercise was to introduce breadfruit trees to the West Indies as a source of cheap, nutritious food for the large slave-labour force working the sugar plantations. The expedition was placed under the command of Captain William Bligh, whom history and Charles Laughton have depicted as a sadistic monster. In fact Bligh was not an excessive flogger. He was an excellent seaman and navigator, but he had two grave faults – he had little imagination, and he commanded strictly by the book. He also had an unpleasant habit of abusing the officers who served under him, often in the most foul and insulting language.

It is possible to argue that Banks himself was indirectly responsible for the celebrated mutiny on the *Bounty*. Once the Government had decided on the enterprise, he was asked to draw up the instructions for the two gardeners sent with the expedition, David Nelson and William Brown.

The target set for the gardeners was to raise one thousand breadfruit saplings on Tahiti. This was achieved over a period of some months, and when they were stowed on board the crew was reduced to very cramped quarters. Banks's instructions meant that the plants had to be constantly moved so that each would receive a reasonable amount of fresh air. The foliage had to be regularly sponged down with fresh water to free them from salt deposits. The plants also had to be con- tinually watered, which meant that the ship's company was put on short rations. It is hardly surprising that the seamen grew to hate the plants which caused so much discomfort and arduous work on top of that involved in working the ship. Set that against the months of idyllic living in Tahiti, and mutiny became virtually inevitable.

What is curious is that Brown, who had spent so much time and care helping to raise the plants, should join the mutineers and help to dump them in the sea.

After his incredible voyage with eighteen men in a twenty-three-foot open boat to Timor, a journey of 3,618 miles, Bligh did face criticism when he finally reached England. But Banks, who was bitterly disappointed by the failure of the breadfruit run, remained loyal to him. Indeed, he went so far as to recommend that Bligh should command the second and successful attempt to take a duplicate consignment to the West Indies, and some years later approved Bligh's appointment as Governor of New South Wales.

Clearly Bligh regarded Banks as a close and valued friend. After the court-martial into the loss of the *Bounty*, he wrote to Banks on 24 October 1790:

I am happy to inform you that on Friday last I was most honourably acquitted respecting the loss of the *Bounty*—The sentence closed with— 'You are hereby honourably acquitted'.

He was worried whether or not he would be promoted to Post Captain, and appealed to Banks for backing.

I am concerned at· losing your kind assistance just at this time, but I hope and beg of you, Dear Sir, to do your endeavours to secure me the rank of Post, for if this opportunity passes off it may be lost for ever.

Bligh was not the only problematical character that Banks had to cope with during his work of organising plant collecting. George Caley, a Yorkshire stable-lad turned botanist, was sent to New South Wales. That he was hardworking and enthusiastic was not in doubt, but he had an evil temper and constantly believed that he was being belittled and done down. Banks was for ever on the receiving end of his irascibility, but never lost patience, possibly because his self-control was rewarded with a steady stream of seeds.

A Polish-born gardener, Anton Pantaleon Hove, was sent to India to collect cotton seeds. William Roxburgh, who really pioneered the study of Indian flora, was another Banks collector. Alan Cunningham went to Brazil, Australia and New Zealand, and was followed later by his brother, Richard.

When William Wilberforce founded Freetown in Sierra Leone as a home for freed slaves, he turned to Banks to find a botanist for the new colony. Banks recommended Adam Afzelius, the Swedist botanist, and provided him with all the equipment he would need.

Banks was always deeply interested in Africa and was a founder member of the African Association. He was closely associated with Mungo Park and his great and finally fatal expeditions to the continent. One of the last Africa collectors he commissioned was James Bowie, who went to the plant-rich Cape.

Quite apart from the men he commissioned directly, Banks's connections with foreign naturalists ensured prolific gifts of plants, seeds and herbarium specimens.

Many foreign botanists had cause to be grateful for his friendship, not least Jaques Labillardière.

Before the French Revolution, Labillardière joined an expedition sent to search for La Pérouse, the explorer, who was overdue. In fact he had died when his ship was wrecked. Although the expedition failed to find any trace of La Pérouse, it was highly successful in putting together a valuable collection of botanical specimens. During the return journey there was a mutiny in which the revolutionary crew turned on the Royalist officers. Shortly afterwards the French vessel was intercepted by a British cruiser and captured. Labillardière and his valuable collection were seized.

When the prize reached England, Banks was asked to catalogue the collection and make suitable selections for the Royal herbarium, which was the particular joy of Queen Charlotte. Normally he would have disapproved of holding a captured scientific collection, since he regarded science as being above war, but because of the mutiny and the fact that Labillardière had joined the revolutionaries, he considered the collection forfeit. But upon less emotional reflections he took a leading part in having it restored to France.

Although he left the day-to-day running of Kew to Aiton, Banks did fulfil a practical role. He supervised much of the germination of exotic seeds, and privately he liked nothing better than experimenting with plants at Spring Grove, the Heston house which he took in 1779.

When he moved there, there was a well-established garden which he developed over the years into a kind of mini-Kew. He experimented with fruit culture, introduced the mulching of strawberries with straw; he grew American cranberries with great success, and many of the papers he wrote for the Horticultural Society, now the Royal Horticultural Society, were based on work carried out at Spring Grove.

A History of the Vegetable Kingdom by William Rhind, gives an account of an experiment by Banks in growing mountain rice in Britain. The Board of Agriculture gave him the seeds of six different kinds of mountain rice sent by the East India Company.

Sir Joseph Banks . . . planted each kind in a separate bed, in a sheltered spot with a south aspect, in his garden at Spring Grove. The grains . . . speedily sprang up, and the plants tillered so much that the beds put on the appearance of compact, dense masses of vegetation; each plant having from ten to twenty off-sets. Although the blades grew vigorously, attaining in a short time the length of two feet, there was never any symptom of a rising stem.

Eventually an early frost in September killed the rice plants. Some grown in a hot house did produce grain, but :

. . . the conclusion to which Sir Joseph Banks arrived from these experiments was unfavourable to the cultivation of rice in this country as a grain-bearing plant; but he was led to consider from the great quantity of its blades, that it would afford excellent green-meat for cattle.

When Banks died in 1820, Kew Gardens sank into a decline. A parsimonious Government was reluctant to part with much money for its upkeep, and Banks's years of work and devotion were dangerously threatened. It was fitting, therefore, that in the nick of time they were placed under the care of William Hooker, the young man Banks had befriended years before, who rescued the gardens and reinforced the Banksian foundations that have made Kew the greatest botanical garden in the world.

Although Banks had an enduring love of flowers and was always entranced by their beauty and intricacy, he also shared with George III a passion for agriculture.

Despite the immense range of his interests and the fact that so much of his time was taken up in travelling, and the mass of work that occupied him in London and at Kew and Windsor, he never relaxed his close involvement in his Lincolnshire estates.

Every year from August to the end of October he retreated gratefully into the life of an English country gentleman, but it was not a period of idleness. Brought up in a family tradition of land improvement, he supervised a continuing programme of drainage and enclosure, of stock and crop improvement, and, of course, gardening. As at Spring

Omai, the young Tahitian 'priest' who was brought to England by Capt Tobias
Furneaux, Master of The Adventure, which was separated from The Resolution during
Cook's second circumnavigation of the World, with Banks and Solander in the painting by
William Parry *(From the Collection at Parham Park, West Sussex)*

When Omai came to England he was the darling of society, and great artists, such as Sir Joshua Reynolds, clamoured to paint his portrait. But his charm, wit and grace degenerated into petty tyranny when he was returned to his native island complete with a horse and full suit of armour *(From the Castle Howard Collection)*

Grove, the gardens of Revesby Abbey were magnificently stocked with exotics.

Farming was however the major interest in Lincolnshire and it was carried out with the same thoroughness and detail that marked all Banks's activities.

In his *General View of the Agriculture of the County of Lincoln*, the great agriculturist, Arthur Young, leaves this picture of the nerve-centre of Banks's farming empire.

In the management of a great estate, I remarked a circumstance at Revesby, the use of which I experienced in a multitude of instances. The liberality of Sir Joseph Banks opened every document for my inspection, and admiring the singular facility with which he laid his hand on papers, whatever the subject might be, I could not but remark the method that proved of such sovereign efficacy to prevent confusion. His office, of two rooms, is contained in the space of thirty feet by sixteen, there is a brick partition between, with an iron-plated door, so that the room, in which a fire is always burning, might be burnt down without affecting the inner one, where he has one hundred and fifty-six drawers of the size of an ordinary conveyance, the inside being thirteen inches wide by ten broad, and five and a half deep, all numbered. There is a catalogue of names and subjects, and a list of every paper in every drawer; so that whether the inquiry concerned a man, or a drainage or an inclosure, or a farm, or a wood, the request was scarcely named before a mass of information was in a moment before me. Fixed tables are before the windows (to the south), on which to spread maps, plans etc., commodiously, and these labelled, are arranged against the wall. The first room contains desks, tables and bookcases with measures, levels etc., and a wooded case, which when open forms a bookcase, and joining in the centre by hinges, when closed forms a package ready for a carrier's wagon, containing forty folio paper cases in the form of books; a repository of such papers as are wanted equally in town and country. Such an apartment, and such an apparatus, must be of incomparable use in the management of any great estate : or, indeed, of any considerable business.

Apart from the land that he farmed directly, Banks also owned a large number of tenant farms, some 268 producing £5,721 a year in rents. He was a benevolent landlord, but was intolerant of sloppy mismanagement. Nobody ever dared approach him for a lease, for the offer had to come from him. Arthur Young wrote of him :

Seeing a tenant of his improving his land by hollow drainage, he gave him a lease of twenty-one years, as a reward and an encouragement, the idea is an excellent one; and if they were thus given only to such as merited reward, they would prove a powerful instigation to good husbandry.

One of Banks's major interests was sheep, hardly surprising in a country which was still heavily dependent on the growing and manufacture of wool.

The wool intererests were split between the farmers and landowners who grew and harvested the fleeces, and the wool merchants and manufacturers. The fact that they shared a common interest in the industry did not prevent a constant enmity between the two sides. This friction came to a head in the early 1780s when the producers wanted to export their surplus wool, a move fiercely resisted by the manufacturers and merchants who wanted to retain a monopoly of the home produce so that they could manipulate the price of the raw material. Reluctantly Banks was drawn in on the producers' side. It meant becoming politically involved and politics was a game he shunned at all costs. But once involved he fought hard for his fellow farmers. It was a battle lost before it started. The merchants and manufacturers had money and political power on their side.

In 1788 the monopolists forced through a Wool Act which made it a criminal offence to export live sheep, rams and lambs, wool, woolsels, mortlings, shortlings, yarn or worsted, made-up wool, woolflocks, cruels, coverlids and waddings.

Nothing that could be reduced and made use of as raw wool could be shipped out of the country, and this included mattresses and beds stuffed with wool, combed wool, or wool fit for combing and carding. Even fuller's earth and fuller's clay (pipe clay used in the manufacture of woollen products) were on the banned list.

Farmers were forbidden to lay up wool in store within ten miles of the Sussex or Kent coast, and if sheep were sheared near the coast the wool had to be carried inland for storage.

The penalties for breaking the regulations enshrined in this infamous Act, which Banks and his friends had fought so hard, were savage. For exporting live sheep there was a fine of £3 for every animal, and twelve months in solitary confinement. For a second offence the fine increased to £5 an animal and two years' solitary imprisonment.

Wharf-owners had to lodge a bond of £200 for wool stored in their warehouse, and this was forfeit if the wool was smuggled by, as the Act put it, 'evil disposed persons (who) may in the night time put the same on board vessels ready for sailing to foreign parts'. Informers received an automatic bounty of £40, and could also claim the vessel and its contents. Smugglers who turned King's evidence within six months of an offence were guaranteed a free pardon, and naval officers involved in smuggling lost all pay and wages due to them, were imprisoned for six months and discharged from the service. And if smugglers resisted arrest they were transported.

With such an Act the farmers were completely at the mercy of the merchants and manufacturers who could set the price of wool at will. But there was one price area which the monopolists could not control, and that was the cost of Merino wool from Spain. The fine Merino wool was essential in the production of fine cloth, and as manufacturing techniques improved, so it became more important.

Banks recognised that if the British growers could produce Merino wool at home they would have a powerful bargaining weapon to use against the manufacturers and merchants. The problem was that the Spanish, having a monopoly, banned the export of breeding Merino sheep. Only the French had acquired an experimental breeding flock through the connexion between the French and Spanish royal houses.

The findings of the French geneticists working with the sheep were printed but kept secret. Banks, however, had close links with men of science in Europe, and in particular with a young French botanist turned zoologist, Pierre-Marie-Auguste Broussonet. Through Broussonet he obtained copies of the findings and eventually the gift of a ram and a ewe from the French Merino flock.

Monsieur Ram and Madame Ewe were brought to Spring Grove, and when they were eventually sheared Banks had the wool made up into two blue coats which he found 'as good as any made of real Spanish wool'.

Naturally he told George III of his modest experiment with the sheep, and between them the two men conceived the idea of 'The Patriotic Plan', which was to cross-breed Merinos with native breeds in order to fine down the British wool so that it would no longer be necessary to import Spanish wool.

Through his French connexions Banks arranged for a fairly large shipment of French Merinos, ostensibly for himself, but in fact for the royal flock at Windsor. The results from these animals were reasonably satisfactory, but it became clear that 'The Patriotic Plan' could not succeed without sheep from a good Spanish flock.

A direct approach to the Spanish was pointless, but Banks did know that Merino flocks were wintered in Portugal, and he was confident that for a price the Spanish shepherds would probably agree to 'lose' a few animals. It was also known that Spanish smugglers regularly ran herds of horses and mules across the border.

Armed with this knowledge he embarked on a lengthy series of secret negotiations which dragged on for months. A number of people had to be involved, which made the enterprise all the more dangerous. One of the most reliable people involved was a tough old seaman, Captain Michael Firth, master of the *Betsy*, who made regular trading runs to Portugal. In March 1788 he sent Banks a message from Dover:

I have got for you two ewes and one ram of the best Spanish breed and if you like them you may have more of the same sorte the next season as the Spanish contrabandys can get me any quantity I want . . .

Thus the true Spanish breed came to England. In the years that followed the flow of imported Spanish Merinos increased, until during the Peninsular Wars the numbers became embarrassingly large.

Once the royal Merino flocks were established, the King distributed breeding animals to farmers and landowners who could be trusted to breed them, and there were regular auctions at Windsor and public shearings, which became social occasions.

Despite the painstaking work carried out on the Merinos they were not a great success in Britain. Where they did thrive spectacularly was in the new Australian colony of New South Wales, a fitting place considering Banks's close interest in the country. Curiously he showed little enthusiasm for the introduction of the breed to New South Wales. When he was sent some samples of wool from the colony in 1803 he declared that it was only equal to 'the second and third piles'. He went on to comment:

I have no reason to believe from any of the facts that have come to my knowledge, either when I was in that country or since, that the climate and soil of New South Wales is at all better for the production of fine wools than that of other temperate climates and am confident that the natural growth of grass of the country is tall, coarse, reedy and very different from the short and sweet mountain grass of Europe upon which sheep thrive to the best advantage.

Of course Banks was completely wrong. Maybe his prejudice was partly that of a sick and ageing man, and partly because the most influential sheep farmer in the colony, Captain John Macarthur, was the very man who led the mutiny against Banks's friend William Bligh, when Bligh was ousted as Governor of the colony.

After examining the Australian wool, he said:

I have never heard of any luxuriant pastures of the natural growth of New South Wales at all fitted for the pasturage of sheep till I read of them in Captain Macarthur's statement, nor did I ever see such in that country. I confess therefore that I have my fears that the Captain has been too sanguine in his wishes to give a favourable representation of the country and that it will be found on enquiry that the sheep do not prosper well there unless in lands that have been cleared and prepared for their reception with some labour and expense.

Continuing to put the knife into Macarthur, in a statement to the Board of Trade, which was considering whether or not to back sheep farming in the new colony, Banks wrote:

I have been informed that the freight of wool from Spain to England costs from one penny to three halfpence a pound on account of the great bulk of the article, a ton weight or 80 tods of wool taking up much more room than 40 cubic feet or a ton of shipping. What the freight of a ton of wool from New South Wales will be I am not able to ascertain but it certainly will add very materially to the actual price when brought to market.

From what I have stated above you will easily conceive that I am not inclined to advise their Lordships to recommend any special encouragement to be given at present either by grants of land or the sending out of shepherds to a prospect which as yet is a mere theoretical speculation.

In such enterprises as the Merino sheep and Kew Gardens, George III valued Banks's expertise and loyalty. A less publicised mission which he entrusted to him was to select and send a collection of plants from Kew to the Empress Catherine II of Russia. On the face of it, it seemed to be little more than a courtesy gift from one monarch to another, but in fact it was a diplomatic exercise of the greatest importance.

For many years Britain had enjoyed a special trading relationship with Russia, and although the trade balance was weighted heavily in favour of Russia it was worth the cost in that it assured a steady supply of strategic supplies such as iron and steel, hemp, sailcloth, pitch, tar and timber, as well as keeping the Baltic seaways open to British shipping. But in the 1700s relationships with Russia became intensely strained, and the tension was increased by Russia's confrontations with Turkey and Poland.

It was not before the early 1790s that relationships were on the mend. Largely responsible for this was one man, Sir Charles Whitworth, later the first Earl Whitworth, who was Envoy-extraordinary and Minister-plenipotentiary at St Petersburg. He learned that Catherine would value a collection of plants from Kew, which had by now earned a world-wide reputation. Such a gift would set the seal on the new Anglo-Russian amity, and it was to Banks that the King turned for the selection and freighting of the collection.

Work of assembling the collection began at the end of 1793, but it was not before the early summer of 1795 that it finally sailed for Russia. As so often happened Banks received little help from official sources. The only ship available was a 100-tonner with very little space for a cargo that needed light and air.

The massive official indifference quite embittered Banks. He confided in a letter:

If I am to do all, write all, direct all and pay all and no human being feel inclined to thank me I shall I fear in due time feel as sulky as a measly sow who has lost her scrubbing post.

In fact he did foot the bill and it took him three years to recover the money from the Government, and even then he was underpaid by some £60.

Despite the difficulties, however, the plants arrived safely in Russia, in all some two hundred and twenty-six species. At the top of the list was *Strelitzia reginae* (bird of paradise flower), now a popular florists' flower, but then a greatly valued rarity. The collection contained many plants which are familiar to most keen gardeners—pelargonium, salvia, antirrhinum, alstroemeria, hydrangea, daphne, erica, begonia, mesembryanthemum and protea, among many others.

That Banks was able to conduct so much work for the King would not have been extraordinary had he confined his activities to the Court, but this was not so. Apart from running his estates in Lincoln-shire and Derbyshire, and conceiving and carrying out agricultural and horticultural experiments, he was for forty-one years President of the Royal Society, and an undisputed director of scientific advance.

CHAPTER 11

OMAI

In 1774, a year after his royal appointment as special adviser and untitled Director of Kew Gardens, Banks, who had been elected a Fellow of the Royal Society during his voyage to Newfoundland and Labrador, became a member of the Society's Council. The Councillorship set him firmly at the centre of scientific development and discovery, and his already established enthusiasm for the Society grew. He rarely missed a meeting and contributed widely and expertly to its proceedings. To those close to him it was clearly only a matter of time before he would take his place in the Presidential chair. In fact four years were to pass before that day.

The four years between his election to the Council and achieving the Presidency were not wasted. Apart from his work at Kew and putting his extensive collections into order, he familiarized himself with the workings and politics of the Royal Society.

There were also diversions, not least among them the arrival of Captain Tobias Furneaux, Commander of the *Adventure*, which had become separated from the *Resolution* during Cook's second voyage round the world. After a fruitless search for the mother ship he had decided to return to England, and with him he brought a young Tahitian, Omai, who was to take London by storm.

With his unique knowledge of Tahiti and the Tahitian language, Banks was enlisted by Lord Sandwich to help look after the young man. Solander went along to meet Omai, who knew Banks instantly, but not Solander, although he did recognize his voice.

Omai was not of the Tahitian nobility, but he did have great presence, a natural dignity, and considerable intelligence. Fanny Burney met him and wrote in her voluminous journal:

He was dressed according to the fashion of his country, and is a very good looking man—my father says he has quite an interesting countenance. He appeared to have uncommon spirits and laughed very heartily many times.

Shortly after his arrival Omai was taken by Sandwich and Banks to meet the King. There are conflicting accounts of his behaviour on this occasion. Banks's sister, Sophia, believed he made an elegant speech, which was unlikely as his English was very limited. A contemporary newspaper account has him falling to his knees, stretching out his hands, and saying 'How do ye do', while another said that he said 'How do, King Tosh', Tosh being his pronounciation of George. Whatever he did say, the King responded kindly and held him warmly by the hand.

His behaviour during his first appearance at court impressed all who saw it, and apart from being a natural curiosity, he became a much-sought-after guest at all the great houses. Men of science also studied him closely, prominent amongst them the eager anthropologist, Lord Monboddo, who rigidly held to the view that somewhere in the world there must be a nation of men with tails—the missing link, no doubt.

Omai was inoculated against smallpox by Baron Dimsdale, who introduced smallpox immunisation, and Banks stayed with him while he got over the effects of the operation. Lord Sandwich had him to stay at Hinchingbrooke, his country seat, where he delighted the assembled company by cooking a shoulder of mutton Tahitian-style in an earth oven. Wherever he was entertained he charmed his hosts with his impeccable manners, coping with gargantuan English meals which were in such sharp contrast to the far healthier diet of his native islands.

Banks took him to a dinner of the Royal Society Club, a feast that challenged the strongest heads and digestions. Barthelemy Faujas de Saint-Fond, who toured England and Scotland in the eighteenth century, described just such a Royal Society Dinner as Omai ate.

The dishes were of the solid kind, such as roast beef, boiled beef and mutton prepared in various ways, with abundance of potatoes and other vegetables, which each person seasoned as he pleased with the different sauces which were placed on the table in bottles of different shapes. The beefsteaks and the roast beef were at first drenched with copious bumpers of strong beer, called porter, drunk out of cylindrical pewter pots, which are much preferred to glasses, because one can swallow a whole pint at a draught.

This prelude being finished, the cloth was removed and a handsome and well-polished table was covered, as if it were by magic, with a number of fine crystal decanters filled with the best port, madeira and claret; this last is the wine of Bordeaux. Several glasses, as brilliant in lustre as fine in shape, were distributed to each person and the libations began on a grand scale, in the midst of different kinds of cheese, which rolling in mahogany boxes from one end of the table to the other, provoked the thirst of the drinkers.

To give more liveliness to the scene, the President proposed the health of the Prince of Wales; this was his birthday; we then drank to the Elector Palatine, who was that day to be admitted to the Royal Society. The same compliment was next paid to us foreigners of who there were five present.

The members of the Club afterwards saluted each other, one by one, with a glass of wine. According to this custom, one must drink as many times as there are guests, for it would be thought a want of politeness in England to drink to the health of more persons than one at a time.

A few bottles of Champagne completed the enlivenment of every one. Tea came next, together with bread and butter and all the usual accompaniements : coffee followed, hardly yielding preference to the tea, though it be the better of the two. In France we commonly drink only one cup of good coffee after dinner; in England they drink five or six of the most detestable kind.

Brandy, rum and some other strong liquers closed the philosophic banquet.

Wherever he appeared in public Omai was perfectly turned out and fastidious in his manners. He expected the same standards of behaviour from those around him. He was quite capable of dressing down a lady of high fashion if he believed she was not observing the correct standards of behaviour and appearance. One morning he met the beautiful Georgiana, Duchess of Devonshire, who was out walking dressed in the most slovenly manner. Her hair was in wisps and rats-tails, her shoes down-at-heel, the trimming on her dress was coming adrift; her hat was askew, and her cloak looked like an old blanket. Omai marched up to her and demanded to know why she was looking such a mess.

Despite being shocked from time to time, Omai enjoyed his stay in England enormously. He enjoyed being the centre of attention, he enjoyed having his portrait painted by such leading painters as Sir Joshua Reynolds, William Parry and Nathaniel Dance. Certainly he was an interesting subject for the artists.

A close botanist friend of Banks, the Rev Sir John Cullum of Hardwick Hall in Suffolk, left this description of the Tahitian :

He is about thirty years old, rather tall and slender, with a genteel make; his nose is somewhat flat, and his lips thick, but on the whole his face is not disagreeable. His ears are bored with a large hole at the tip; his complexion swarthy; his hair of considerable length, and perfectly black. The back of his hands are tattooed with transverse lines, and his fingers with round ones;

the lines are not continuous, but consist of distinct bluish spots; his posteriors are the only other parts tattooed. He walks erect, and has acquired a tolerably genteel bow, and other expressions of civility. He appears to have good natural parts; has learned a little English; and is in general desirous of improvement. Particularly he wishes to learn to write, which he says would on his return enable him to be of the greatest benefit to his country. But I do not find that any steps have been taken towards giving him any useful knowledge; Mr Banks seeming to keep him as an object of curiosity, to observe the workings of an untutored, unenlightened mind.

The latter comment is not entirely fair. It is true that Banks and others wanted to study Omai's response to a sophisticated society, but attempts were made to give him some kind of basic education, but these largely failed.

Continued the Rev Sir John:

When he is serious, and observing what others are saying, his look is sharp and sensible, but his laugh is rather childish. When he wants you to understand something he has seen he uses very lively and significant gestures; and is in truth a most excellent pantomime. He is pleased (as many of more improved understanding often are) with trifling amusements, and is unhappy when he has nothing to entertain him. When I dined with him, with the Royal Society, a small magnifying glass had been newly put into his hands; he was perpetually pulling it out of his pockets, and looking at the candles etc., with excessive delight and admiration. We all laughed at his simplicity, and yet probably the wisest person present would have wondered as much if that knick-knack had then for the first time been presented to him. He had seen hail before he came into England, and was therefore not much surprised at the first fall of snow; which he called, naturally enough, white rain. But he was prodigiously struck, when he first saw and handled a piece of ice; and when he was told that it was sometimes thick and strong enough to bear men, and other great weights, he could scarcely be made to believe it.

He is entirely reconciled to the European manners and customs. He conforms to our diet, which he likes very well; and denies (against self-conviction) that his countrymen eat human flesh. He drinks wine, but is not at all greedy of it; and has never been intoxicated since he was in England. He likes the English women, particularly those of a ruddy complexion, that are not fat. He submits most readily to the slightest control, and has not the least appearance of a fierce and savage temper. I observed him play with a gentleman who sat by him, and encouraged him, with all the cheerful and unsuspecting good-nature of childhood.

One of the most delightful accounts of Omai, and indeed of Banks, at play, has been left by George Colman the younger, the son of George Colman, the playwright, impresario and minor landowner.

After staying with Lord Sandwich, Banks, Constantine Phipps (Lord Mulgrave's heir), George Colman, young George (then twelve), and Augustus (Constantine's youngest brother, a boy of George's age), set off for Mulgrave Castle in Yorkshire in Banks's enormous coach.

Young George takes up the tale of the journey which was led (almost commanded) by Banks:

The coach in which we rumbled . . . was the ponderous property of Sir Joseph, and as huge and heavy as a broad-wheeled waggon; but, however ill-constructed for a quick conveyance over the rough roads and sharp acclivities which we had to encounter, its size was by no means too large for its contents. It carried six inside passengers, with much more than their average luggage;—for the packages of Captain Phipps, who intended to make some stay at Mulgrave, and who was ardent in his professional studies, were laid in like stores for a long voyage;—he had boxes crammed with nautical lore,—books, maps, charts, quadrants, telescopes etc., etc.,—Sir Joseph's stowage was still more formidable;—unwearied in botanical research, he travelled with trunks containing voluminous specimens of his hortus siccus in whitey-brown paper; and large recepticles for further vegetable materials, which he might accumulate in his locomotions. The vehicle had, also, in addition to its contingent loads, several fixed apper-tenances with which it was encumbered by its philosophical owner :—in particular there was a remarkably heavy safety-chain—a drag-chain upon a newly constructed principle, to obviate the possibility of danger in going down hill,—it snapped short, however, on our very first descent; whereby the carriage ran over the post-boy, who drove the wheelers, and the chain of safety very nearly crushed him to death. It boasted, also, an internal piece of machinery with a hard name—a hippopedometer, or some such Greek coinage,—by which a traveller might ascertain the precise rate at which he was going, in the moment of his consulting it :—this also broke, in the first ten miles of our journey : whereat the philosopher to whom it belonged was the only person who lost his philosophy.

Such mishaps were only partly responsible for the slow pace of the journey.

Our progress under all its cumbrous circumstances, was still further retarded by Sir Joseph's indefatigable botany :—we never saw a tree with an unusual branch, or a strange weed, or anything singular in the vegetable world, but a halt was immediately ordered :—out jumped Sir Joseph; out jumped the two boys (Augustus and myself) after him; and out jumped Omai after us all. Many articles 'all agrowing, and agrowing', which seemed to me no better than thistles, and which would not have sold for a farthing in Covent Garden Market, were pulled up by the roots, and stowed carefully in the coach, as rarities. Among all our jumpings, the most amusing to me was the jump of a frog down the throat of the same Sir Joseph;—he held it in the palm of his hand (having picked it up in the grass) till it performed this guttural somerset, to convince his three followers, and two boys, and the savage, that there is nothing poisonous in this animal as some very ignorant people imagine.

In fact the creature must have been a toad as it was Banks's party piece to hold a toad to his lips to prove its harmlessness.

The rumbling journey took the coast road with a stop at Scarborough, even then a popular watering place. It was young George's first sight of the sea, and early on the morning after their arrival he ran to the beach 'to take a dip, as the Cockneys call it'.

I was on the point of making my maiden plunge from a bathing-machine, into the briny flood, when Omai appeared wading before me. The coast of Scarborough having an eastern aspect, the early sun-beams shot their lustre upon the tawny Priest, and heightened the cutaneous gloss which he had already received from the water :—he looked like a specimen of pale moving mahogany, highly varnished; not only varnished, indeed, but curiously veneered;—for, from his hips, and the small of his back, downwards, he was tattooed with striped arches, broad and black, by means of a sharp shell, or a fish's tooth, imbued with an indelible die, according to the fashion of his country. He hailed me with the salutation of Tosh, which was his pronunciation of George,—and uttered certain sounds approaching to the articulation of 'back', 'swim', 'I', 'me', 'carry', 'you'. This attempt at the English language became intelligible to me from his 'suiting the action to the utterance', or rather elucidating the utterance by the action, and the proposition was, that, he should swim out to sea with me.

Delighted, the boy leapt onto Omai's back, and the Tahitian

. . . walked a considerable way before the water came up to his chin;—he then struck out; and having thus weighed anchor for this my first voyage, I found myself on board the Omai, decidedly not as Commander of the vessel, but as a passive passenger who must submit, without effort, to the very worst that could happen. My wild friend appeared as much at home upon the waves as a rope-dancer upon a cord; but, as soon as he had got out of his depth, my apprehensions were aroused, and I began to think that, if he should take a fancy to dive, or to turn round, and float, with his face towards the sky, I, who was upon his back, must be in a very awkward situation.

The further they swam from the beach, however, the happier George became, especially as Omai chatted away and nonchalantly combed his wet hair out of his eyes. When they returned to shore,

Augustus was vexed that he was not with us . . . my father looked a little grave at my having been so venturous; the noble Captain and the Philosopher laughed heartily, and called me a tough little fellow; and Omai and I were, henceforth, constant companions.

From Scarborough they made their way to Whitby where the route to Mulgrave lay down a precipitous hill called Up-Gang and then across three miles of track with quicksands on the one side and a sheer cliff face on the other.

When we got upon the sands, the wind had risen, the sea roared, and it was almost dark;—the horses took fright, dragged the carriage into the surf, and the evening marine trip threatened to be much less propitious than my morning's excursion, upon the back of Omai.

With great skill the post-boys forced the horses towards the cliffs, avoiding the quicksands, and by nightfall the party arrived at Mulgrave Castle.

Life at Mulgrave was a gentle mixture of fun and study. Although Banks and Constantine Phipps 'distained to shoot at any bird or beast more common than a Penguin or a Bear', there was plenty of grouse on the table from the neighbouring moors. Omai, on the other hand, who had been terrified by firearms on his native island, took to shooting with unfettered enthusiasm.

Omai, indeed, prowled about the precincts with a gun . . . he popped at all the feathered creation which came in his way; and which happened, for the most part, to be dunghill cocks, barn-door geese, and ducks in the pond.

His slaughter of domestic birds was by no means inconsiderable . . . and had it not been that he was naturally a tender-hearted barbarian, it is probable that, after having killed off a farmer's live stock, he might have taken a shot at the farmer himself.

He even stalked partridges and caught them by hand; was dragged round a field by a startled horse he grabbed by the tail, and had an unsuccessful encounter with a bull, which he respectfully called 'man cow'.

For George and Augustus there was a crash course in botany organised by Banks, who put them into 'active training . . . by sending us into the woods, early every morning, to gather plants'.

'We could not easily have met with an abler master,' wrote George, who regarded Banks as a latter-day Dioscorides.

Although it was somewhat early for us to turn natural philosophers, the novelty of the thing, and rambling through wild sylvan tracts of peculiarly romantic beauty, counteracted all notions of studious drudgery, and turned science into a sport.

We were prepared over-night for these morning excursions by Sir Joseph. He explained to us the rudiments of the Linnaean system, in a series of nightly lectures, which were very short, clear and familiar; the first of which he illustrated by cutting up a cauliflower, whereby he entertained the adults (Omai excepted) as much as he delighted the youngsters.

For a while young George Colman, inspired by Banks, 'got a Botany mania', but apparently it did not last. Years later he self-teasingly wrote :

I can still distinguish a moss-rose from a Jerusalem artichoke; and I never see a boiled cauliflower, without recollecting the raw specimen, and the dissecting knife in the hands of Sir Joseph; and thinking on the fructification, sexual system, pericarpium, calyx, corolla, petals etc., etc., etc.

The other consuming occupation at Mulgrave was the opening of ancient burial barrows. Each operation was conducted with the greatest care, for both Banks and Phipps were serious antiquaries, and not grave robbers. Work on a single barrow would take days, so a tent was pitched at the dig and large quantities of food were brought along.

Sir Joseph made very palatable stews in a tin machine, which he called by a hard name, and which is now very common.

One day they barbecued a hog :

. . . which I thought very nasty; for I took a prejudice against him while he was roasting :—he was put down to a blazing fire in the field, where he was burned, scorched, and blackened, till he looked like a fat Protestant at the stake, in the days of Bishop Bonner.

But at Hinchingbrooke, Omai was the one who shone at *al fresco* cookery, using a Tahitian-style earth oven.

He cooked fowls instead of dogs, which last he would have preferred in his own country, as the greater delicacy. For part of his combustibles, and the layers to cover the stones, he had other materials than the husks and leaves of the cocoa (coconut); for plantain leaves, to wrap up the animal food, he was supplied with writing paper, smeared with butter;—for yams he had potatoes;—for breadfruit, bread itself,—the best home-made in Yorkshire

. . . and as to Omai's dish, in the eating, nothing could be better dressed, or more savoury :—the smouldering pebble-stones and embers of the Otaheitan oven had given a certain flavour to the fowls, a soupçon of smokiness, which made them taste as if a ham accompanied them.

The Yorkshire holiday continued along in this gentle happy way until mid-September, when the party broke up.

Banks continued to oversee the care of Omai until the Tahitian returned home in 1776 in the hands of Cook in the *Resolution*. He was laden with gifts. Sandwich had a suit of armour made for him at the Tower of London, impressive no doubt, but uncomfortable to wear in the tropic heat of a Pacific island. Banks arranged more practical equipment—suits of light clothes, tools, kitchen equipment, furniture for a house that was to be built for him by the ship's carpenters. There was also assorted iron and beads, ready cash among the islands. Reluctantly he was given firearms, but not enough to satisfy Omai, for despite his charm and gentleness he had formed a plan to avenge himself upon the warlike Borabora clan who years before had driven him and his family from their native island of Raiatea into exile on Tahiti.

Upon his arrival home Omai did not behave particularly well. His character underwent a change for the worse. Cook saw to it that he was supplied not only with a musket, a fowling piece, and pair of pistols, cutlasses, powder and shot, but also with livestock—a small breeding herd of pigs, a pregnant goat, two horses, ducks, geese and turkeys.

Such riches, along with his newly-built house and its furnishings, set him apart from the rest of the islanders. His unique position turned his head and he began to take a high-handed attitude towards his fellow Tahitians. Cook had not set him a particularly good example. With his now almost manic intolerance of the tiresome Tahitian habit of stealing, he responded with extraordinary savagery, ordering severe floggings, ear-cropping and head-shaving,

Sadly Omai did not enjoy his wealth and position for long. He appears to have become involved in some inter-island war, lost many of his possessions, and eventually died of disease within a short time of Cook's departure.

About a year before his return home, Omai was a guest with Banks on Lord Sandwich's yacht, the *Augusta*, during a trip from Deptford to Plymouth and back, during which Sandwich inspected the naval dockyards along the way. The short cruise marked the complete rapprochement between Banks and Sandwich after the *Resolution* quarrel. Banks, as usual, kept a journal, a cheery, light-hearted account of a happy period.

The cruise started, not noticeably successfully, on 2 June 1775, with the First Lord's yacht in collision with another ship.

Arrived off Greenwich. Here our yacht fell desperately in love with a Dutch vessel and in spite of all our efforts to prevent her proceeded to such familiarities that Sir Richard (Sir Richard Rickerton, Commander) ordered her to an anchor and as a punishment for her libidinous inclination and effectively to prevent the generation of so foul a monster as would have sprung from such illicit amours, confined her during the rest of the ebb.

Martha Ray, Lord Sandwich's beautiful and talented mistress, joined the party for the first part of the journey down the Thames.

By 5 June they reached Chatham Dockyards 'neat and clean as a private house' and the following day, while Sandwich was busy with official duties, Banks and a party went on a noisy trip up the River Medway 'shooting at gulls and herns which came in our way'. At Snathling they shot lapwings on the marshes, and a turtle dove, which proved to be 'very juicy and good'.

Two days later there was further exploration of the marshes where they found crabs:

... which appeared to be amorously inclined. We were much amused by the vigorous attempts of the males and the prudery of the females, which they seemed to possess in a high degree.

At Queensborough the scene changed to a graveyard where the party examined the inscriptions on the tombs. Banks copied down one which took his fancy:

> Life is a city full of crooked streats;
> Death is the market place where all men meets,
> Was life a merchandise and men could buy
> Rich men would ever live and poor men die.

Early in the voyage the *Augusta* challenged a naval vessel to a race to Dover. She lost, and the party having paid its gambling debts renewed the challenge for the leg to Spithead. They lost that race also.

A day was spent ashore in Dover, and when they returned to the yacht in the evening the ferrymen were so drunk that one fell over the side.

LINCOLNSHIRE,} To the Constable of *Beesby-*
LINDSEY. } *in the said Parts.*

BY Virtue of an Order from the Deputy Lieutenants in
and for the said County, at their General Meeting for
that and other purposes assembled and unto me directed,
you are hereby required to make out a fair and true list in
Writing of all Men usually and at this Time dwelling within
your Parish between the Ages of Eighteen and Forty-five
Years, distinguishing therein their several Ranks and Occu-
pations, and where the true Names of such Persons are not
to be procured, the common Appellation of such Persons shall
be sufficient; and which of the said Persons labour under any
Infirmities incapacitating them from serving as Militia Men:
And also which of them (if any) is a Peer of this Realm, or
a Person who shall serve as a Commissioned Officer in any
Regiment, Troop or Company in his Majesty's other Forces,
or in any of his Majesty's Castles or Forts, or Non-Com-
missioned Officer, or private Man serving in any of his Majesty's other Forces, or a Commissioned Officer serving or who
has served Four Years in the Militia, or a Member of either
of the Universities, Clergyman, Licenced Teacher of any
seperate Congregation, Constable or other Peace Officer, Ar-
ticled Clerk, Apprentice, Seaman, or Seafaring Man, or Poor
Man who has more than one Child born in Wedlock. Which
List so fairly and truly made as aforesaid, you are hereby
required to return and verify the said Return upon Oath, to
the Deputy Lieutenants Justices of the Peace for the said
County, at their *next* Subdivision Meeting for that
purpose to be held on the *fifth* Day of *November*
next ensuing the Date hereof at the *George Inn* in
Horncastle in the said County; and you are hereby
further required to affix a true Copy of the said List so to be
made out as aforesaid, on the Door of the Church or Chapel belonging to your respective Parish, Township or Place;
and if such Place being extraparochial hath no Church or
Chapel belonging thereto, then on the Door of the Church
or Chapel of some Parish or Place thereto adjoining, on some
Sunday Morning next before the said *fifth* Day of
November which Sunday shall be three Days at least before the said *fifth* Day of *November* And also
Notice in writing at the Bottom of such List of the Day
and Place of such Meeting, that all Persons who shall think
themselves aggrieved by having their Names inserted or by
any others being omitted, may then appear and Appeal,
and that no Appeal will be afterwards received. Herein fail
not. GIVEN under my Hand and Seal the *Thirteenth*
Day of *October* in the Year of our
Lord 179*4*

Jn.º Longstaff

CHIEF CONSTABLE

One of the Militia census orders that sparked off the violent Lindsey Riots. The Lincolnshire
villagers believed they were being tricked into extra militia duties, with the threat of being
drafted overseas to fight in the Napoleonic Wars (*From the local History Collection, Lincoln
Library, by courtesy of Lincolnshire Library Service*)

The Library at No 32, Soho Square, which housed Banks's huge collection of scientific books and manuscripts, and his great Herbarium, now at the Natural History Museum in London (*British Museum, Natural History*)

In the pleasant, crowded disorder of the study at No 32, Soho Square, Sir Joseph Banks conducted his voluminous correspondence with the leading men of science of his day, and met and advised a constant stream of visitors (*British Museum, Natural History*)

On 16 June they dined with one Mr Peter Taylor at Purbrook. The food was dreadful, but the wines and spirits flowed plentifully and 'some of our party were so cheery that I know not how they found their way home'.

For the next few days they remained at Southampton, fishing, shooting and botanising. They were entertained to wild music on a Russian ship, and watched a smuggler being chased and caught in rough weather. At Omai's insistence they went to a play.

The party reached Plymouth on 27 June, visited the Eddystone Lighthouse, and took a musical trip up the River Tamar. Omai again insisted on going to the theatre.

It turned out the worst acted we had seen for some years, but as many of us were of the opinion that plays should be either very well or ill-acted, we went home not at all displeased.

By 8 July they were on the homeward journey, stopping at the Isle of Wight for sport of a different kind—a picnic with 'lively and entertaining' women. There was eating, drinking and dancing, indeed 'the most successful party of pleasure I remember to have partaken of'.

The holidaymakers arrived back, rather ingloriously, at Deptford on 12 July and ran aground on a mudbank close to where they had collided with the Dutchman. Next day Banks took his leave of 'our beloved yacht' and signed off his journal with the poignant note: 'I have been happy.'

CHAPTER 12

PRESIDENT OF THE
ROYAL SOCIETY

Shortly after the return of the jaunting party, Cook arrived back in the *Resolution*, and Banks became involved in the scientific results of the expedition, proving, despite popular gossip to the contrary, that he and Cook were on speaking terms. If anyone had cause to be incensed it was probably Cook, who had been on the receiving end of Banks's wrath. In fact he had generously written from the Cape of Good Hope in 1772 to Banks:

Some cross circumstances which happened at the latter part of the equip-ment of the *Resolution* created, I have reason to think, a coolness betwixt you and I; but I can by no means think it was sufficient for to break off all correspondence with a man I am under many obligations to.

In his turn Banks kept in the background during Cook's triumphant return, merely offering his help where it could be useful. He was also busy, because in 1776 he bought 32 Soho Square, which was to be his great London house for the remainder of his life.

32 Soho Square (sadly the house no longer exists, having been replaced by a particularly ugly office block) was a large, comfortable building of practical elegance. Its very heart was the library where Banks housed his huge scientific library, the finest of its kind at the time. Some idea of its extent can be gauged from Jonas Dryander's catalogue which filled five octavo volumes and 2,464 pages. Besides the library there was the herbarium, enormous through Banks's personal collecting, and vastly added to by the collections of others. And there was the museum, the mineral collection, the insects, fish, shells, birds and animals, the scientific instruments, and the artefacts from his extensive travels, and the folios of drawings and paintings.

Banks did not hoard this great treasure for private pleasure. The doors to his house were always open to men of science, travellers and explorers. The constant stream of visitors were free to browse among the papers and books, and study the collections, and many a happy enthusiast left with gifts for his own collections.

Every Thursday a breakfast was held at Soho Square, a formal occasion at which some subject of current scientific importance would be discussed, very often accompanied by demonstrations and lectures. A light meal of rolls, and tea or coffee would be served to the many people gathered in the library and museum, while Banks would have a more elaborate meal in a private room with a smaller, specially invited group of guests.

Sunday evenings were more relaxed affairs to which women were invited, but it is hard to believe that even at these soirées the conversation drifted far from science.

Perhaps the experiments were more entertaining. Doubtless there was music, and travellers' tales from Solander and Banks, and other adventurers.

But never a day passed in the house without visitors to the bright and pleasant rooms. The glamorous young explorer was maturing into a leading man of science. Anyone, from home or abroad, with a serious interest in the subject, was automatically drawn to Soho Square—and not only them, but sailors bearing curiosities for sale or as gifts.

Those unable to call, wrote. The correspondence that flowed in and out of the house was prodigious. Most of it was serious, but some was bizarre, even absurd.

In November 1780, for example, Banks received a statement, sworn before Samuel Brown, Mayor of King's Lynn in Norfolk, concerning an unfortunate man, Archibald Wilson Taylor, who complained of stomach pains and nausea after eating watercress twice a day for five weeks. Taylor insisted there was something living in his stomach. His doctor prescribed a strong emetic, and in due course the patient began to retch. After several strains something stuck in his throat. It was, the statement swore, a toad measuring two and a half inches by one and a half. A servant threw the evidence on the fire.

Another man wrote to say that he could provide Banks with a pair of unicorn horns.

Harry Smeathman, a botanist and aeronaut, sent the latest reports of Montgolfier's balloon displays—Banks was greatly interested in flying —and outlined an idea for a winged balloon that could be steered 'Aerostatic Vessels', he called them, and begged Banks's help in obtaining Government support for the project.

In the midst of all his activities Banks found time to become involved in a public row about plucking live geese for pen quills. Pointing out to those who complained that the practice was barbarous, that many geese who were regularly plucked lived to be twenty or more, he added that the complainants

. . . wrote this sentiment with a quill which they buy at an easy price from the Lincolnshire feather merchant, retire to rest upon a bed stuffed from the breasts of geese whom they compassionate, without once reflecting that they themselves are the real causes of the existence of the custom, for, if they did not purchase the feathers the Lincolnshire man would not torment his geese by procuring them.

No problem was too trivial or too problematical for him to deal with. He was the complete enquirer, ever receptive to new ideas and information.

With his reputation as a botanist firmly established, and now well in the mainstream of the scientific life of the country, it was no surprise, in 1778, when Sir John Pringle retired from the Presidency of the Royal Society, that Banks's name was advanced as his successor.

The Presidency of the Royal Society was, as now, a powerful and prestigious position. Apart from Banks there was only one other contender, Alexander Aubert, a wealthy London merchant and amateur astronomer, who built three observatories—at Austin Friars, Highbury and Lewisham.

Banks was only thirty-five, but he had been a Fellow of the Society since 1766, and had served on the Council in 1774 and 1775 and was serving on it at the time of the election of the new President. He was also a successful, well-known, even glamorous, public figure. There was another, important factor that acted in his favour. In 1775 the Royal Society had been asked to assist in the development of an efficient lightning conductor that could be used to protect ammunition dumps. The most effective conductor—one with a pointed tip—had been invented by Benjamin Franklin. He was opposed by a group who claimed that a conductor with a blunt end was better.

The blunt-and-pointed argument rumbled on and had not been resolved when the American colonies rebelled, and Franklin was among the rebels. That was enough for George III; blunt-ended conductors were in, and he all but ordered the Royal Society to drop its support for Franklin's design.

Sir John Pringle did not endear himself to the King when he drily remarked : 'Sire, I cannot reverse the laws and operations of nature,' a comment that in the King's eyes was tantamount to an act of treachery against state and monarch.

Despite the absurdity of the situation, there was a serious side to it. The King was Patron of the Royal Society, and his continuing patronage was essential to its successful operation. Banks was a close and trusted friend of the King, and the man most likely to cool the royal wrath.

In spite of all these advantages, the election was a heated, noisy affair. Banks was not without his enemies, but at the end of the day he was elected with 220 votes, an almost unanimous result.

Solander had been confident of Banks's victory from the start. When Sir John Pringle resigned he wrote to his friend and travelling companion :

If you cannot find out a man of high rank who will accept the Chair you must listen to the voice of the people. All talk of you.

When his election was secure, Banks was elated. He arrived breathless and late to occupy the President's chair at the Anniversary Dinner (without, some of the stuffier Fellows thought, the proper dignity fitting his new position), collapsed in his chair and announced : 'I believe never did a President of the Royal Society run so fast.'

Banks lost no time in imposing his forceful personality upon the Royal Society. Great changes were sweeping the country. Science and technology were taking giant steps forward. Industrial production was becoming increasingly mechanised, and there was growing a clamorous demand for new methods and raw materials.

He saw himself as the captain of a great enterprise; the taskmaster and bear-leader of a company of men winning advance and advantage in this great surge forward. Everything must radiate from the power-house of the Royal Society.

Curiously, since his own life and affairs were so ordered, he took little interest in the day-to-day running of the Society, which was often chaotic, but he never allowed his presence and authority to be absent. During the forty-one years of his presidency he missed only thirty-three out of 450 meetings. He was domineering and blunt, sometimes even rude, thus making enemies of the men who suffered from the rough edge of his tongue. His detractors accused him of manipulating the Society, and charged him with packing the Council with his friends, which was untrue.

One unpopular reform that he introduced governed the election of Fellows. His over-riding criterion was that any person who successfully practised science, particularly through original research, should be elected regardless of wealth or rank. Rich men of position and title who patronised science or even involved themselves in research should be only admitted after careful investigation. Despite this edict the number of purely scientific councillors remained woefully small.

For the greater part of his long term of office, Banks was able to rule with benign despotism in an atmosphere of relative peace and tranquillity, except for a period towards the end of 1783 when there was a determined effort to topple him. The incident, which developed into a major row, began when Dr Charles Hutton, the Professor of Mathematics at the Artillery College at Woolwich, who was in charge of the Royal Society's foreign correspondence, was accused of failing in his duties. Hutton lived out of London and was said to have fallen behind with his Society work, which involved translating foreign correspondence and scientific papers and documents. It was decided that in future the Foreign Correspondence Secretary must live in London, and thus Hutton resigned. His resignation produced the charge that he had been forced to quit.

In December 1783 the Council proposed a vote of thanks to Hutton for his past services. Banks, somewhat brutally, opposed the motion on the grounds that Hutton had not performed his duties efficiently.

Banks was defeated and later that month Hutton submitted a written defence of his conduct which was read and accepted by the Society. This gave one of Banks's bitterest enemies, Dr Samuel Horsley (later Bishop of St Asaph, and a mathematician), the opportunity to launch a savage attack on the President and his administration. He was supported by Dr Nevil Maskelyne, Mr P. H. Maty, Secretary of the Royal Society, and a number of others.

The position was now such that it could be resolved only by a vote of confidence in Banks. The motion was carried after an angry meeting in January 1784. The anti-Banks faction, however, still had some fight in it. An attempt was made to overturn the ruling that the Foreign Correspondence Secretary must live in London, thus opening the way for Hutton's reinstatement. This failed.

In February, Dr Horsley and his group accused Banks of interfering with the election of councillors and the selection of candidates for Fellowship. This lead to a further furious debate.

A month later Maty, who must have been an incautious gambler, offered the Society an anonymous pamphlet entitled *An Authentic Narrative of the Dissensions and debates in the Royal Society*. Banks refused to propose the customary vote of thanks for the document on the grounds that it was misleading and offensive to the Society. So Horsley proposed the vote of thanks and was only supported by Maty and Hutton.

Opposition to Banks was now crushed. Maty resigned and his place was taken by Sir Charles Blagden, an old friend and staunch supporter of the President.

The Presidency of the Royal Society was not merely a matter of sitting magisterially in court dress at the Society's meetings. It involved an almost endless round of committee work. Banks was on the Board of Visitors of the Royal Observatory at Greenwich; a trustee of the British Museum; an exceptionally active member of the Board of Longitude. When there was an explosion at a gas works in Westminster in 1801 he was called on to the committee of inquiry; and he was involved in investigating standards of length.

As well as dealing with weighty matters of importance, Banks also had to deal with the bizarre.

In 1782 a man, James Price, who was both wealthy and a clever chemist, announced to an astounded nation that he had discovered how to transform mercury into gold and silver. Such a claim might well have been laughed to scorn if Price had not had a sound reputation, and had not conducted a convincing public demonstration in his laboratory near Guildford before a distinguished audience of local dignitaries, including Lord Palmerston, Lord Onslow and Lord King. Furthermore the gold he seemed to produce by mixing a red powder with mercury—a white powder was used for silver—proved on assay to be indeed pure gold.

Everyone was taken in, even the University of Oxford, which awarded him an honorary degree, everyone, that is but a handful of Fellows of the Royal Society, including Banks. They thought that Price's claim was absurd; and the matter was made worse by the fact that Price was an FRS.

At the start it was decided to take no action in the hope that the whole charade would collapse and that Price would fade into obscurity. The opposite happened. He wrote a book about the chemical reactions that occurred during the transmutation process, but carefully avoided describing the composition of the essential powders. The book sold out and interest in Price's claims grew.

The one fact that clearly indicates that Price was a fraud comes out in a note written in Banks's hand on the back of a letter. It reads :

Dr Price's declaration about a year before his death.
    The invention of extracting gold from mercury is Dr Price's own, but that of extracting silver from it, was communicated to him by another person, who has laid him under an injunction not to publish it.
    As the former was deduced by analogy from the latter, he considers himself bound to conceal that also.
    So he said, but would allow nothing but the former words to be wrote down as his declaration.

Finally the Royal Society had to act. It told Price that he must perform his experiment before experts from the Society. Price began to wriggle. The process had been witnessed already by respectable men, he argued. Preparing the powders was a lengthy business and bad for his health. And anyway, he declared, the transmutation of mercury into gold was not a practical proposition, because it cost more to produce than it was worth.

The Royal Society was adamant, and Price was forced to agree. He went home to Guildford to make his preparations. For the next six months nothing was heard of him and it was assumed he had fled in shame. Not at all. He had been in Germany supervising the translation of his book, which again was a great success.

Shortly after his return to England he informed the Royal Society that all was ready for the demonstration. Three Fellows travelled down to Guildford, not, as it turned out, to see a remarkable piece of chemistry, but to witness a tragedy.

Price welcomed them into his laboratory, walked to his work bench, swallowed a strong dose of laurel water he had prepared beforehand and collapsed and died.

Such were the varied distractions of the President of the Royal Society.

On top of all his other activities there was not a new learned society mooted to which Banks was not asked to lend his name. He helped to found the Linnaean Society, the first specialist scientific society in Britain. When it became the leading body for botany and zoology he became alarmed that it would undermine the authority of the Royal Society. For this reason he opposed the formation of such organisations as the Royal Institution, the Astronomical Society and the Geological Society. But later, when it was agreed that the new societies would be subordinate to the Royal Society, he relented and lent them his full support.

The Horticultural Society, now the Royal Horticultural Society, famous throughout the world for its annual Chelsea Flower Show, benefited from his zeal, and from a number of learned papers by him.

Indeed the list of societies to which he gave his support seems endless—the Society of Arts, the Engineers' Society, the Dilettanti Society, the Society of Antiquaries and the Society for the Improvement of Naval Architecture, and many others.

Such tireless work brought its rewards. In 1781 Banks became a Baronet, and in 1795 he received the Red Ribbon of a Knight of the Order of the Bath. As he was given the Order by George III, the King murmured: 'I have many years wished to do this.'

The Baronetcy came as a pleasant delayed wedding present. Banks was married in the spring of 1779 to Dorothea, the eldest daughter of a wealthy Kent landowner, William Western Hugessen, who lived at Norton.

Dorothea was a considerable heiress, no great beauty, but a generally agreeable woman. She must have had a placid, accommodating nature, since she shared her home, and her husband's affections, with his sister, the formidable Sarah Sophia. One visitor described her as a 'comely and modest young lady'. Sadly the couple had no children.

High office and public respect and admiration did not protect Banks from the attacks, scorn and ridicule of the popular lampoonists of his day. Indeed, his position fuelled their pens.

When Hawkesworth's great account of the voyage of the *Endeavour* was published, Banks was singled out for special attention. Major John Scott, a prolific satirist and pamphleteer, took particular delight in Banks's relationship with Purea, then known as Oberea. He depicted the stay on Tahiti as one long orgy, and even suggested that Hawkesworth's scholarly official account was nothing less than a dirty book.

> One page of Hawkesworth, in the cool retreat,
> Fires the bright maid with more than mortal heat;
> She sinks at once into the lover's arms,
> Nor deems it vice to prostitute her charms;
> 'I'll do', cries she, 'What Queens have done before,'
> And sinks, from principle, a common whore.

But it was Banks's supposed affair with Purea that really fired Scott's imagination. He published an epic poem under the title: *An Epistle from Oberea, Queen of Otaheite to Joseph Banks Esq, Translated by T.Q.Z. Esq, Professor of the Otaheite language in Dublin, and of all the languages of the undiscovered islands of the South Sea; And enriched with Historical and Explanatory Notes.*

Throughout there are constant references to sex between Purea and Banks, who is called by his Tahitian name, Opano. A heartbroken Purea addresses him:

> With you, thrice dear Opano, oft I lay,
> Within the wigwam 'till the dawn of day.
> Perhaps Opano (be the omen vain)
> If ere thy ships shall reach these shores again;
> You'll seek the wigwam where we fondly lay,
> And in its place will find my sad Morai.
> Yet think at least my copious tears you see,
> And spare one thought from Botany for me.
> And when with curious search thine eyes explore,
> The waving forest, or marshy shore;
> When in strong gin thy skilful hands shall steep,
> Some unclass'd fowl or monster of the deep;
> Think of the raptures which we once have known,
> And wast one sigh to Otaheite's throne.

This was followed by a new lampoon—*An Epistle from Mr Banks, Voyager, Monster-Hunter and Amoroso, To Oberea, Queen of Otaheite, Transposed by A.B.C. Esq, Second Professor of Otaheite, and every other unknown Tongue. Enriched with the finest passages of the Queen's letter to Mr Banks.*

It was written in the style of a confession by Banks of his behaviour on Tahiti. He starts off by denying that he has forgotten Oberea for some European girl, because in her letter she said:

> Though now some European maid you woo,
> Of waists more taper, and of whiter hue;
> Yet oft with me you deign'd the night to pass,
> Beneath yon bread-tree on the bending grass.

Banks then says :

> I own the plants thy love has given to me—
> But what a plant did I produce in thee !
>
> And, well I ween, blest produce of thy charm,
> My image lives and prattles in thy arms.
> Oh, plunge the infant in the briny lake,
> And give him vigour for his father's sake;
> So shall, when years have well matur'd his size,
> Numerous Opano's in thy country rise;

Again and again Scott has Banks recalling nights of love and lust.

> All hail ! Sweet Oberea, queen of charms,
> Whom oft I've clasp'd within my wanton arms !

Much was made in the poem of the description in Hawkesworth of an erotic dance performed before Banks and others, and here he has Banks in an agony of self-reproach, accusing himself of abandoning the King's orders in the pursuit of dubious pleasures.

> Oh ! how the mem'ry pains my aching thought !
> The gallant sons of Britain's warlike land,
> In curious crouds around the beauty stand,
> While as she turns her painted bum to view,
> With fronts unblushing, in the public stew*,
> They searched each crevice with a curious eye,
> To find exotics—where they never lie.
> Oh shame ! were we, great George, thy gallant crew,
> And had we—damn it—nothing else to do,
> But turn thy great design to filthy farce,
> And search for wonders on an Indian's a - - -?

Another popular lampoonist, John Wolcot, who wrote under the name of Peter Pindar, took particular delight in poking fun at Banks after he became President of the Royal Society.

---

*Meaning, 'being in a sweat and state of excitement'.

In 1796 he took a swipe at Banks in *A Satire: In Four Dialogues.*
In a footnote he claims that

... it is an incontravertible fact that Sir J. Banks proposed the plan of a throne
for himself, and benches for the foreign Princes and Ambassadors beneath
him, whose heads might be on the same plane with the most noble
President's ten toes. Dr Horsley, the present Bishop of Rochester, by a well-
timed ridicule, put an end to the vision of Vanity.

He wrote :

> Thus, when the President of frogs and flies,
> And weeds and birds-nests, wish'd in pomp to rise,
> And fill (himself) a throne sublime and fair,
> And give his hammer's arm a Jove-like air;
> Th' uncourtly Doctor, hostile to the scheme,
> Gave a loud horse-laugh, and dissolv'd the dream !

Wolcot gathers strength in *Sir Joseph Banks and the Emperor of
Morocco: A Tale by Peter Pindar Esq.*

> A nutshell might with perfect ease enclose
> Three-quarters of his sense, and all his learning.

Referring to Banks's firm, sometimes dictatorial handling of meetings
of the Royal Society, Pindar paints a picture of the Fellows falling
asleep during the reading of a learned paper :

> Down goes the hammer, cloath'd with thunder !
> Up spring the snorers, half without their wigs;
> Old greybeards grave, and smerk-fac'd Prigs,
> With ell-wide jaws displaying signs of wonder.

In another place he has Banks praying to God for more insects and
creatures.

> Since monsters are my great delight,
> With monsters charm thy Servant's sight,
> Turn feathers into hair :
> Make legs where legs were never seen,
> And eyes, no bigger than a pin,
> As broad as saucers stare.

He asks God for headless flies which he would discover and become famous.

> These headless flies should have a name—
> My name—Sir Joseph Banks!

But Wolcot was at his most vicious when Banks was made a Privy Councillor. He exclaimed:

> Ye Gods! Sir Joseph on the Council Privy?
> Inventive Newspapers, I can't believe ye!

And the verses continue:
> His Majesty is surely wise;
> And wants no talk on butterflies,
> On eggs and bird-nests, newts and weeds:
> He wants a man to talk on wars,
> On dread invasions, wounds and scars,
> On stumps, and carcases, and heads.
>
> After a butterfly to scamper,
> And with a net his captive hamper,
> Sir Joseph is expert, and must delight;
> But, as for politics!—O Heav'n!
> The Board must very hard be driv'n,
> To choose a swearing Tadpole Knight!
>
> To give a breakfast in Soho,
> Sir Joseph's very bitterest foe
> Must certainly allow him peerless merit;
> Where, on a wag-tail, and tom-tit,
> He shines, and sometimes on a nit,
> Displaying pow'rs few Gentlemen inherit.
>
> I grant he is no intellectual lion,
> Subduing ev'ry thing he darts his eye on;
> Rather, I ween, an intellectual flea,
> Hopping on Science's broad bony back,
> Poking his pert proboscis of attack,
> Drawing a drop of blood and fancying it a sea.

The lengthy poem continues in the same vein :

> From Joseph Banks unto Sir Knight,
> Then Privy Counsellor in spite
> Of nature, brain and education !
> If, for the last, he hands has kiss'd;
> There's not a reptile on his list
> E'er knew a stranger transmutation.

Wolcot imagines the scene during a debate of the Privy Council :

> Gods ! if amidst some grand debate,
> All for the good of our great state
> A moth should flutter, would the man sit quiet ?
> Forgetting state affairs, the knight
> Would seize his hat with wild delight,
> And, chasing, make the most infernal riot :
> O'erturning benches, statesmen, ev'ry thing,
> To make a pris'ner of the mealy wing.

There is a parting dig in a footnote :

Ridicule enjoys a second feast on the occasion. Her first treat was his elevation to the chair of the immortal Newton.

It is not possible to tell whether Banks was hurt or angered by these lampoons. He never appears to refer to them, and probably regarded them as an occupational hazard.

But one furious attack he had to take seriously. It appeared in the influential *Annual Register*, edited by William Cobbett, in April 1802.

At the end of 1801 Banks was elected a foreign member of the French Institut National. The French were still intensely unpopular in Britain, and Banks, in accepting the honour, wrote a letter to the Institut which was not only tactless for British consumption, but almost fawning in its wording.

Citizens,—Be pleased to offer to the National Institute my warmest thanks for the honour they have done me in conferring upon me the title of Associate of this learned and distinguished Body.

Assure at the same time my respectable brothers that I consider this mark of their esteem as the highest and most enviable literary distinction which

I could possibly attain. To be the first elected to be an Associate of the first Literary Society in the world surpassed my most ambitious hope, and I cannot be too grateful toward a Society which has conferred upon me this honour, and toward a nation of which it is the literary representative. A nation which during the most frightful convulsions of the late most terrible revolution never ceased to possess my esteem; being always persuaded, even during the most disastrous periods, that it contained many good citizens who would infallibly get the upper hand, and who would re-establish in the heart of their countrymen the empire of virtue, of justice, and of honour.

Receive more especially, citizens, my warmest acknowledgements for the truly polite manner in which you communicated this agreeable intelligence.

When the letter was published, an article in the *Annual Register*, signed by Misogallus (who, it is suggested, was none other than Dr Horsley), pulled no punches.

Now, Sir, notwithstanding my disgust at this load of filthy adulation, I shall trouble you with some remarks upon it. Supposing your acceptance of the nomination to be perfectly consistent with your dignity (which, however, I deny) there would be no material objection to the first and concluding paragraphs of your letter, which would have been amply sufficient for the purpose of acknowledgement : but the intermediate part is highly reprehensible; it is replete with sentiments which are a compound of servility, disloyalty and falsehood; sentiments which never ought to be conceived by an English heart, never written by an English hand, and least of all by yours, distinguished as you are by repeated (out of respect to his Majesty I will not say unmerited) marks of royal favour, and elevated to a station in which the country might be excused for looking up to you as the jealous guardian, not the betrayer, of its literary credit. Your 'respectable brothers' of the French Institute may perhaps be intoxicated by the incense which you have lavished before their Altar of Atheism and Democracy, for, although they were companions of the respectable Bonaparte in his expeditions, and plundered libraries and cabinets with as much alacrity, and as little scruple, as he displayed in treasuries and in churches, I do not believe that the ungrateful nations whom they robbed ever composed such a brilliant eulogium on their talents and their virtues. No, Sir, it was reserved for the head of the Royal Society of London, to assure an exotic embryo academy that he is more proud of being a mere associate of the latter than president of the former; that he considers their election of him as 'the highest and most enviable literary distinction which he could possibly attain'; and that he deems them the first literary society in the world.

Misogallus goes on to suggest that the Institut National were merely repaying Banks for organising the return of Labillardière's seized collections.

Thus, Sir, you imposed an obligation on the French, which they have repaid, it seems, to your equisite gratification. By the sacrifice of what duties and what principles that obligation was imposed, it is not for me to say; but I will, without hesitation, assert, that your acknowledgement of its discharge has brought disgrace upon your country, and discredit upon the Royal Society, the guardianship of whose honour was confided to you by your sovereign.

The writer also points out that the date on Banks's letter of acceptance, 21 January, was the anniversary of the execution of Louis XVI.

Banks weathered the storm with little harm to his reputation, although the piece in the *Annual Register* was used in an abortive attempt to oust him from the Presidency.

Engraved by Ridley

Rt HONble Sr JOSEPH BANKS K.B.

Pub by J Sewell Cornhill Oct 1 1802

Despite the many clashes between Britain and Europe during his lifetime, Sir Joseph Banks managed to maintain close contacts between himself and Continental scientific colleagues. He was one of the few Englishmen able to negotiate with the French during times of war

This portrait of Sir Joseph Banks, drawn by T. Phillips RA in 1816, is the frontispiece to the bound volumes of Banks's letters, which bear the legend:

  'He was a man, take him for all in all
  We shall not look upon his like again'
  (*Natural History Museum*)

CHAPTER 13

TROUBLES IN LINCOLNSHIRE

Despite the fact that his public business occupied so much of his time, Banks was always ready to play a leading part in his home county.

In October 1796 he was in Lincolnshire attending to the business of his estates when violent rioting broke out in the county. The establishment had been shaken rigid by the French Revolution, and was in a state of war with France, who had made peace with all her enemies except Britain and Austria. Britain was jumpy. Her professional army and navy were fully occupied, and it fell to the counties and parishes to provide, under statute, a 'voluntary' backstop to fend off an invasion. According to the Militia Notice published at the time,

60,000 men will be ready in case of necessity on the shortest notice, properly armed and cloathed and in readiness to join the Militia of their own counties.

It ended with the stirring call, 'God save the King, and protect Old England.'

The normal system of recruiting for the militia was to make each parish responsible for raising a certain number of men. This was usually done by means of a draw, which at least gave everyone a fair chance of getting out of service. It was possible to pay someone to take your place, or to buy your way out. But, since most of the men involved, particularly in the country, were ill-paid labourers, there was little chance of escape. It was true that the men were provided with a uniform and arms, and paid a shilling a day for exercises; but service was unpopular, because it meant giving up what little free time they had to training, and there was always the danger of being drafted into active fighting.

There had been trouble in several parts of the country when people agitated against militia service, and the landed gentry, ever fearful, suspected that the unrest was being whipped up by British republicans. In fact there was probably some basis for this fear.

In the autumn of 1795 precepts were issued by the deputy lieutenants in Lincolnshire for the purpose of replacing men of the Northern Battalion of the Royal Lincolnshire Militia who had died. But instead of the summonses being sent to those parishes where men had died, they were sent out to all the parishes. This was a complete departure from the normal practice, and was almost certainly due to a bureaucratic error. Even when the summonses were issued there was doubt in the minds of the acting magistrates and deputy lieutenants, but not one of them took the trouble to find out if a mistake had been made.

Needless to say the people from the parishes were thoroughly alarmed by what was happening. To them it looked as though the Government had decided to increase the militia force, and that even more men than usual would be caught in the net. On the day the returns of men were to be made at Spilsby, a huge crowd gathered in the town and staged a protest march, which so unnerved the magistrates that they postponed the meeting until there were troops in the area.

Banks was asked to help with what was developing into a dangerous situation. With his obsession for recording everything that came his way, he kept a unique diary of the events which followed.

Along with a local magistrate and deputy lieutenant, Thomas Coltman, he was largely responsible for putting down the rioting that took place. Indeed, but for the two men the situation could well have got seriously out of hand, because the other magistrates and deputy lieutenants appear to have been a particularly feeble bunch of men. In May 1796, when the precepts were again issued, the magistrates cancelled the meetings for the returns 'as Mr Coltman was at that time at Bath in an ill-state of health' and the magistrates 'were deprived of that assistance they had so long been used to look up to'.

It was a bad move. The second cancellation was seen by the country people as a victory, and they were convinced that if they put up enough opposition the meetings would never be held and they would be free from service in the militia.

Another reason for the unrest probably came from the fact that discipline in the militia service had been very slack. The (by then late) Colonel of the Northern Battalion, had discharged the men before their period of service had expired as well as given them their uniforms.

Banks writes:

Infinite confusion arose from this circumstance when the men were summoned to resume their arms and told that they were to serve during the continuance of a war which had just commenced. They pleaded the discharge given them by their Colonel and when as many of them as could be found were mustered they made a most motley appearance. Very few had retained their uniform so that most of the North Lincolnshire Battalion met their Colonel in smock frocks.

To make matters worse, a very junior clerk in the Militia turned up at the Louth Quarter Sessions to get the magistrates to sign the orders for the recruiting meetings.

He told them that the hurry of holding these meetings was so great that it was necessary one only should be held for each town and that to effect this it was ordered that the appeal should be held on the same day as the ballot.

This the magistrates remonstrated against, but he assured them it was necessary, and at last prevailed upon them to sign these unusual orders. He was asked why the summonses were to be general when so few men were wanted, but he could give no explanation of the conduct of the deputy lieutenants who had ordered this mode of precepting.

Clearly someone had made an error, but the magistrates were unwilling or afraid to institute an inquiry before signing the orders. Only Mr Coltman, who was chairman of the Quarter Sessions, made any real effort to sort out the blunder.

He talked over the situation several times with Banks, and expressed the fear that there would be riots at the meetings. If, he said, he could discover exactly how many men were required, he was sure he could defuse the situation. As it was, the local people were more and more convinced that they faced a general call to arms. But nobody could tell Coltman what was required for the area.

Coltman was a very well-respected man, and what he said was believed.

The first sign of real trouble was at a meeting held at Caister in Norfolk on 29 October when a huge mob, armed with staves, gathered in the town. The deputy lieutenants who were to have conducted the meeting did not dare to face them. Banks records:

The mob therefore, quite unrestrained, seized the constables and took from them their lists and destroyed them in their presence, says the latter that they had rather lose their lives than enter into the new militia, but that if the gentlemen would stand forward they would stand true to their King and their country.

Five days later on 3 November a town crier appeared in Spilsby, and bellowed to the crowds that 'the lads will meet at Horncastle on Saturday and show them they won't pay fines nor go into the militia'.

A large crowd gathered round the bellman, and it was reported that many of the men said they had got scythes and clubs, and swore they would die on the streets rather than join the Militia.

On the Saturday Coltman, some of the deputy lieutenants, and Weller, a magistrate, rode to Horncastle early in the morning hoping to get there ahead of the mob. Weller was stopped by a crowd, but he was allowed to explain the situation as best he could, and he was asked to join in shouting 'God save the King', which he did, before being set free.

Banks did not attend, because he was still suffering from a severe attack of gout, but he was kept well informed of what happened.

By midday the streets of Horncastle were seething with men, most of them carrying heavy sticks. They kept up a constant chant of : 'God bless the King; No Pitt; No militia; Oh, the justices.'

It was quite impossible to go ahead with the meeting, and anyway the vital figures that Coltman wanted had not arrived. When the clerk to the militia did finally turn up on the edge of the town the riot was at its height, and he was ordered to leave.

Some of the mob were contacted by the deputy lieutenants and the magistrates, and they set out their terms for joining what they were now calling the 'new Militia'. The terms were that the gentry should join up with them, and that they should be paid for the time spent training. If these terms were met, they said,

... we will spill the last drop of our blood fighting the French, but we will not be compelled against our will to fight for the rich. We would sooner die in the streets.

The mob said that they had been told that it would cost them from three to five guineas to buy their way out of service, and they could not afford this kind of money. They said they were willing to pay a guinea. This, in fact, was false information which had been put around by agitators.

By the afternoon the magistrates decided they could not go on with the ballot, and left the town. Once they had gone most of the mob broke up quietly and went home, but a hard core stayed behind and went from house to house demanding money which they spent in the pubs.

Two days later another meeting was scheduled to be held in Alford, but at the last minute the constables were told not to go near the town, and the meeting was scrapped. This was the news the rioters had been waiting for, and they arrived in force. Because it was market day some constables were in town, and they were caught by the mob and beaten up. One man, who was hit by a thrown cudgel, escaped on a horse, but was chased back to his house and forced to give the rioters ten pounds. They also broke into his home and stole food and drink. A magistrate in town was beaten and made to hand over five pounds.

At nightfall the mob began systematically terrorising people living on the edge of Alford.

On 9 November, a widow, Mrs Dashwood, was beseiged by a mob. She wrote a letter to Coltman:

I have this morn had a visit from above two hundred who came up in front of the house. I threw up the window and as well as I could harrangued them for about half an hour or hour.

She said that the rioters thought they were to be drafted into the regular army and sent to fight abroad,

... misunderstanding instilled into them by the agents of old Nick which are spread all over the county in order to excite disturbance and confusion.

The rioters were now sure that they had the upper hand, and reports were pouring in of major disturbances being planned, of the fensmen armed with their great fowling guns being mobilised, and of blacksmiths being asked to make pike heads that could easily be fitted on to pitchfork handles.

The magistrates and deputy lieutenants appealed for support from the army, and a cavalry regiment, the Somersetshire Fencibles, was despatched to Lincolnshire. After a forced march they arrived on 11 November and were quartered at Spilsby and Horncastle.

Banks and Coltman went to the town for a council of war, only to find that the commanding officer had gone to Alford.

We therefore spent our time till night in getting information against ringleaders, and Mr Coltman determined himself to attend after dark and with the soldiers to take some prisoners. We conceived that doing so we should strike a terror into the mob that they would have all Sunday to consider, and we thought it most likely that they would, on consultation, drop all thoughts of meeting us at Spilsby on Monday, the market day. But if we took our prisoners on Sunday night we thought they might inconsiderately attempt a rescue and bring on mischief.

With the Fencibles' Quarter-Master and twenty men, Mr Coltman rode to Bolingbrook, where they seized two men who had been named as leaders of the rioters. By this time the commanding officer caught up with the search party. He must have been an emotional man, because it was said that when he arrived at Spilsby to find the party had left 'he shed tears', and leaping on his best horse set off in pursuit.

The party now galloped on to a named house in a neighbouring town, surrounded it and took a prisoner. Another house was surrounded, and the terrified women in it said that the wanted man was six miles away courting. He was found and dragged away from his girlfriend.

Put up on horses, the prisoners were taken to Spilsby and lodged in the town cage.

Although it was late at night new information came in about the servant of a constable who had stolen the list of men needed for the Militia. The house was seven miles from Spilsby, so once again Mr Coltman and his troops mounted up. But this time the information was incorrect and the man was not arrested.

Thus ended the night in which Mr Coltman had rode nearly fifty miles. Deep roads fatigued his best horse who fell with him, and sprained his shoulder, though not violently.

The lightning raids had a sobering effect on the rioters, but Banks was determined to make a public spectacle of the prisoners. The following morning he and Mr Coltman went to Horncastle to arrange with the commanding officer for a troop of cavalry to be standing by to escort the men.

We determined to come to Spilsby as usual, to take no military escort and to carry on the business exactly as the customary justice meeting held in Spilsby on a Monday is conducted and unless disturbed by a mob, to show no particular anxiety on the occasion.

It was a courageous plan. Banks wanted a psychological victory in which he would treat the rioters with contempt, and exhibit the prisoners as ordinary criminals. The show of force was reserved as a final intimidating blow to morale.

The reports of this day were that the mob were resolved to rescue the prisoners and were arming themselves with the long guns which our fenmen use to shoot wild duck. The military at Spilsby kept strict watch all night, the men in their clothes and the horses saddled.

In the early pre-dawn hours of the fourteenth the fensmen were heard firing their guns.

Mr Coltman and myself, however, determined on our own opinions that the country would not meet us, and to go unarmed and unattended more than usual.

At half-past eight they set out in Banks's great lumbering coach, stopping for breakfast with the Rev Edward Walls, a Lincolnshire landowner. At 11 a.m. they were in Spilsby and taking their places on the bench.

Our examinations were long and we did not wish to shorten them or show any signs of haste so that it was near dark before we had signed the commitment of three of our prisoners. One whose crime seemed to us to have originated more in ignorance than ill-intention, and who had an excellent character from his master, we discharged with much good advice which brought showers of tears from him.

We had previously settled the mode of sending these culprits to Lincoln in order to preclude all hopes of rescue and to diffuse a terror of our proceeding over the county. Relays of cavalry were ready at Horncastle and Spilsby. They (the prisoners) were placed upon troopers horses, with the constable and his warrants upon a fourth, and set out, with swords drawn, at a quick pace from the midst of a crowd who did not express a single murmur, or indeed anything but a quiet and astonished anxiety. They arrived at Horncastle in 50 minutes and were, as I have been informed, at Lincoln in three hours, without the swords ever being sheathed.

The following day another ringleader, who had been hiding in the loft of a tenament block in Alford, was captured after a struggle, during which a sick woman in the house had a violent fit.

The prisoner was charged with extorting money in a riotous manner, a capital offence, and committed. Mr Walls appears to have given him a prayer book or a Bible 'to prepare himself for his fate', a kind but comfortless gesture.

Surrounded by troopers, their drawn swords glinting dully in the thin November sunlight, the man was carried off to Lincoln.

The war of nerves was beginning to have some effect, but the hard-core of the rioters had also spread a fear of their own. The people of Alford were so intimidated that it was impossible to get information about ringleaders. Even a constable of the court, Basset, who had been badly beaten up and robbed, refused to name his attackers. Meanwhile more rumours of planned uprisings in the county were coming in, which Banks tended to discount.

They did get information on another leader in Alford, but when they got to his house he had fled, although he could only just have been ahead of the troops, because one shoe and a pair of breeches were found abandoned in the house.

The arrests and the presence of the troops had the effect of steadying the nerves of the local gentry. At Horncastle forty-six men, 'all the persons of property', offered themselves as special constables, and acted as the magistrate's body guard. They also volunteered to form a yeomanry cavalry.

During the following days, the sixteenth, seventeenth and eighteenth, there was no further rioting, and Coltman grasped the opportunity to complain publicly about the lack of communication between the officers of the Militia, and the civilians who had to carry out recruitment. These were genuine grievances, and by being voiced by a leading county personality it was hoped that the mob would see that in reality the gentry were, at least to some extent, on their side.

On the nineteenth fresh information was brought to Banks about a planned uprising at Lincoln. Three ringleaders, Catliff, Walker and Taylor, were still at large, and they had put it around that the mob was too strong to be put down by the military. At the same time a newly made pike-head had been found on the turnpike road between Spilsby and Louth.

Banks set out for Lincoln in a bid to put down the expected riots, which in fact never took place.

Within a few days Catliff was under arrest, and was turned into a local hero through the pig-headedness of a Fencibles officer, Captain Wade, who conveyed him to Lincoln in a chaise, rather than on horseback under a guard of troopers with drawn swords. The rioters spread the word that Catliff 'had gone to gaol like a gentleman in a post-chaise'.

Wade had refused to lend horses because he said that one of his had been lamed while carrying the first batch of prisoners to Lincoln.

'I am sorry for his ill-judged obstinancy,' Banks wrote. 'It had done us harm.'

Taylor was arrested a few days later, but Walker appears to have escaped altogether.

These two arrests brought about the complete collapse of the troubles, and by early in December recruitment for the Militia was going ahead peacefully.

There is a postscript to this episode which shows Banks as a basically humanitarian man.

Catliff was not only one of the ringleaders in the riots, but probably the major one. He also had a long record for theft. Under the circumstances it seemed inevitable that he would be condemned to be hanged, but Banks intervened, and the judge was persuaded to deport him.

The Rev Walls seems to have put the idea of clemency into Banks's mind. In a letter giving an account of the trial of the ringleaders he wrote : 'All were found guilty—Catliff was sentenced to death, but I hope he will be reprieved and only for transportation.'

Today this would not seem a particularly attractive alternative to hanging, but Banks, who was principally responsible for the establishment of the penal settlement at Botany Bay, believed that deportation and the chance of a new life in a new country were better, not only than hanging, but also than rotting in an over-crowded gaol in Britain.

The remaining prisoners, described by Coltman as 'inexperienced lads' who 'had no felonious designs' were given short prison sentences.

CHAPTER 14

PLANS FOR BOTANY BAY

Banks's interest in penal colonies seems on the surface to be somewhat macabre, particularly in the light of history in which they emerge as grim and cruel places. But his motive was largely humanitarian, and closely linked to his enduring interest in the future of Australia.

The disaster and humiliation of the American revolution, which brought an end to the British penal settlements in that country, and the complete failure of a prison settlement in West Africa, where both convicts and administrators died like flies from disease, left Britain's gaols and hulks dangerously overcrowded.

Faced with this crisis the Government set up a special Committee of the House of Commons to attempt to find a solution. Banks was called to give evidence. He had no doubts at all that Australia was the ideal country, and that Botany Bay was tailor-made for a penal colony.

When he appeared before the Committee he spoke long and eloquently of the land he had helped to discover. His enthusiasm for Botany Bay was infectious, for it was there he had put together one of the richest collections of plants made during the *Endeavour* voyage.

He was able to back his arguments with the most meticulous detail. Certainly his performance was impressive, so much so that he was offered a seat in the Commons, which he refused.

But the interest aroused by the Committee was short-lived, and it was eight years before the first convict convoy sailed for Australia.

Meanwhile a new scheme was advanced for the colonisation of Australia. It came from James Mario Matra, who as a midshipman on the *Endeavour* had become a close friend of Banks, despite being accused of being responsible for the brutal ragging of Orton, the ship's clerk.

On his own evidence he appears to have been responsible for preventing a mutiny on the *Endeavour*. After Bligh's remarkable survival from the *Bounty* mutiny, he wrote:

Something like what Bligh's people did was designed by most of the people in the *Endeavour* . . . When the scheme was discovered, the only successful argument against it was the Pox, the disease being there, their getting it being certain of dying rather most probably, was what I insisted on, and it turned the Scale . . .

Curiously neither Banks or Cook mention anything of mutinous plans in their journals covering the period at Tahiti, where the scheme must have been laid.

Matra's background seems a little vague. He is generally thought to have been an Irishman who had for a time lived in America, but had lost everything there during the revolution. There is also some evidence to suggest that he was of Corsican origin.

He was bright and energetic, and in 1783, a year after the final separation of America from Britain, he wrote an impassioned plea to the Government appealing for the foundation of a new colony in Australia for the Loyalist Americans who had fled to England following the surrender of Cornwallis' 7,000-strong army at Yorktown.

The majority of the American colonists who had remained loyal to the Crown arrived in Britain with little more than the clothes they stood up in. They had lost their homes, farms, businesses, possessions and fortunes. They were impoverished and disgruntled, and since the country was in the midst of political and constitutional upheaval, their future looked bleak and hopeless. They did get some support out of public funds, but the most pressing question was that of their ultimate settlement.

Matra conceived the idea of resettling them in Australia, which would become

. . . an asylum to those unfortunate American Loyalists, whom Great Britain is bound by every tie of honour and gratitude to protect and support, where they may repair their broken fortunes and again enjoy their domestic felicity.

In his address to the Government he claimed that his plan had met with the approval of Banks. Doubtless this was true. He had heard of Banks's continuing efforts to develop Australia, and wrote to him saying:

I have heard a rumour of two plans for a settlement in the South Seas; one of them for New South Wales to be immediately under your direction, and in which Sir George Young, Lord Sandwich, Lord Mulgrave, and Mr (George) Colman, and several others are concerned . . . I have frequently revolved such plans in my mind, and would prefer embarking in such to anything that I am likely to get in this Hemisphere.

In fact he never got to Australia again, but did well for himself in later years as Secretary to the British Embassy in Constantinople, and afterwards as British Consul in Tangier.

All those he mentioned in the pressure group were men of influence who were trying to keep alive an idea which had apparently been shelved by the Government.

Despite invoking the name of Sir Joseph Banks in his appeal to the Government, Matra did not get very far. He was virtually unknown, and had no influence. But the scheme was not totally dismissed. It aroused great interest in many circles, and Matra was swamped with inquiries from would-be settlers.

His lack of success was due as much as anything to timing. Great Britain was in a terrible state. She had lost her most important overseas territory, the Fox–North coalition government was in a shambles, and the King, still smarting from the drubbing at the hands of the American rebels, was threatening to abdicate and retire to Hanover. He was prevented from taking this catastrophic step—it would probably have led to internal revolution—only by the intervention of his closest and most trusted friends, amongst them, Banks.

In 1784, after the collapse of the Fox–North coalition, the new administration began to show a keener interest in the settlement of Australia. Lord Sydney raised again the possibility of a penal settlement.

But another two years were to drag by before a firm decision was taken. The catalyst for that decision was a short, clear, undated and unsigned document entitled *Heads of the Plan for Botany Bay*. There can be very little doubt that it was written by Banks. It bears the hallmark of his direct, uncluttered approach to problems. Even the style of writing is markedly similar to that of his journals and letters. Knowledge of the Pacific area, of the climate, conditions, flora and soil of Botany Bay; the enthusiastic recommendation of New Zealand flax (Banks brought the plant back to Britain) could only have come from someone familiar with that part of the world. In the final paragraph there is a hint of Banks's broad concept of the colonisation of both Australia and New Zealand and of linking them with India and the Far East.

It may also be proper to attend to the possibility of procuring from New Zealand any quantity of masts and ship timber for the use of our fleets in India, as the distance between the two countries is not greater than between

Great Britain and America. It grows close to the water's edge, is of a size and quality superior to any hitherto known and may be obtained without difficulty.

This observation is typical of an economic botanist, and Banks was among the first of that breed.

The opening paragraph of the *Heads of the Plan* is characteristic of Banks's habit of coming bluntly to the point.

Heads of a plan for effectually disposing of convicts and rendering their transportation reciprocally beneficial, both to themselves and to the state, by the establishment of a colony in New South Wales, a country which by the fertility and salubrity of the climate, connected with the remoteness of its situation (from whence it is hardly possible for persons to return without permission) seems peculiarly adapted to answer the views of the Government with respect to the providing the remedy for the evils likely to result from the late alarming and numerous increase in felons in this country, and more particularly the Metropolis.

The document continues with a kind of shopping list of requirements for settling a new colony. Two companies of marines to guard the convicts, made up of men chosen for their artisan skills as much as for their military ability; tools to build shelters, and to break the virgin soil; medicines and medical instruments.

It included instructions for taking on livestock and seeds at the Cape of Good Hope or any other suitable port of call, and there were to be sufficient stores to last the colony for at least two years. Banks also explained how, when the troops, convicts and civilian settlers had been landed, the ships could commute to the Cape or the Molucca Islands for fresh supplies and livestock. There is one odd and almost sinister note :

. . . or the tender, if it should be thought advisable, may be employed in conveying to the new settlement a further number of women from the Friendly Islands, New Caledonia etc., which are contiguous thereto and from whence any number may be procured without difficulty.

Whether they were to be slaves, free-women for labour or troop's comforts, is not made clear.

Pitt, the Prime Minister, showed immediate interest in the plan, but his interest was solely with the cost of the undertaking. He asked for a detailed account, and he wanted it in a hurry. After years of delay and prevarication the whole enterprise took on an extraordinary urgency and the arrangements were put in the hands of junior officials of the Admiralty who had no great experience in equipping a major expedition to the other side of the world.

Banks was not asked to help with the arrangements. Despite the many years that had passed since the *Resolution* row, the Admiralty had not yet forgiven him. It was a mistake that he was not involved, for his knowledge of the area and his great powers of organisation might well have prevented what turned out to be a near disaster.

The haste with which the convoy was put together was due to the Government, doubtless influenced by Pitt, trying to underwrite the cost of the adventure by timing it so that the ships could drop the convicts, soldiers and settlers at Botany Bay, and then sail on to China in time to pick up a cargo of tea. It was a decision that was to create terrible problems for the embryo colony.

So appalling were the arrangements that when the ships put to sea it was discovered that no clothing had been taken aboard for the 150 women convicts. They had to travel in the rags they were wearing when they were brought from prison to the docks.

But far more dangerous was the discovery, once under way, that there was no small-arms ammunition of any kind for the 178 marines and their 16 officers who had the job of guarding and controlling 500 rebellious and resentful convicts. The marines had to bluff their prisoners until the convoy reached Rio de Janeiro, where the first Governor of the new colony, Captain Arthur Phillip of the Royal Navy, was able to persuade the Portuguese Viceroy to sell him 10,000 musket balls.

Captain Phillip had had endless trouble with the Admiralty while the convoy was fitting out. He wrote a stream of letters to the First Lord, Lord Sydney, pointing out that there were no tools for the repair and maintenance of small arms, no surgeon's instruments, no anti-scorbutics. He even had to point out the quite obvious fact that five dozen razors and six scythes were hardly sufficient for such a large expedition.

Vainly he argued that it would be suicidal folly simply to dump a large group of convicts and their guards on an alien and largely unknown shore. He wanted time to build huts, plant vegetables and set up at least the makings of a workable colony before landing the convicts. No, said the Admiralty, the ships must leave with all speed for China after the landing. On top of all these difficulties there was a powerful lobby in Britain trying to scuttle the idea of a penal settlement. They conjured up visions of a new Alsatia—a nest of pirates preying on shipping in the South Seas and the Far East.

Despite all, Phillip finally set sail with his convoy of six transports, three store ships, HMS *Sirius*, the *Tender* and the *Supply*, in May 1787.

The first Governor was a remarkable man, and his ability is best illustrated by the fact that when the convicts arrived at Botany Bay in January 1788, only 36 male convicts had died. By comparison, two years later when the second consignment of convicts was sent out, 263 out of 983 men died on board, and 82 died within six weeks of going ashore.

With such inadequate planning in the first place it was hardly surprising that the colony suffered terribly from the start. The convicts were so rebellious that they preferred punishment to work. Either through incompetence or sabotage, the first seeds planted failed. Of the entire colony, convict and free-man alike, only Phillip's servant knew anything about growing crops and vegetables.

Inevitably illness broke out—scurvy and dysentery—and this was coupled with near starvation. Captain Phillip fell ill, but by sheer will-power remained on his feet. Such was the quality of his leadership that he shared the same discomfort and wretchedness as the rest of the people.

At home the Government showed a massive disinterest in the distress of the colony. Phillip did, however, draw comfort from knowing that he had at least one powerful ally in Banks. He wrote him long letters setting out the problems and difficulties he was experiencing, and not only did Banks reply with good advice, he also devoted much of his energies in trying to obtain help from the Government. He became so involved in the construction of the colony that he was asked again and again to enter politics with the promise of a place in the Administration. Wisely he refused. 'I could not take office and do my duty,' he said. 'I prefer to be friendly with both sides.'

Banks's greatest difficulty was setting in the minds of the Government his concept of the new colony. He saw it as a flourishing agricultural community where hard-working men and women would prosper, and hardened criminals would be reformed into industrious and successful members of society; but the politicians were far too pressed by problems at home and the gathering threat from Europe to concern themselves with dreams.

Certainly the reality of the colony was a far cry from Banks's ideals. Although the first governors were men of integrity, corruption soon set in, and as far as the administrators in Britain were concerned the new colony was simply a convenient dumping ground for the overflow from the prisons. Transportation was merely a bludgeon to enforce the law.

Banks argued constantly that only convicts who were trained artisans and farmers should be sent to the colony, or at least they should make up a high proportion of the transportees. But when the transports left for New South Wales they carried a motley cargo of thieves, poachers, confidence tricksters, and intellectuals who had been found guilty of sedition.

Many of the naval officers who commanded the transports had scant regard for the health and lives of the convicts in their care. The mortality rate on the long voyage was horrifying. For the officers the losses were something of a bonus since they could sell the resulting surplus supplies at a premium in the colony, which for years tottered on the edge of starvation.

Against this background Banks toiled ceaselessly for improvements.

When Phillip was replaced by Captain John Hunter, Banks was delighted with his first letters. They justified everything he had claimed for Australia. Hunter enthused about the climate, the richness of the soil, and the fine condition of livestock and crops.

In a letter dated 12 October, 1795, he described how five cows and two bulls that had escaped into the bush in 1788 were rediscovered near the Hawkesbury River. They had increased into a large herd and were in superb condition.

Hunter's honeymoon period in the colony was short-lived, and soon Banks was receiving letters describing an environment of lawlessness in which murder and robbery were commonplace. The colony, he said, was 'a mere sink of every species of infamy'.

One of the abuses which really horrified Banks was the treatment of women convicts on their arrival. They were paraded on the dockside for the settlers to pick out servants, and for the male convicts to select 'wives'. Many of the women ended up as little more than unpaid prostitutes. This abuse was not stopped until as late as 1809, and this was largely due to a report that Banks wrote on the conditions in New South Wales, and the reforms that were required.

Before that, however, Hunter's successor, Captain Philip Gidley King, brought about some improvements. He was a tough, fair man, whose discipline was fiercely resisted by both the settlers and the soldiers in the garrison, who preferred the free-booting style of life that had grown up since the first landing.

His concern for the women convicts was clearly expressed in a letter to Banks :

Those (the women) who did not go with one man were sent to be hut-keepers, that is to take care of huts in which there were from two to ten men. If a virtuous woman, as there may be among female convicts, should fall to that unfortunate lot of being a hut-keeper, I leave you to judge.

Although there was little King could do to help the women, he was able to save many of the young girls and children, who were orphaned, illegitimate or abandoned, from exploitation by establishing an orphanage.

King was not popular, and after little more than four years at his post, he asked to be relieved. Banks was given the job of finding a successor to the Governorship, which carried a salary of £2,000 a year.

Banks selected Captain William Bligh. Despite the *Bounty* mutiny and the loss of the breadfruit plants, Banks retained a high regard for Bligh's integrity, and determined sense of duty. He considered him the right man to set the colony on the straight and narrow. 'I know of no one but Captain Bligh who will suit,' he said. But what he failed to recognise was that Bligh was far too cold and aloof a man to come to terms with the fiercely independent spirit that had been generated in New South Wales.

Bligh's attitude is perfectly illustrated in a letter he wrote from Government House, Sydney, to the Hon Charles Greville in 1807.

You can form no idea of the class of persons here who consider themselves Gentlemen. The Colony seems to have been in a distracted state; and this, I am sorry to say, has been caused by the want of proper dignity at Government House, where every person was admitted, and the Governor irritated by conversations, and troubled by letters of complaint, which he should have refused to listen to. The liberty which persons took was irksome; if a request made was not complied with, altercation took place, and ill-will followed; further attempts were then made to gain the object; and at last the Governor consenting he was turned into ridicule, while the parties themselves became envious of each other and a few individuals, such as two or three, have been by that means able to disturb it . . .

He went on to say :

The arduousness of my situation is more than can well be described—Magisterial, Civil, and Criminal Courts all ultimately rest with me in decisions; besides all concerns of Government, in public works and issues of stores, and distribution of convict servants—nothing can be trusted to be done but under the Governor's orders.

Almost from the moment he arrived, the colonists tried to get rid of Bligh. They accused him of everything from dishonesty to cowardice. Within less than a year of taking up his appointment the crisis came to a head. Bligh arrested Captain John Macarthur, a difficult and argumentative man, but also the colony's richest and most successful sheep farmer, for some relatively unimportant technical breach of the law.

Macarthur refused to be tried by the Judge-Advocate, who, he claimed, was drunk; and in this he gained the support of Major George Johnston, the commander of the New South Wales Rifles. At the same time the colonists, whipped up by Macarthur's supporters, rioted, and demanded his release. Johnston agreed, and Bligh faced his second mutiny.

The soldiers burst into Government House, and eventually found Bligh hiding in a small bedroom. He was seized and placed under arrest.

Eventually Johnston was ordered home, where he was court-martialled and cashiered. Macarthur was also sent to Britain under arrest, but no charges could be proved against him, and, after a period of exile, was allowed to return to Australia, taking with him Merino sheep.

Bligh, who was relieved of his Governorship, had to face a court of inquiry, which cleared him of all blame for the mutiny. Indeed, he remained in the navy, rising to the rank of vice-admiral.

As for Banks, he never lost sight of his vision of a thriving pastoral land in the South Seas. In a letter to Governor Hunter he once wistfully expressed the wish that he could 'ask for a grant of land on the banks of the Hawkesbury River'.

CHAPTER 15

LAST YEARS

Banks never relaxed his grip on the mass of affairs that occupied his life, not even when gout took such a hold on him that he would be confined to bed for days in agony. Towards the end of his life he was more or less tied to a wheelchair; his limbs and joints were horribly deformed by the disease, and he almost lost the use of his hands, as well as of his legs.

Outwardly he disguised the pain and suffering, but there were moments of near despair when he was ready to try any cure. In a letter to his physician and friend, Sir Everard Home, he asked for a new drug so that he could act as a guinea-pig in the search for a remedy.

Despite the crippling effects of the disease, he kept pace with the unceasing flow of correspondence which continued to arrive daily. His mind remained fresh and agile.

Only six months before his death he found the energy to write a long, chatty letter to William Marsden, the orientalist. The only note of complaint is about the intense cold. He tells Marsden that the bird he has sent is not a rarity; enquires about a hole he has cut in the ice, for fishing perhaps, and urges Mrs Marsden not to 'despise the comforts of a flannel petticoat'.

Infirmity did not prevent his looking ahead. In 1817, only three years before his death he modernised his greenhouses at Spring Grove, and installed the latest development, steam pipes.

His influence in all areas of science and exploration remained undimmed to the end. Few people cared, or even dared, to make a move in either field without consulting him. In 1815 an expedition up the Congo River was being contemplated. and Sir John Barrow, Secretary of the Admiralty, wrote to Banks saying: 'We can do nothing without your assistance; you will perhaps be good enough to cast about for a proper person as a naturalist.'

Barrow sent him some botanical drawings by two young Scotsmen he thought would be suitable. Banks was as firm and blunt as ever:

I cannot say that I feel any inclination to engage the services of the Scotch lads. The drawings sent are such as no botanist can reap advantage from.

He was also worried that their botanical knowledge was confined to 'Scots plants' and that their experience 'must be chiefly confined to moors and glens'.

Despite such toughness, Banks had a reputation for kindness and generosity. Early in his life he had said that he regarded his great fortune as being available for those deserving help, as well as for his own comfort and amusement. This apparent openhandedness brought its problems from time to time and then he had to curb what was a naturally generous spirit.

In 1794 he turned down a request from the distinguished engineer, James Watt, to support a new medical innovation known as 'Factitious air treatment'. He replied to Watt that he had read all the papers on the treatment, but

. . . had not been able to deduce from them a favourable opinion of the probability of their success, for the proofs yet given do not in my mind afford sufficient evidence that the use of them will be advantageous to the practice of medicine.

He added that he thought it better to throw his weight behind the establishment of conventional hospitals.

Watt accepted the explanation, but not all Banks's supplicants were so easy to put off. One, in particular, became an increasing nuisance over a period of fourteen years. He was Thomas Christopher Banks, a genealogist who claimed kinship with Sir Joseph. At the start of the correspondence Banks was kind. He took an interest in Thomas's work, and he and his sister, Sarah Sophia, even subscribed money for one project. Indeed, at one stage Banks seemed convinced by Thomas's evidence that they were related, and in a letter dated May 1813 even refers to 'our ancestor'.

In 1818 Thomas, who had never been particularly successful, fell on hard times. His wife died, and with her a small income, and he also 'experienced several severe losses in other quarters'.

On 7 September he wrote to Banks:

I am now placed in a state of embarrassment peculiarly affecting to me. To relieve me and enable me to pursue a line of life which may at once be profitable and honourable, I want the sum of £500. To crave your liberality to advance me this sum, I am conscious is a point of nice delicacy. But I beg to be understood, that I do not ask it *as a gift*, but as a loan . . .

The letter goes on to describe at length how a relative, a mutual relative, one Captain Francis Banks, had ruined his father, and how promises of an income for Thomas were not kept. He claims that Captain Banks had made him heir to a share in a Banks family lead mine in Derbyshire, but says the will was destroyed.

Two days later Banks replied that he had no objection to making the loan

. . . was it convenient to me at this time to disburse the money; but that is not the case. Like other persons who live upon a good income and who, having no inducement to save, measure their expenses as near as they can to the extent of their means of defraying them, I felt rather severely the diminution which the price of all the produce of the land experienced on the return of Peace, and I have not yet repaired the injury I received by the temporary reduction of my income below my expenditure.

Thus he turned down the request for a loan of what was, in 1818, a large sum.

On the eleventh Thomas wrote again :

. . . I particularly stated that I had no right to ask so great a favor at your hands; and I by no means should have made the application, had I not considered that the losses and injuries which our family had sustained from a near connection with yours . . .

Under these circumstances and imagining that, while you have the happiness of a large fortune, without children to provide for I flattered myself I should not be too bold in representing to you my situation; although not an acknowledged relative; yet in point of name and character, I might derive the satisfaction of partaking a *minimum* of your expanded generosity, which I have heard you have bestowed in many a maximum upon others . . .

Thomas Banks struck just the wrong note in suggesting that Banks carried some kind of moral responsibility for the debts of Captain Banks, which had ruined Thomas's father. Neither did he take kindly to the suggestion that he gave more liberally to strangers than to his family. It all had the odour of moral blackmail.

Banks replied on 13 September :

Sir, I am now for the first time charged with the losses and injuries supposed by you to have been suffered by your family in consequence of a near connection with mine : and I, who never before knew that any connection between our families had ever taken place, do not feel myself or any of my predecessors guilty of the charges made against us or some of us, of withdrawing property from yours.

I thought I had given you sufficient reasons in my last for declining the loan you proposed to me. I am not in the habit of lending money for interest; but, as the securities you offer me are, no doubt, good, I cannot, I think, hesitate in believing that some person who deals in money will supply you with what you want.

Thomas, with an injured air, wrote back denying that he claimed any special relationship or favours :

I have never wanted to attach myself to any family for base interest; I am satisfied in point of who I am, unless trampled upon by any inferior of pretended superiority assumed by acquired wealth—I do not wish to say, that I have often done acts of kindness, friendship and liberality; but well I know, I have done unto others, as I would they should do unto me, tho' I never have experienced, that others have done unto me, as they would wish to be done unto themselves.

Just to seal the insult there is an acid postscript :

To evince the little inclination I have had to make occasions merely to press myself upon your notice, I have only to remark, I have never before told you, your carriages bear the arms with false colours—viz. A Cross Or, between four *Fleur di Lis* Or, instead of Arg.

Not all of Banks's private correspondence was of such a disagreeable nature. His relationships with his friends were normally of the warmest character.

One of his most enduring friendships was with Sir William Hamilton, and his lovely mistress, Emma, who eventually became Lady Hamilton and later Nelson's mistress. Banks and William Hamilton corresponded for over twenty years, often on the most intimate and personal subjects.

In 1786, for example, writing from Naples, Hamilton refers to the fact that he has seduced Emma away from his nephew, Charles.

My *Visitor*, for you must know I have one, is as handsome as ever, and in tolerable spirits considering all—it is a bad job to come from the nephew to the uncle; but we must make the best of it; and I long to see poor Charles out of his difficulties.

In the spring of the following year he wrote to Banks:

Emma is tolerably reconciled to her banishment, and really contributes much to my happiness—she begins to speak Italian well, and will sing well; so that her education will be improved at least by her visit to me.

Banks was devoted to Emma, and became increasingly concerned at Hamilton's refusal to marry her. When the liaison became a topic of particularly vicious gossip and scandal, he asked Hamilton outright why he would not marry his lovely young mistress.

The reply he received in April 1790 is a measure of the closeness of the friendship:

To answer your question fairly, was I in a private station, I should have no objection that Emma should share with me *le petit bout de vie qui me reste,* under the solemn covenant you allude to as her behaviour in my house has been such for four years as to give her universal esteem and approbation, but as I have no thought of relinquishing my employment, and whilst I am in a public character I do not look upon myself at liberty to act as I please and such a step I think would be imprudent and might be attended with disagreeable circumstances, besides as amidst other branches of natural history I have not neglected the study of the animal called woman, I have found them subject to great changes according to circumstances, and I do not like to try experiments at my time of life. In the way we live, we give no scandal, she with her mother and I in my apartment, and we have a good society, what then is to be gained on my side? It is very natural for her to wish it and try to make people believe the business done, which I suppose has caused the report in England.

I assure you that I approve of her so much that if I had been the person that made her first go astray I would glory in giving her a public reparation, and I would do it openly, for indeed she has infinite merit, and no Princess could do the honours of her palace with more care and dignity than she does those of my house, in short she is worthy of anything, and I have and will take care of her in proportion as I feel myself obliged to her; But as to the solemn league.

Amplius Considerandum Est

Now, my dear Sir, I have more fairly delivered you my confession than is usually done in this country, of which you may make any discreet use you please—those who ask out of mere curiosity I should wish to remain in the dark—Adieu, and believe me ever sensible of your friendship and kindness to me.

Eventually the couple did marry, very largely as a result of Banks's efforts. Certainly Emma was very fond of Banks, and took notice of what he had to say. She indicated her affection in a letter she wrote in 1797 to congratulate him on the appointment to the Privy Council.

As I am inclined to love all his (William's) friends how rejoiced I was at your happiness and welfare, for indeed I do not consider you as one of his common *friends*, and therefore love and esteem you more than you think I do.

Banks enjoyed the company of younger people, and was always, or nearly always, ready to give them help, encouragement and sound advice. Certainly they were assured of a welcome at Soho Square.

The explorer, William Scoresby the younger, first met Banks in 1807 after his father suggested he should call on the old man when he was passing through London. The meeting resulted in a friendship that lasted until Banks's death.

In the preface to *An Account of the Arctic Regions*, Scoresby wrote:

By means of some valuable instruments etc., furnished me by Sir Joseph Banks, whose friendly suggestion and encouragement I am happy to acknowledge, and whose kindness and liberality I shall ever remember with gratitude, I was enabled to make some experiments on sub-marine temperature, the result of which proved novel and interesting.

Allan Cunningham, the plant collector, received some firm advice in 1817 just before embarking on an expedition along the north-west and west coasts of New Holland. Perhaps when he wrote the following words, Banks had in mind his youthful arrogance over the *Resolution*.

As the vessel employed in this service is very small your accommodation on board her cannot but be very limited, as, however, the whole of the crew will be under the same circumstances, I trust that the great importance of the business in which you are employed will induce you to be content with the room that can be afforded to you.

Arguably the best advice he ever gave to a young man was given to James Edward Smith, an enthusiastic young botanist and naturalist, in 1783.

After Carl Linnaeus died, his son, another Carl, inherited his father's huge herbarium, and collections of insects, shells, minerals, as well as a large scientific library. The collections were in a poor condition and young Carl worked tirelessly to restore and preserve them. Banks, in fact offered to buy everything for £1,200, but Carl thought this a 'cruel offer' and rejected it.

Suddenly, in 1783, the young Carl died, and Linnaeus's widow found herself with the collections on her hands, with neither the money, the will or the ability to cope with them. She wanted a buyer, and Banks was approached. The offer arrived at Soho Square during one of the famous Thursday breakfasts. Among the guests was young Smith. After reading the letter Banks turned to him and advised him to make an offer for the Linnaean collection.

Smith offered one thousand guineas and it was accepted. Despite loud and angry protests from Sweden's scientists and academics, the collections were shipped to London. It was an impressive cargo—19,000 specimens of plants, over 3,000 insects, 1,500 shells, about 800 pieces of coral; there were 2,500 mineral specimens, and as many books, as well as thousands of letters. The Linnaean Society was founded in 1788, and to this day looks after the unique collections.

Banks liked to lead and direct, he liked to inspire and encourage, and most of all he liked to be at the centre of events. He was fortunate to be extremely rich, and thus have the leisure to order his life according to his choice, without the pressures of earning a living. But it was not wealth alone that enabled him to follow such a varied and significant career. Part of his success, at least, he owed to the two women in his life—his wife, Dorothea, and his sister, Sarah Sophia.

The two women worked tirelessly in his interest. They shared the same house in, it would seem, an atmosphere of peace and tranquillity. If there were rows, they were certainly not serious enough for Banks to note in either letters or journals, although often he refers, teasingly, to 'my ladies, who are a little mad'.

Of the two, Sarah Sophia emerges as the more dominant personality. She had a loud, even strident voice, was tall and imposing, and cut an unmistakable figure striding along the streets or through the parks, always accompanied by a servant carrying a long cane.

Dorothea, on the other hand, was on the tubby side, with soft oval features, large gentle eyes, and silky curly hair.

Sarah Sophia collected cartoons, visiting cards, medals and newspaper cuttings, drove a four-in-hand with the skill and confidence of a man, and was skilled in archery and fishing.

Dorothea collected old china, and was regarded as an expert on the subject.

But what they both had in common was a selfless devotion to Banks and his career.

When he was promoting British Merino wool, his ladies wore dresses made from the product. Sarah Sophia had three dresses made from the wool, which she nicknamed Hightum, Tightum and Scrub.

Invitations to social events which arrived at the Banks household were always addressed to Sir Joseph, Lady and Miss Banks. Both ladies enjoyed social occasions, although their enthusiasm was not always shared by Banks. Despite her gentleness Lady Banks could keep her end up at even the most boisterous rural frolic, such as one in Lincolnshire in 1780. Describing it in a letter, Banks said that she,

Thank God . . . escaped pretty well as only one pot of porter was thrown over her gown, tho' she danced between more pots of porter and bowls of negus than couples in the country dance.

For many years there was a fourth member of the household, Daniel Solander. He and Banks were like brothers, and the Swede was adored by the two women. He was cheerful and entertaining, and when laughter rang through 32 Soho Square, it was a certain thing that Solander was behind it. Tragically in the Spring of 1782 he was struck with paralysis, and despite the most devoted nursing by Lady Banks, he died within a few days.

While the atmosphere in Banks's homes was relaxed and easy, their running was ordered, and routines were strictly adhered to. In a letter to a Norfolk landowner, Samuel Tyssen, in 1805, Banks says:

We shall be happy to see you at dinner at Spring Grove on Tuesday next in your way to Oxford; only remember that we are punctual persons, and that our hour is half past four.

Perhaps infirmity, the loss of close, dear friends, and the sharpening awareness of death inevitably impress a sadness on old age. Certainly there is a sadness that hovers over Banks's last years.

He had to stand by helplessly and see the King, with whom he had shared and done so much, and whose friendship he had enjoyed over so many years, fall increasingly under the illness porphyria, which crippled his mind and reason. In fact it was during this period that the two men had their one and only row. George III accused Banks of breaking faith with the public by selling some of the royal Merino flock privately, instead of at auction, as had been advertised. The accusation was unfounded, but Banks was deeply wounded by the King's anger.

In the end, happily, the misunderstanding was cleared up, and the King expressed his grief that Banks had taken the matter so much to heart.

Added to all this there was the frustration of his own infirmities. So immobilised was he by gout that he had to be carried to his chair at the Royal Society. The thunder was muted, but when he offered his resignation on the grounds of failing health, it was refused.

Age, illness and overweight placed the annual journey to Revesby at risk, a threat that distressed Banks, so that it was with almost childish gratitude that he wrote to Home after the doctor gave his permission for the trip to go ahead in 1817. 'Your permission to visit Lincolnshire gives me spirits to undertake the journey,' he said. But now there was none of the rush and urgency of past pilgrimages to the family home. It was undertaken in slow stages, a process that Banks found irksome, but not his ladies. He wrote to Home :

My ladies, who are both rather crazy, approve much of this leisurely mode of travelling : we shall therefore return in the same manner.

The following year Banks and his ladies were returning home from a dinner party when their drunken coachman overturned the coach. The three large occupants were trapped, and for half an hour lay all of a heap at the bottom of the vehicle. Sarah Sophia received a bad cut on her head, while Banks was in agony from the need to urinate.

Once rescued he passed a huge quantity of urine, and during the process vented a stone, which according to a sketch he made of it measured about three-quarters of an inch long, by a quarter wide 'resembling a small branch of coral'.

Only three years before, the Banks family were attacked by Corn Bill rioters who smashed the windows at Soho Square, broke down the front door and wrecked the hall furniture. Describing the incident to James Smith, Banks said :

I have, Thank God, suffered as little from the miscreants as could have been expected. The windows and doors of my house and the hall table and chairs was all they destroyed.

He added that the rioters did not dare enter the inner rooms of the house through fear of being arrested and hanged as burglars.

Although his ladies bore up well face-to-face with the rioters, the effect of the coaching accident was far more serious. Just over a month later, on 27 September, 1818, Sarah Sophia died following a slight illness. Her death was a tremendous blow to Banks. Apart from his journeys, they had rarely been apart, and she had been a loyal, enthusiastic and loving companion.

He survived her for less than two years, dying on 19 June 1820, and being buried without fuss, or pomp and ceremony, in Heston parish churchyard. At his request his grave was not marked with either a stone or tablet.

Sir Joseph Banks left no heir to carry on his work. With his death he seemed simply to fade out of history.

He did not leave any great published works to perpetuate his memory, and indeed his letters and papers were eventually disposed of in a disgraceful manner by Lord Brabourne, to whom they passed in 1882. All the Banks papers had been placed in the safe-keeping of the British Museum, but Brabourne repossessed them and sold them at auction at Sotheby's for a total of £182 19s. Those that were not bought by autograph dealers, were distributed throughout the world. They are to be found in Australia, New Zealand, Canada and America, as well as Britain.

The sale not only broke up the collection of letters and manuscripts; it also broke up the record of the life's work of a great man. More than any other single act it condemned him to a shadowy place in history—a cruel fate for one who was so positive, and played such a vital role in laying the foundations of a modern, technological society.

SELECT BIBLIOGRAPHY

Beaglehole, J., ed. *The Endeavour Journal of Joseph Banks, 1768–1771,*
   Public Library of New South Wales and Angus and Robertson
Brooke, J. *King George III,* Constable (1972)
Bulletin of the British Museum (Natural History) Historical Series, 'Sir
   Joseph Banks and the plant collection from Kew sent to the Empress
   Catherine of Russia, 1795' (London, 1974)
Burney, F. *Diaries*
Cameron, H. C. *Sir Joseph Banks,* The Batchworth Press (1952)
Carter, H. B. *His Majesty's Spanish Flock,* Angus and Robertson (1964)
Coats, A. M. *The Quest for Plants,* Studio Vista (1969)
Colman, G. the Younger, *Random Records*
Creasy, Sir E. *Memoirs of Eminent Etonians,* Chatto and Windus (1876)
Delany, Mrs *Life* and *Correspondence*
Lee's *Botany*
Lyon, Sir H. *The Royal Society*
Lysaght, A. M. *Joseph Banks in Newfoundland and Labrador, 1766,* Faber
   (1971)
McCormick, E. H. *Omai – Pacific Envoy,* Auckland University Press and
   Oxford University Press (1977)
Maxwell-Lyte, Sir H. *The History of Eton*
Rhind, W. *A History of the Vegetable Kingdom,* Blackie and Son (1872)
Smith, E. *The Life of Sir Joseph Banks,* Bodley Head (1911)
The Town and Country Magazine, September 1773
Young, A. *General View of the Agriculture of the County of Lincoln*

INDEX